EDUCATING THE GIFTED

Suppose that Abraham Lincoln, George Washington, Martin Luther, William Harvey, Oliver Cromwell, Nicholas Copernicus, Andrew Jackson, and Michael Faraday were all students in your local high school this year! If your high school is of average size . . . and your community of average intelligence, as far as native endowment is concerned, that probably is actually the case every year.

> —Ernest M. Ligon, *A Greater Generation,* 1948

We cannot measure the demands upon our people in the second half of the 20th century . . . by what was demanded of them at the beginning of the first half of this century. We are entering upon an era which will test to the utmost the capacity of our democracy to cope with the gravest problems of modern times—and on a scale never yet attempted in all the history of the world. We are entering upon this difficult and dangerous period with what I believe we must call a growing deficit in the quantity and quality of American education. . . .

We have to do in the educational system something very like what we have done in the military establishment during the past fifteen years. We have to make a breakthrough to a radically higher and broader conception of what is needed and of what can be done.

> —Walter Lippmann, in an address before the National Citizens Commission for the Public Schools, San Francisco, 1954.

EDUCATING THE GIFTED

an axiomatic approach

Virgil S. Ward
University of Virginia

Charles E. Merrill Books, Inc.
Columbus, Ohio

dedication to
**VIRGINIA SCOTT AND
MILAN AND BONNIE PETTY**
for reasons that those
who have known us will
understand

preface

This work develops a systematic theory of differential educational experience for the gifted. The theory is predicated upon the behavioral characteristics of the group as a whole and upon their anticipated adult roles. These roles typically involve leadership and reconstruction at the frontiers of culture, as distinct from mere participation in the status quo. The principles pertain to the general education of persons of superior intellectual ability rather than to the specific training of particular aptitudes manifest in gifted people. They are intended to cover that broad span of school years from the intermediate grades through the general college.

Lewis M. Terman and his colleagues, in the continuing development of the "Genetic Studies of Genius," offer what Terman himself called a factual "prolegomenon" to educational endeavor. The present work relates to this idea in comprising what the author holds to be a necessary intervening step, i.e., the derivation from those facts which distinguish the gifted as a group of a comprehensive educational theory through which practical programs and curricular modifications for the gifted can be made truly appropriate to their needs. In the absence of such intermediate principles it is logical to expect what actually exists, a growing miscellany of practices in schools across the nation which perhaps fail to serve the needs of the gifted as often as they succeed.

The principles, which are presented in the logical form of proposition and corollary, are rendered coherent by the underlying conception of *general education for the intellectually superior individual.* The work concentrates more upon the quality of educational experience than upon administrative arrangements. There is an attempt to derive *a theory of experience internal to the learner,* in contrast to *a theory of practice external to the experiencing subject.* Such direct communication to teachers in terms of requisite teaching-learning processes has been recognized as a deficient area in the literature on the gifted, which is predominantly concerned with pupil identification and administrative programming.

The book is intended to serve two main practical purposes. The first purpose is to afford insight for classroom teachers, supervisory personnel, and administrators into essential qualities which enriched curricula must possess. Without such insight changes in assignments and activities involve for the brighter pupil, not a different quality and plane of experience, but merely "more of the same"; and proposed courses and administrative arrangements fail to accord intimately with their specific objectives. The second intention is that the principles serve as an extensive check-list for instructional provisions already in effect, again to determine whether the modifications of the regular school program do, indeed, possess potential for a higher quality of educational experience for the gifted youngster.

This work has been developed at two different periods of the author's concern with the education of gifted persons. Part I represents current thought given to the problem as a result of a variety of experiences in the field. Much of the remaining parts in which the formal principles are stated was developed a decade ago in a graduate thesis (University of North Carolina, 1952). The original set of principles was devised deductively for the most part. As they now stand, they comprise a fair representation of the empirical substance of excellent practices emerging here and there in pioneering schools. Promising practices have been observed and generalized upward into principles; the analyses of unpromising practices has given rise to additional principles; and there has been left intact from the earlier thought other principles which educational practice has not yet reflected, at least to the author's knowledge.

The college or university instructor of courses on the gifted will want, first, to interpret the full meaning of the various propositions, with an open declaration of agreements and disagreements, and, next, to examine selectively contemporary practices with respect to their adequacy in terms of pertinent points in this theory. This constant reflection upon principles that underlie given practices comprises the virtue of an attempt to mediate between an accumulated body of psychological fact and direct educational practice. Both good and bad practices offer appropriate opportunities for exercise of thought, and the instructor's own imagination and educational philosophy are called into play through interpretation, criticism, and application.

Virgil S. Ward

acknowledgments

A number of long-standing personal friends have contributed over the years to the author's understanding of the educative process. These include, among others, Munroe Faucett, Clinton Prewett, George Holmes, and John Doby. A debt of gratitude is due many former teachers; among them are Elizabeth Matheson, Virginia Greever Plack, Kenneth Coates, Harold MacCurdy, and Irvin Wolf. From professional colleagues and friends, special indebtedness is acknowledged to Jack Birch, William Geer, Ernest Newland, and Leon Reid, the latter having been more than any other person responsible for encouraging the publication of this book. Mr. John H. Sandberg, an able assistant in the author's recent work with the gifted, handled a number of technical details connected with the preparation of the manuscript. For their valuable assistance in reviewing the manuscript, acknowledgment is made to Dr. John Horrocks, The Ohio State University, and Dr. Arthur Coladarci, Stanford University.

A teacher is always indebted to his own students. The author acknowledges that small number of exceptional students who have helped through their love of learning to keep his own alive. Their accomplishments will always be for their teacher a matter of continuing pride, far beyond that warranted by his share in their personal development.

xiiAcknowledgments

Finally, a very special acknowledgment is made to the author's immediate family. Without their patience, his work could not have been carried on; without their confidence and respect, no achievement would be satisfying.

Virgil S. Ward

contents

Part One The Superior Student in an Educational Perspective 1

Introduction 3

Chapter 1 Characteristics of the Gifted 10

Chapter 2 The Nature and Significance of Education
for the Gifted 28

Chapter 3 Toward an Educational Theory 48

Part Two General Principles of the Educational Design 78

Chapter 4 The Logic of Special Education for the Gifted 79

Chapter 5 Meeting Individual Differences 86

Chapter 6 The Principle of Economy 102

Chapter 7 The Teacher of the Gifted 108

Part Three Principles of Intellectual and Academic Development 121

Introduction 123

Chapter 8   The Role of Intellect   126
Chapter 9   The Role of Knowledge   141
Chapter 10   Instruction in the Methods and Sources
             of Knowledge   156
Chapter 11   Meaning and Communication in the Instruction
             of the Gifted   161
Chapter 12   The Foundations of Civilization as
             Educational Content   170

**Part Four   Principles of Personal, Social, and Character
Development   181**
Chapter 13   Personal, Social, and Character Development
             in the Gifted   183
Chapter 14   Applying the Scientific Method   194
Chapter 15   Instruction in the Principles of Behavior   200
Chapter 16   Total Planning for Personal Integrity   212

Bibliography   223

EDUCATING THE GIFTED

part
one

THE SUPERIOR STUDENT
IN AN EDUCATIONAL
PERSPECTIVE

*Education may be defined as a process of
continuous reconstruction of experience with
the purpose of widening and deepening its
social content, while, at the same time,
the individual gains control of the methods
involved.*

—John Dewey

introduction

The social significance of special education for men of great abilities impressed Plato more than two thousand years ago. The timelessness of man's central concerns is suggested by the intense preoccupation in America today with the problem of educating those among contemporary youth who are the most educable. This book deals with the problem of educating individuals of superior intellectual ability by suggesting a conception of the educative process which differs from that governing the sequence of experiences through which persons of ordinary ability can and should proceed.

Special education for the intellectually gifted is justified by the educationally significant capacities that set these persons at a distance from the middle ranks and by the probable types of social responsibility which they are destined as a whole to assume by virtue of their superior endowments.

This book is intended to sketch a foundation in basic principles for the educational experience of children and youth who form the topmost level of brightness—possibly the upper 1, 2, or 3 per cent of the general intelligence scale—and who are intrinsically motivated toward academic, scientific, or other intellectual accomplishment. The educational levels considered include the intermediate grades through general college. Children falling within the group superior to the average,

3

but short of the extreme upper limits of ability—variously termed "moderately gifted" or "academically talented"—will be, according to individual personality, variously suited to an educational program governed by these principles. Where developmental and educational experiences have been constructive, young people falling within the top 10 per cent of the ability scale will benefit from the educational experiences described as appropriate for the top group, but to a diminishing degree, of course, as ability and motivation lessen.

In aiming high, it is intended that this work differ from much of the thought and activity going on at the moment in this area. The overall character of much of the present work in the interest of the brighter pupil, with some notable exceptions, is chiefly in the nature of improvements in the curriculum as it is presently known. These improvements include additions and deletions in standard subject matter, condensation of subject matter into briefer time expanses, and location of certain subject matter downward in the grade sequence so as to allow advanced entry into subsequent levels of the school system. Such essentially administrative rearrangements are excellent in themselves and necessary, but they scarcely comprise the whole task or even the most significant aspect of it.

This description applies in the main to the most recent and best organized single effort in the movement of the gifted, that in behalf of the "academically talented student." All responsible educators value the support and momentum being given to the improvement of the American educational system through the vigorous efforts of Dr. James B. Conant in his current studies of American schools and through the National Education Association's Project on the Academically Talented Student in the American Secondary School. As an indication, however, that the thinking connected with this recent movement is centered in present educational thought and practice and avowedly so, we cite from Dr. Conant's introductory remarks at the 1958 conference which initiated the studies and promotional efforts in the NEA project:

> What is needed, most of us feel, is a careful consideration of the secondary school education of all those boys and girls who have the ability to study effectively and rewardingly advanced mathematics, foreign languages and tough courses in chemistry and physics. You will note that I have just ventured to give a definition of the "academically talented youth"—in the jargon of modern philosophy, it is an operational definition. And this question of defining the type of pupil

whose education we will be considering has given us all a good deal of trouble, I must admit. There are some of us here who are primarily interested in the really unusual pupil, who often fails to do well in school just because he or she is too able and is not challenged by the work. These pupils—not more than 2 per cent of the high school population—are often labelled as the "gifted," and I, for one, think this is the proper use of the word. The much larger group, some 15–20 per cent of a typical American comprehensive high school, perhaps as much as 50 per cent of some atypical high schools and more than 90 per cent of secondary schools which are on a selective basis, are the group who should be going to college. . . .[1]

It is insufficient thus to consider the curriculum for the gifted in terms of traditional subjects and instructional processes. Furthermore, Dr. Conant's operational definition of the abler pupil as one who can handle "tough" courses involves a surprisingly meager conception both of the abilities of the superior student and of the imperative need for a radical reinterpretation of the educative process.

Academicians, also, seem to be saying with one voice that educational ills can be remedied by increasing the dosage of traditional educational medicines unwisely abandoned in late years for "progressive" placebos. Such proposals for improving the education of persons who must reckon effectively with world problems of unsurpassed complexity are seriously lacking in imagination. It would be regrettable, indeed, if the present public concern for education produces nothing but superficial adaptations under the traditional framework of education—mere additions, deletions, and changed proportions within established educative processes and subject matter.

We prefer the imaginative boldness that runs through a series of commanding questions posed by Margaret Mead concerning the inadequacy of present concepts and practices in education to reckon with the character of present times. These questions are included in support of the plea that education of the gifted in the contemporary world be reconceived, radically, and largely apart from present practice. Mead inquires:

> Is our present historic idea of education suitable for people in the mid-twentieth century, who have a life expectancy of 70 years, and who live in a world of automation and global communication, ready to begin space exploration and aware of the possibility that we can bring about the suicide of the entire human species?

As all these present and pressing concerns of the human race are new, is it not possible that a system of education may be out of date which was designed for small societies that were connected by horse-drawn coaches and sailing ships, and where any war could threaten only small sections of the human species at any one time?

Is it not possible that the problem of the educational system's obsolescence goes beyond such issues as methods of teaching reading or physics, or the most desirable age for leaving school, or the payment of teachers, or the length of summer holidays, or the number of years best devoted to college, or even the comparative advantages of working while going to high school or college?

Is not the break between past and present—and so the whole problem of outdating in our educational system—related to a change in the rate of change? For change has become so rapid that adjustment cannot be left to the next generation; adults must—not once, but continually—take in, adjust to, use, and make innovations in a steady stream of discovery and new conditions.

Our educational system, besides being the oldest system of universal free primary education in the world, bears the marks of its long history. But is it not possible to think that an educational system that was designed to teach what was known to little children and to a selected few young men (after which they could be regarded as "educated") may not fit a world in which the most important factors in everyone's life are those things that are not yet, but soon will be, known?

Is it not equally possible that our present definition of a pupil or a student is out of date when we define the learner as a child (or at best an immature person) who is entitled to those things to which a child is entitled—moral protection and a meager subsistence in a dependency position—and who is denied those things which are denied to a child—moral autonomy, sex and parenthood, alcoholic beverages, and exposure to hazards?[2]

This book describes no single plan for educating the gifted, such as those developed in various metropolitan centers and offered for the guidance of others who choose to pattern their efforts similarly. Instead, the work is theoretically oriented and makes an explicit attempt to depart from those established practices which do not promise to realize the full potential of the most educable children and youth of school and college age. Experience internal to the learner is the main concern, and necessary discussions of the external programs accompanying various practices proceed in terms of this primary interest.

These principles should afford a set of broad criteria by which existing programs may be evaluated and in terms of which classroom teachers can study their daily attempts at enriching experience for able youth. These principles stand or fall to the extent that they are evident in the practices of schools that have developed truly appropriate experiences for the gifted, that they provide guidelines for the development of initial practices in other schools, and that they provide theoretical sanction for enrichment activities devised by individual teachers through their own private insights.

That these principles attain to the majestic stature demanded by Margaret Mead's questions it would be presumptuous even to hope. They do aim, however, toward a more fundamental re-examination of the curriculum, not only as it is here and now, but *as it can be and as it should be* in view of the abilities of the young people concerned and the most likely demands to be made upon them during their life span in a dynamic world of material and social change.

In the development of these principles, special consideration will be given to our increasing knowledge of the educative process. This is an exciting era in the history of the behavioral sciences. Experiments based upon rigorous thought and design are yielding empirical results that parallel the insights of visionaries in earlier periods of educational thought. Especially pertinent to education of the gifted are forward thrusts in thinking about the *nature of mind*—creativity and other higher mental processes, with particular respect to the power of experience for fundamental effects upon these processes; a corresponding firm dissatisfaction with present conceptions of "intelligence" and related instruments of measurement (although older concepts and instruments remain useful in the absence of effective substitutes); attempts to discern the multiplicity of dynamics which make for human achievement; and new respect for ethereal aspects of personality and experience, such as unconscious mental processes, teleological possibilities, and possible qualitative differences in mental stuff, delicate subtleties which only yesterday were inadmissible into the masculine world of empirical science.

But principles which promise to guide educational practices soundly cannot be based merely upon dissatisfaction with present conceptions or modes of action or upon fragmentary reaches into frontiers of knowledge, no matter how exciting. Even if the inevitable lag between thought and practice might be abridged, the probability of error and inadequacy is too high when consequences extend beyond the dependable present. Accordingly, the propositions presented in this work recognize only the more stable researches in the behavioral sciences and the more enduring philosophical thought that underlies educational practice. No attempt has been made to summarize interesting and potentially significant contemporary experimentation which has not yet been adequately tested for significance and reliability.

The thought of John Dewey, the factual "prolegomenon" embodied in the continuing *Genetic Studies of Genius* initiated by Lewis M. Terman and presently conducted by his associates, and the researches into the nature of creativity and the "faces of intellect" going on for more than a decade under the leadership of J. P. Guilford are stable lines of development such as should constitute bases for educational principles. Catherine Patrick's analysis of conditions reported to favor creative thinking (see p. 136), for instance, was made for publication in 1946 and based on literature dated as far back as 1906. Yet little exists in later research on this important quality of behavior which suggests an alteration in Patrick's conditions as guidelines to educational practice, and nothing at all sufficient to negate them.

Part I of this work describes the characteristics of the intellectually gifted and makes suggestions toward a theory of general education which pertains to these characteristics, to present world conditions, and to the social role of reconstruction which the gifted tend to assume. Parts II, III, and IV explicate this philosophy in terms of principles which pertain to the instruction of abler youth from childhood through general college or university instruction.

Specifically, Part II, entitled "General Principles of the Educational Design," is concerned with the total program of education for the gifted, its roots in biological and sociological fact, and the nature of its aims.

Part III, entitled "Principles of Intellectual and Academic Development," relates to the content and methods through which general understandings about man and nature should be transmitted and acquired. This part explores a range of ideas held to be applicable to the development of the cognitive aspects of mind per se. This section is of special significance since it is in general intellect that the subject of this work differs most markedly from other persons and most requires special education.

Part IV is entitled "Principles of Personal, Social, and Character Development." These dimensions of personality are familiarly referred to as *non-cognitive*, or *dynamic*. It is widely accepted that education of the "heart" is as essential as education of the "mind." In the present treatment of these dimensions of personality, however, the relationship of general intellect to behavior as a whole is of principal concern, for again, it is in intellectual potential that our subject differs most critically from other persons. These aspects of human behavior are treated at all only out of faith in their importance in total behavior and development. They are considered, further, in full awareness that the harvest of behavioral science in these areas affords the educator far less exact information upon which to base educational thought and practice.

chapter one   CHARACTERISTICS OF THE GIFTED

WHO ARE THE GIFTED?

New movements inevitably become involved in conflicts over terminology. The current emphasis upon education for the gifted is no exception. In an attempt to economize upon ideas of definition, rather than to recapitulate the endless original arguments in support of one term or set of terms over another, it is submitted that the issue of whom to consider gifted involves two basic points of view.

The somewhat older position, assumed by Lewis M. Terman in his *Genetic Studies of Genius* (before there was any argument on the matter) and prevalent until very recently, considered the term "gifted" to apply to those persons of school age who fall at the top 1 per cent level in general intellectual ability, as measured by the Stanford-Binet Intelligence Scale or comparable instrument.[3] The contrasting position has been successfully promoted in American schools by Paul Witty, whose recommendation as recently stated is "that our definition of giftedness be expanded and that we consider any child gifted whose performance, in a potentially valuable line of human activity, is consistently remarkable."[4] This point of view includes children exceptionally endowed in specific *aptitudes*, as in some form of art, in mechanics, in academic disciplines such as natural science or foreign language, or in interpersonal relationships. It has even been interpreted, and with reason, to refer to superior athletic ability. This position has become widely accepted in the post-World War II re-emphasis upon education for the gifted in American schools.

Among school systems and experimenters using the IQ as a central criterion for identification, there have been varied practices in cut-off points. Terman's fairly high cut-off point (137 IQ as adapted to the 1937 Revision of the Stanford-Binet Scale) has been paralleled by some positions suggesting a criterion as low as IQ 112 or 115.[5] The Cleveland Public Schools, in which systematic provisions for the brighter child have probably pertained over a longer period of time than in any other American school system, take an intermediate position, admitting to its "Major Work" classes children of 125 IQ and above.[6] All such positions are, of course, arbitrary or *ad hoc*, and the merits of each can be argued with some validity.

Educational expediency urges that where IQ is a central criterion, the cut-off point be sufficiently low to include numbers large enough to make practicable the effort and expense involved in adapting the school program; and educational theory suggests that the cut-off point separate children who promise to profit more than at present from special educational provisions. A position assumed by the Educational Policies Commission in 1950 seems appropriate for both points of view. The Commission writes:

> In this statement, the term "highly gifted" is used to designate those who are in the top 1 per cent of the total population with respect to intellectual capacity (that is, roughly, individuals with an IQ above 137). Similarly, the term "moderately gifted" will apply to individuals who fall within the top 10 per cent below the top 1 per cent (that is, between 120 and 137 IQ).[7]

This point of view is harmonious with the concept of the academically talented to which we have already referred. The material cited from Dr. Conant (p. 4) refers to two levels of capacity for learning, holding that the top 2 or 3 per cent of the general school population should be termed "gifted" and including some 15 to 20 per cent within the group termed "academically talented."

No other attempts to enter into the semantics of this problem have added substantially to these basic ideas which ground definitions either in (1) general intelligence or (2) specific aptitude, and recognize both a level of ability sufficiently above average to warrant certain differences in educative processes and another level, yet rarer and higher, which warrants still more radical educational differentiation.[8]

Throughout the present work the terms *superior* and *gifted* will be used interchangeably with roughly synonymous terms which are varied to avoid monotony. These two terms and their synonyms will always refer to general intellectual ability, beginning at the topmost level and descending the scale of learning capacity as the student's native potential, personality structure, and developmental status require.[9] Thus, the educational theory and principles derived in this volume are based on the earlier point of view assumed by Terman. A detailed argument for this position is undertaken later in Part I (pp. 28–40). Since most of those who are specifically talented are also above average in IQ, however, the ensuing prescriptions toward general education for brighter youth would include many from the talented group as well.

This fairly flexible conception of the level of intellect required for special educational experiences appears to be consistent with a point of view developed by David C. McClelland and his colleagues in an extensive study of the nature and role of talent in society. They suggest that factors other than intelligence may account more critically for academic success than high intelligence alone. Their idea is stated as follows:

> But the question of the linearity of the relationship of intelligence test scores to even so simple a criterion as school performance has not been studied as it deserves. Let us admit that morons cannot do good school work. But what available evidence is there that intelligence is not a threshold type of variable; that once a person has a certain minimal level of intelligence, his performance beyond that point is uncorrelated with his ability? Several studies suggest that if such a minimal level is set fairly high, ability may no longer play a crucial role in success.[10]

With respect to the fairly high cut-off point on the intelligence scale for designating those who should have special educational experiences, it should be remembered that an increasing percentage of individuals in the upper levels of the secondary school, and of the general college as presently organized, would come within any given upper intellectual level. Thus, if 15 per cent (or 10, or 5) of elementary school children qualify at present for a significantly adapted curriculum, a larger percentage of high school students would so qualify because of the loss of those pupils unable to ascend this far, and an even larger percentage of those in college. It may well be that the common school curriculum as presently conceived fails to exact greater excellence in thought, judgment, and other higher mental processes as students progress through the grades. It is the writer's observation that the quality of reasoning which will "pass" a modestly intelligent freshman in the average college course will serve him for the same purpose as a senior. The standards of expectation for student behavior should take better account both of the maturing intellectual processes and of the sequential levels and areas of study previously accomplished by the student. It may be objected that a curriculum which truly challenges individuals who exceed a "threshold" level in perceiving, learning, and thinking will place moderately gifted students at a slight relative disadvantage. This reversal of role might be wholesome, however, in contrast to the spuriously high accomplishment of the latter group in an undifferentiated sequence of experiences.

THE INTELLECTUALLY SUPERIOR INDIVIDUAL

The planning of educational procedures for any selected segment of the population is dependent upon a knowledge of the principal characteristics which distinguish the designated group. The present section contains a selection of the major facts which research and educational experience have revealed to be characteristic of intellectually superior children and youth. Lewis M. Terman, upon whose *Genetic Studies of Genius* we draw for the data concerning the characteristics of intellectually superior persons, conceived this magnificent longitudinal study as a necessary background for a "direct attack upon the pedagogy of gifted children." Terman and Oden state:

> One other thing should be made clear: the investigation as planned was not a direct attack upon the pedagogy of gifted children; it was instead a search for the basic facts that would provide a necessary prolegomenon to further advances in this field of special training. Information must precede reform. It was lack of information that made this region the darkest Africa of education. Once the physical and mental characteristics and the developmental tendencies of intellectually superior children have been definitely established, then, and only then, is it possible to plan intelligently for their education.[11]

In the laying of this necessary factual basis, Terman's work unquestionably stands supreme. All of America is indebted to this able scientist and his co-workers.

Prior to abstracting from these studies the educationally significant characteristics of gifted persons, however, another historic contributor to thought in this field should be recognized. In the manner of observing the gifted child in an educational setting, and contributing to educational theory the rich insights and inferences which she derived from these observations, few would deny Leta S. Hollingworth perhaps an equal place with Terman in the history of this phase of American education. Working independently on the west and east coasts respectively, Lewis Terman and Leta Hollingworth, with the large number of students and co-workers whom they guided and inspired, deserve major credit for carving out the scientific facts and insightful observations necessary to the development of a theory of special education for the gifted.

Very briefly, Hollingworth's work, though in the beginning concerned with the psychological characteristics of the bright and dull, subsequently assumed more and more the character of educational promotion and experimentation. She organized two major educational projects for gifted children in New York City, one in 1922 and another in 1936, and supervised numerous small-scale research studies of other students of the problem. Her diligence in promoting educational efforts in behalf of intellectually superior and talented students remains unexcelled to the present day. Because her best-known contributions were in an educational context, however, Hollingworth's theories will be used chiefly in those sections of this work that deal with the educative processes.

Terman's *Genetic Studies*, on the other hand, will be drawn upon immediately and quite extensively, since they comprise the largest body of systematic data yet gathered on gifted persons. These genetic studies consist to date of five volumes reporting initial and follow-up findings pertaining to some fifteen hundred California children testing within the upper 1 per cent of the general school population in general intelligence. Instituted in 1921, the project is reported in a series of which the fifth volume, by Lewis M. Terman and Melita H. Oden, *The Gifted Group at Mid-Life* (Stanford, California: Stanford University Press, 1959) is a thirty-five-year follow-up study. The mean chronological age of the "Main Experimental Group" when first tested was about ten years, and the mean Binet IQ for this group of approximately one thousand children was 151, with a range from 135 to 200.[12]

The essential findings concerning these intellectually superior youngsters were derived from a comparison of the main experimental group and a control group made up of a random sample of children of comparable age. A second group, less systematically selected and followed and consisting of 365 subjects from smaller urban communities, afforded other comparisons; and a third experimental group of 444 subjects admitted to the study on the basis of group tests, and including for the most part students of high school age, permitted still others. Intermediate follow-up studies were made (prior to the 1955 study reported in Volume V) in 1927–28, 1940, and 1945.[13]

Since the academic world came to depend upon the investigations and inferences of Hollingworth and Terman, it is immediately apparent that fundamental differences which might have been revealed in the results of these two investigators, who were using the soundest procedures known and working with sufficient numbers to render their results worthy of some generalization, would have been significant and disturbing. With respect to the similarity of their findings, however, Hollingworth herself stated in an address before the National Committee on Secondary Education in 1939:

> I shall not dwell here upon the present knowledge of gifted children as organisms. Our findings in follow-up studies on tested children in New York City confirm in all particulars Professor Terman's researches on the Pacific coast. Since these several studies have been carried on in complete independence, one in the East, the other in the West, for nearly twenty years, we may certainly feel justified in the conclusion that we are arriving at truth about the mental and physical traits and development of highly intelligent persons, coming as we do to the same results.[14]

In like manner, had any of the minor, independent researches consistently resulted in radically different findings, a legitimate question might have been raised as to the validity of the larger studies. Catherine Cox Miles, however, in an encyclopedic survey of the history of research and study performed on gifted children, states that the minor investigations are generally confirmatory of the major ones. In no instance, apparently, were findings reported which were sufficiently contradictory to raise questions about the data accumulated by Terman.[15]

The Main Body of Facts

In the 1947 report, Terman and Oden offer a summary of their findings in the form of a "composite portrait" of the hypothetical gifted child.

First of all, we have seen that despite many exceptions to the rule the typical gifted child is the product of superior parentage—superior not only in cultural and educational background but apparently also in heredity. As a result of the combined influence of inheritance and environment, the typical member of our group is a slightly better physical specimen than the average child of the generality: the evidence obtained from anthropometric measurements, health histories, and medical examinations is unanimous and conclusive on this point.

Educationally, the average gifted child is accelerated in grade placement about 14 per cent of his age, but in mastery of the subject matter taught he is accelerated about 44 per cent of his age. The net result is that a majority of the members of our group, during the elementary school period, were kept at school tasks two or three full grades below the level of achievement they had already reached. In the earlier years, at least, the school appears to play only a minor role in the education of the gifted child, for among those of a given age there is almost no correlation between achievement test scores and length of school attendance. Notwithstanding this gross neglect of their educational needs, the vast majority of gifted children like school and prefer the hard subjects to the easy ones.

The interests of gifted children are many-sided and spontaneous. They learn to read easily, read more and better books than the average child, and largely educate themselves. At the same time, they make numerous collections, engage in all kinds of childhood activities, and acquire far more knowledge of plays and games than the average child of their years. Their preferences among plays, games, and amusements follow fairly closely the normal sex trends with respect to masculinity and femininity of interest, although gifted girls tend to be a little more masculine in their play life than average girls. Perhaps the most significant thing about the play preferences of gifted children is that they reveal a degree of interest maturity two or three

years beyond the age norm. . . . 90 per cent of the gifted subjects
score above the average of unselected children in intellectual interests and 84 per cent of them score above the average in social interests.
In activity interests the gifted differ little from unselected children of
the same age.

A battery of seven character tests showed gifted children above
average on every one. As compared with unselected children they are
less inclined to boast or to overstate their knowledge; they are more
trustworthy when under temptation to cheat; their reading preferences, character preferences, and social attitudes are more wholesome; and they score higher in emotional stability. On total score of
the character tests, the typical gifted child of nine years tests as high
as the average child of twelve.

Ratings on 25 traits by parents and teachers confirm the evidence
from tests and case histories. The proportion of gifted subjects rated
superior to unselected children of corresponding age was 89 per cent
for 4 intellectual traits, 82 per cent for 4 volitional traits, 67 per cent
for 3 emotional traits, 65 per cent for 2 aesthetic traits, 64 per cent
for 4 moral traits, 61 per cent for 2 physical traits, and 57 per cent for
5 social traits. Only on one trait—mechanical ingenuity—were they
rated as low as unselected children, and this verdict is contradicted
by the results of mechanical aptitude tests.

There are two facts which stand out clearly in the composite
portrait: (1) the deviation of the gifted subjects from the generality
is in the upward direction for nearly all traits. This is another way of
saying that desirable traits tend to be positively rather than negatively
correlated. There is no law of compensation whereby the intellectual
superiority of the gifted is sure to be offset by inferiorities along non-
intellectual lines. (2) The amount of upward deviation is not the same
in all traits. It is greatest in those aspects of behavior most closely
related to intelligence, such as originality, intellectual interests, and
ability to score high in achievement tests. In school achievement
the superiority is greatest in the abstract subjects and least in pen-
manship, spelling, and routine arithmetical computations. This un-
evenness is no greater in amount for gifted than for average children,
but it is different in direction; whereas the gifted are at their best in
the "thought" subjects, average children are at their best in subjects
that make least demands upon concept manipulation.

The reader is cautioned, however, to bear in mind the limitations
of composite portraiture. The method is useful in calling attention to
central tendencies and in providing a basis for generalization as a
guide in educational practice, but it would be unfortunate if this

emphasis should lead one to overlook the wide range of variability within the gifted group on every trait we have studied. Gifted children do not fall into a single pattern but into an infinite variety of patterns. One can find within the group individual examples of almost every type of personality defect, social maladjustment, behavior problem and physical frailty; the only difference is that among gifted children the incidence of these deviations is, in varying degrees, lower than in the general population. . . .[16]

The admirable array of data thus handily summarized allows the educator to infer reliably about the gifted child in general with respect to such educationally significant factors as family and socio-economic status, physique and health, personality and character, interests, and educational achievement. Fortunately, Terman's data provide us with a picture of harmonious integration among all major and significant traits found in the typical intellectually superior individual. Positive deviations in mental capacity are apparently attended as a rule by positive deviations in non-intellectual dimensions of personality and character as well. Truly, the sound mind tends to be integral with the sound body.

But what of the gifted children as they grow into adulthood? The question of adult status is obviously a significant one for education, lest the school program be planned for a group whose present promising characteristics are reduced to insignificance as the years pass.

Terman's longitudinal studies disclose data which enable us to generalize with respect to the gifted group's maintenance of biological superiority and characteristic attainment subsequent to the school years. The obtained measures and record of accomplishment of the group present a picture of general superiority—of similarly, though slightly reduced, deviant intellectual status; of occupational choices that lie in the upper levels on a standard scale; of higher earned income; and of superior achievements in the realms of art, science, and practical human endeavors. In socio-economic status, 86 per cent of the employed men in 1955 were in the top two classifications on the Minnesota Occupational Scale. The topmost classification on this scale, by way of indicating the positions of prominence and probable leadership attained by the gifted, includes lawyers, members of college or university faculties, engineers, physicians, chemists, authors, teachers below the college level, clergymen, artists or composers, and architects.

Classification II includes owners and executives in industry, officials and executives in banking and finance, and other groups.[17]

In the service rendered during World War II the group also attained positions of prominence and leadership. A summary of ranks in both the Army and the Navy is given in the 1947 report, the data representing only partial accomplishments since it was gathered prior to the end of active service by some of the group:

Approximately one-half (49.5 per cent) of the men in the Army entered as privates, and 46.1 per cent entered as commissioned officers. Seven men (3.4 per cent) entered as cadets or officer candidates, and 2 (1.0 per cent) as noncommissioned officers. The ranks in the Army at time of report (chiefly late 1945), or at time of discharge for those who had left the service previous to reporting, were as follows: privates or privates first class, 6.9 per cent; noncommissioned officers, 22.1 per cent; officer candidates, 1.0 per cent; and commissioned officers, 70.0 per cent.

Of men in the Navy, 13.8 per cent entered as seamen, 19.8 per cent with a petty officer rating, 3.4 per cent as cadets, and 62.9 per cent as commissioned officers. Their ranks in late 1945, or at the time of their leaving the service if before reporting, were as follows: seamen, 3.4 per cent; petty officer rating, 21.6 per cent; commissioned officers, 75.0 per cent.

The officer ranks in the Army ranged from second lieutenant to brigadier general, and in the Navy from ensign to captain. Above the rank of lieutenant in the Army were 41 captains, 33 majors, 23 lieutenant colonels, 2 colonels, and one brigadier general. Above the rank of lieutenant (junior grade) in the Navy were 40 lieutenants, 7 lieutenant commanders, 4 commanders, and one captain. The three men in the Marine Corps included one private first class and 2 first lieutenants.[18]

And of *non-military service in the interest of the war effort* this description is given:

Some took jobs as skilled workers in war plants, others were in significant scientific or technical work, and a sizeable number worked in the field of personnel, labor relations, wage standards, price control, *et cetera*. The gifted men were well represented in the activities of the Office of Scientific Research and Development, the Office of War Information, the Office of Price Administration, the State Department, the Labor Department, and various other agencies of the government.[19]

These facts clearly denote the utility of high intelligence in adjusting to the special demands of an unaccustomed war regimen.

The gifted individual's elevated status as an adult is further corroborated by brief descriptions of *individual contributions of members of the group* while yet in their young adulthood. From a large number of such sketches, the following are selected to illustrate the types of accomplishments that are obscured in the statistics of occupational brackets and other measures of socially significant achievement:

> A physicist who is extremely gifted in administration as well as in science is director of one of the great laboratories devoted to the applications of atomic energy.
>
> During the last year of the war, a historian served as director of a large project for the Office of Strategic Services, in which position he directed the work of more than a hundred social scientists engaged in research on the cultural, economic, political, and social conditions of the people in one of our enemy countries. He is now assistant director of a great foundation.
>
> A professor of physiology was co-director, during the war, of what was perhaps the most important investigation that has ever been made of the physiological, biochemical, and psychological effects of prolonged semistarvation. The report of this research will run to several volumes.
>
> A professor in one of the applied physical sciences served throughout the war as director of a government research laboratory which employed hundreds of scientists and technicians, spent millions of dollars, and created devices that so reduced the efficiency of enemy radar as definitely to shorten the war. This man has received two of the highest honors that can come to a scientist; the presidency of his national scientific society, and membership in the National Academy of Sciences.
>
> A professor of pharmacology in a medical school has published more than a hundred research contributions before the age of thirty-five and is the executive head of his department.
>
> Two of our men have won national recognition as writers of fiction. One of these has published seven detective novels. The other, a graduate in engineering, has published dozens of articles and short stories based upon technological themes, three novels—one of which has been compared favorably with the best of its *genre*—and a book on

inventions. His *magnum opus* to date, a scholarly book on witchcraft and magic, has just been completed.

One of our men is a relatively young motion-picture director who is rapidly becoming known as among the most talented in the country.

Several of our women have taken a doctorate in science and have done creditable research. One is a metallurgist who holds a very responsible position in an industrial firm. One is a bacteriologist who holds the rank of assistant professor in a leading medical school. . . .[20]

When the magnitude of such contributions is considered, and it is recalled that the contributors are among only one thousand of the intellectually superior persons as identified at ten and eleven years of age, of one state in the United States, the question of devising an educational scheme commensurate in design with the extreme capacities thus represented must be accepted as of tremendous social consequence. These accomplishments, it should be noted, took place at a time when educational efforts to meet the needs of such individuals were not on the whole extraordinary. The promise of special education for increasing such spontaneous human achievements will be discussed later.

Contrary Instances

We have thus far discussed the mental and behavioral characteristics of the intellectually superior individual from the positive side alone. The sensitive observer may from his own experiences have reflected here and there upon instances of people with brilliant minds who did not present this fortunate array of related personality characteristics. The attempt here has been to round out a description of the individual of high intelligence in ideal developmental and situational circumstances. There are, of course, persons of superior biological endowment for whom the experiences bearing upon their development have served not to polish these native endowments, as with a good home and school, but rather to tarnish them. It is in the nature of scientific generalization that the picture of an entire class be drawn from the facts which are true for the larger and more representative segments of the class and that exceptions be noted as aberrations of the "natural" state manifested in the majority instance. It seems entirely plausible that when the gifted individual displays aberrant personality traits, or fails to achieve in a manner commensurate with his potential for achievement, the causes lie in his past or present environment.

Terman's researches, once more, provide us with a fair survey of the facts concerning the nature and frequency of instances which vary from the expected pattern of behavior in the intellectually superior individual. His "C" group, the lowest 20 per cent in terms of their use through adult achievement of their superior intellectual ability, provides an interesting study of gifted individuals who at the time of the 1945 follow-up had not fulfilled the brightest promise of their youth. The group, numbering 150, could not be termed failures in an absolute sense, since it included twenty-five who were in the professional, semi-professional, and managerial occupations. Only a half dozen had been chronically unemployed, but many more were in occupations which make little demands upon general intelligence. The judges who studied the group in an attempt to distinguish the successful from the unsuccessful used as the primary criterion "the extent to which a subject had made use of his superior intellectual ability." Some of the group were in humble occupations by choice (outdoor work, sales work, civil service); many of them "were well adjusted and contented." Often the difference between a "C" and an "A" is little more than a difference in level of aspiration. Nonetheless, this group stands as evidence that not all who possess superiority use it under the conditions governing the subjects of this study.

As compared to the "A" group, which comprised the top 20 per cent with respect to full use of their superior characteristics, fewer of the "C's" were graduated from college or made honors. Only 9 per cent of the "C's" were in the professions, as compared with 70 per cent of the "A's". The earned income of the "A's" was more than two and a half times that of "C's." The two groups were approximately equal in childhood intelligence, but their family backgrounds differed decidedly. Even in childhood, teachers' and parents' ratings had revealed significant differences in personality, all ratings for the "C" group being lower except that for health. "Evidence of social maladjustment in the "C" group increased steadily from 1922 to 1940." Leadership was more often displayed by the "A" group. As measured by the Strong Test of Occupational Interests, 23 per cent of the "C's" but only 5 per cent of the "A's" earned a rating below B for the occupation in which they were engaged. On self-ratings and ratings by wives and parents, the "A's" were far higher than the "C's" in perseverance, self-confidence, and integration toward goals; and in appearance, attractiveness, alertness, poise, attentiveness, curiosity, originality, and, to a somewhat lesser degree, in speech and in friendliness. "Everything considered, there is nothing in which the "A" and "C" groups present a greater contrast than in drive to achieve and in all-round social adjustment."[21]

The "C" group shows that qualities other than intellectual capacity are essential to success as conceived at present. Mere possession of superior intellect does not assure that it will be used to its fullest extent. Very happy features of the current movement for special education of the gifted are the clear recognition that youngsters presently "underachieving" are nonetheless still *gifted* and direct attacks upon the causes of these defects in motivation and opportunity.

Historical Men of Genius

The contemporary picture of gifted individuals need not stand alone. One of the works projected early in the series of *Genetic Studies* examines the behavioral characteristics of famous men and women of past years. Through an ingenious device called "historiometry," Catherine Morris Cox classifies according to IQ, 301 eminent men and women living between 1450 and 1840. The IQ has been estimated on the basis of reported childhood accomplishments. Selected from the total, the following names fall within the categories of intelligence measures frequently included in current treatises on education for the gifted. This list, it will be recognized, is the source of the statement cited from Ernest Ligon on the frontispiece of the present work.

ESTIMATED INTELLIGENCE OF HISTORICAL MEN AND WOMEN OF GENIUS

IQ 120–130

John Adams, Henry Fielding, William Harvey, Joseph Haydn, Ben Jonson, Lavoisier, James Madison, Rossini, Joseph Addison, Johann Sebastian Bach, John Dryden, Helvetius, Abraham Lincoln, Linnaeus, John Locke, Horatio Nelson, Joshua Reynolds, Jonathan Swift, George Washington.

IQ 130–140

Honore de Balzac, Robert Burns, Heinrich Heine, Christian Huygens, Washington Irving, Moliere, Sir Isaac Newton, Sir Walter Raleigh, Jean Jacques Rousseau, G. Savonarola, Benedict Spinoza, Beethoven, Edmund Burke, John Calvin, Charles Darwin, Erasmus, Alexander Hamilton, Immanuel Kant, G. Lessing, G. Mazzini, Sir Thomas More, Napoleon Bonaparte, William Penn, Racine, Adam Smith, Edmund Spenser, William M. Thackeray, Leonardo da Vinci, Wagner, von Weber, John Wesley.

IQ 140–150

Louis Agassiz, Robert Boyle, E. G. Bulwer-Lytton, Thomas Carlyle, Alexander Dumas (Pere), William Hamilton, Johann Kepler, Montaigne, Tom Moore, William Pitt (1708–1778), F. Schiller, William H. Seward, James Watt, U. Zwingli, Francis Bacon, William E. Channing, G. J. Danton, Charles Dickens, B. Disraeli, R. W. Emerson, J. G. Fichte, B. Franklin, Galileo, Edward Gibbon, Handel, von Humboldt, Thomas Jefferson, Laplace, Michelangelo, John Milton, Daniel Webster.

IQ 150–160

George Berkeley, Lord Byron, L. N. M. Carnot, de Chateaubriand, Auguste Comte, Descartes, Hegel, Hugo, Longfellow, Mendelssohn, Mozart, Ernest Renan, George Sand, Walter Scott, William Wordsworth, de Condorcet, David Hume, Samuel Johnson, Madam de Staël-Holstein, Alfred Tennyson, F. A. Wolf.

IQ 160–170

Phillip Melanchthon, de Musset, William Pitt (1759–1806), Alexander Pope, John Q. Adams, Thomas Wolsey.

IQ 170–180

Thomas Chatterton, Voltaire, Samuel Coleridge, Albrecht von Haller, F. Schelling.

IQ 180–190

Jeremy Bentham, T. B. Macaulay, Blaise Pascal, Johann W. Goethe, Hugo Grotius, Leibnitz.

IQ 190–200

John Stuart Mill[22]

Concerning the accuracy of childhood promise in foreshadowing the eminence achieved by these men, Cox writes:

Youths who achieve eminence are distinguished in childhood by behavior which indicates an unusually high IQ. . . . . Accounts of the early years of our subjects are full of examples of early mental maturity. In their reported interests, in their school standing and progress, and in their early production and achievement, the members of the group were, in general, phenomenal. Later achievement was foreshadowed in youthful behavior, and it is probable that early manifestations of superior intelligence would have been found in every case had the records of all been faithfully kept.

The child is father of the man: the gifted youth will be the leader of the future. . . . Heredity sets limits, but within these limits the adequate training of the most gifted—and so also of their less distinguished fellows—may raise them to the designed stature of men unmarred by the defects of insufficient experience, and thus realize in each one the complete development of inborn worth.[23]

These remarks on the potentiality of the environment in helping to fulfill the promise of youth are an invitation to the designing of school experiences commensurate with the capacities and the needs of children who will someday contribute outstandingly to the progress of the race.

Summary of Positive Intellectual Characteristics

Individuals occupying the top levels of the intelligence scale will as a group, despite contrary instances, manifest broad clusters of educationally significant traits. We close this section with a summary of these traits gathered at large from the literature on gifted children. In the exposition of educational principles outlined in subsequent parts of this work, continual reference will be made to these mental and behavioral qualities. Teachers will recognize in these four groups of mental and behavioral processes the basic stuff which allows, and makes mandatory, an educational regimen distinctively different from that possible for the generality of persons.

MENTAL CHARACTERISTICS OF HIGHLY INTELLIGENT PERSONS

Learning Capacity

Accurate perception of social and natural situations, with insight into part-whole relationships. Independent, rapid, efficient learning of fact and principle. Fast, meaningful reading, with superior retention and recall; advanced reading ability.

Power of Thought

Ready grasp of principles underlying things as they are; sensitivity to inferences in fact, consequences of propositions, and applications of ideas.

Spontaneous elevation of immediate observations to higher planes of abstraction; imagination; meaningful association of ideas; forceful reasoning; original interpretations and conclusions; creative ideas.

Discriminatory power, quick detection of similarities and differences among things and ideas; able in analysis, synthesis, and organization of elements; critical of situations, self, and other people.

Intellectual Drive

Mental endurance; tenacity of purpose; stubbornness, sometimes contrarily expressed as reluctance to do as directed; capacity for follow-through with extensive, but meaningful plans.

Curiosity about things and ideas; intrinsic interest in the challenging and difficult; versatile and vital interests; varied, numerous, and penetrating inquiries, boredom with unnecessary routine and sameness.

Breadth and Depth of Knowledge

Intensive, detailed understanding of matters of interest, not necessarily related to amount of schooling.

Breadth of knowledge and wealth of general information characterized often by truly remarkable peak areas of aptitude and understanding.

Practical intelligence must be brought to bear upon the potential in educational experience to bring to flower the capacities of contemporary youth for advancing human culture in a manner similar to that accomplished by famous men and women in past years. We shall discuss the realities of this "promise" subsequently, as an educational perspective is developed. At present, it is sufficient to suggest that the rigorous application of imagination, and of knowledge of those behavioral sciences most pertinent to educational and developmental processes, to the planning and implementation of an increasingly excellent educational program will improve significantly upon the yield presently gained through formal schooling. Certain (genuine) feats of intellect by persons in our own times have been paraded across the living rooms of America in recent years through the media of radio and television. Teachers are beginning to realize a potential for learning in some of their pupils which extends far beyond the requirements of the standard curriculum in school. The "flesh-and-blood" manifestation of significantly superior human abilities all around us is enough to suggest that the proper shaping of educational experiences can lead to increased attainments beyond those directly provided for by curricula designed, or developed by accident and tradition, for the generality. We must now proceed to an examination of certain perspectives upon an educational process specifically pointed toward the needs of the gifted.

chapter two | *THE NATURE AND SIGNIFICANCE OF EDUCATION FOR THE GIFTED*

Thus far the intellectually superior individual has been characterized with no attempt having been made to explain why this basis was selected from which to review the educative process rather than the position that the school should attempt to identify all sorts of talents and to develop these specific abilities through its various curricular offerings. The position taken on this point must be defended in detail since it is of critical importance as a basis for the ensuing educational theory.

GENERAL INTELLECTUAL SUPERIORITY AS A BASIS FOR EDUCATIONAL PROGRAMMING

At first glance, a conception of differential education based upon general intellect might appear to be quite narrow. Actually this is not the case. There are lines of logic and of empirical fact which establish general intellect as far and away the most justifiable quality upon which to base educational practice. The broad inclusion of specific aptitudes, on the other hand, is difficult to justify on the grounds either of psychological conception and instrumentation (trait definition and measurement) or of the educational process through which such loosely

28

identified traits are supposedly developed. Claims should be more than optimistic verbalisms and should be supported by more than simply well-intentioned efforts. Particulars of both psychological science and educational process must implement and validate all purported objectives. Difficulties in these respects that are inherent in the broader claims so frequently made today will be pursued in an attempt to suggest that general intellect is still the fairest basis for differential general education.

First, the relationships between the nature of general intelligence and the nature of specific aptitude must be examined in order to determine whether there are distinctive properties in aptitudes, presently known and operable in the behavior of children, such that a theory of education developed around general intelligence alone fails to discharge the public responsibility. This phase of the argument will be based on psychological theory. *Second*, the argument in terms of educational theory will examine phases of the educational process as organized in American culture and make suggestions toward the nature of general education as distinct from special training. These two levels of argument will comprise the brief that areas of specific aptitude, apart from general intelligence, can at the moment be neither identified nor developed.

Psychological Theory: General Intelligence and Specific Aptitudes

Is there justification in psychological theory for the claim that specific aptitudes can and should become the basis for academic programs in the American school—i.e., do the processes involved in the behavioral expression or manifestation of specific aptitudes differ from those expressing general intellect? Or, again, is there substance to such claims at the level of instrumentation—i.e., do psychological tests exist which enable us to appraise these differences with sufficient precision that pupil identification procedures for specific aptitudes become distinguishable from those used to identify general intellectual superiority?

The continuing search for more adequate conceptions of the nature of intelligence has resulted thus far in a closer rapprochement between definitions of intelligence and aptitude. The search for a basic catalogue of specific mental properties, "primary mental abilities," has been pursued most profitably through statistical treatments which collect around central axes all items in tests which appear to accomplish an identical purpose; succeeding analyses continue to the point at which all significant clusters of behavior evoked by known intelligence test items are formulated. Such studies of the measurement of mental qualities permit standard texts on educational measurements to refer to "aptitude" as "specific intelligence." To think of general intelligence as a sum of all specific capacities and, conversely, of aptitudes as detailed measures of specific aspects of this intelligence is about as far as educational practice can go with what is firmly known in psychology today.

The more recently developed intelligence tests include items which educe behavior in the major categories of these specific testable traits. Factors variously designated tap verbal and ideational processes and also processes involving quantitative, configurational, and spatial realities, two broad categories found to subsume most of the traits more narrowly defined. Hence, a general intelligence test that labels its various subordinate dimensions and a "battery" of aptitude tests do essentially the same thing; they both evoke practically all reliably known and significant behaviors, both general and specific. That their sub-categories are labeled variously is more a tribute to deficient terminology in the field of psychology than it is to differences, de facto, in behavioral qualities.

Further, the search for behavioral processes exclusively pertinent to given single areas of vocational application, or even to basic modes of mind used in inquiry after knowledge, has been largely unrewarding to date. General intellectual adequacy (efficiency, power) appears to pertain very much alike to all of the diverse pursuits of engineering, doctoring, legalizing, or theologizing. Again, high intelligence would seem to be a prerequisite for both, but not a distinguishing factor between, the able and productive natural scientist and the able and productive philosopher. In these facts lie the breakdown of numerous claims that certain school procedures identify and pertain more to the specific talent of an individual than to his general intelligence.

We choose two illustrations of this point.[24] Paul F. Brandwein's work with young people in the natural science program of Forest Hills High School in New York City was generally conceded to be one of the more admirable attempts to develop specific abilities in the contemporary movement of education for the gifted. Nonetheless, the very traits indicated as critical to the selection of pupils for this program of education in natural science could with equal validity be used in the selection of promising students for history, sociology, or linguistics, if personal interests ran in any of these veins. Brandwein states, for example:

> Hence, the base level of the Genetic Factor was set operationally at 135 IQ, reading score of fifteenth year plus (based on the ninth year), an arithmetic score of twelfth year plus, and a scholastic average at the ninth year of 90 percent or above.[25]

That these criteria pertain to productivity in the natural sciences cannot be denied. It can be denied, however, that they pertain exclusively to such productivity (with the possible but not necessary exception of mathematics) and are distinguishable from traits which pertain to the excellent pursuit of disciplines other than the natural sciences. The same criticism applies to other interesting new designations used by Brandwein for familiar psychological traits, such as *predisposing factor*, *persistence*, and *questing*.

Social leadership as a specific trait displays, if anything, even further difficulties at the level of definition. The following citations from a chapter on this topic by Robert F. DeHaan indicate the status of the search for specific identifying characteristics:

> . . . there is no single physical-factor group of factors which differentiates leaders from nonleaders.

> Intelligence is another trait which is often supposedly associated with leadership. . . .

> Self-confidence is another attribute which is often thought to be associated with leadership. Social ability, will, initiative, persistence, ambition, dominance, surgency also appear to be related to leadership. . . .

> It is clear then that leadership is not a unitary trait or ability but, rather, that it is made up of personal abilities and traits (which in some way make a person prominent and, thereby, eligible for the position as head of a group) plus consistent performance as a socioemotional specialist and a task specialist.

> Developing the socioemotional aspect of leadership behavior often comes closer to being psychotherapy than education proper. The person who is most sensitive to the needs and feelings of others, who can give and receive affection, release tension, show agreement in a

group and facilitate a feeling of group solidarity can probably best perform this aspect of leadership behavior.[26]

This heterogeneous assemblage of popular conceptions (*will, prominence, social ability*) and loosely suggestive psychological conceptions (*show agreement in a group, facilitate a feeling of group solidarity*) could also be considered useful to the medical doctor in his bedside manner with patients, to the school teacher in his relationships with pupils in the classroom, and, possibly above all, to mothers in the general practice of motherhood. Thus, where a distinctive and exclusive trait or trait cluster still remains to be identified, it is illusory to claim that education for such traits is possible.

Again, from a somewhat different point of view, psychological theory supports a reasonably close relationship between general intelligence of a high order and extraordinary aptitude in specific areas. High general intelligence involves perceptual efficiency, adequacy in evolving and manipulating higher syntheses of ideas, and more complex and subtle inferences based upon such complex syntheses. Higher mental processes of this nature are the cognitive essence of creative acts in whatever field they might occur. Students of the problem of creativity have noted the all-round brilliance of such specifically creative individuals as Mozart, Newton, Cellini, and Rembrandt. The generalization is effectively stated by Terman:

> Granting that both interest patterns and special aptitudes play important roles in the making of a gifted scientist, mathematician, mechanic, artist, poet, or musical composer, I am convinced that to achieve greatly in almost any field, the special talents have to be backed up by a lot of Spearman's *g*, by which is meant the kind of general intelligence that requires ability to form many sharply defined concepts, to manipulate them, and to perceive subtle relationships between them; in other words, the ability to engage in abstract thinking.[27]

It may be noted further that the accomplishments of historical men of genius in areas other than those of singular merit are often such as to justify the designation of "genius" even in the tangential area of interest (e.g., Thomas Jefferson). This fact suggests once more the tendency toward non-specificity of truly great human abilities.[28]

Contesting the propriety of educational programs for particular genius, McClelland and his colleagues state:

> But the whole orientation of such an approach is wrong. It places far more emphasis on talent potential as a fixed attribute of a few people than we have any reason to suppose is true. Rather, talent potential may be fairly widespread, a characteristic which can be transformed into actually talented performance of various sorts by the right kinds of education. If so, the emphasis should shift from identifying talent potential to *studying the process by which talent becomes actual*, by which it develops. Such a focus requires above all a knowledge of theory—an understanding of what we are measuring, how it develops under different circumstances, and how it is related to the ultimate criteria of talented performance which we want to predict. Until we achieve these goals, our ignorance of the process by which talented performance develops will remain an outstanding gap in current talent research.[29]

This possibility that specific aptitudes are largely dependent upon the nature of the individual's experience adds a new dimension to the present claim against the soundness of programs purporting to deal with aptitudes already manifest at given age levels. It is doubtful that sufficient evidence exists to support as fact the possibility suggested by these investigators; but the mere *possibility* of the truth of the proposition indicates an order of primacy in scientific inquiry and in social programming. The question whether aptitudes are biologically inherent for the most part—psychological realities that must be respected as they are—or can be originated and developed within generally able individuals through particular experiences must be resolved as a necessary first step, and a fascinating one indeed, before practical endeavors are systematized toward training aptitudes as they presently tend to emerge. The reversal of this order suggests the idea developed by Henry E. Garrett[30] that specifically designated aptitude tests which overlap seriously with one another establish through their titles "traits by fiat." And possibly even closer to the McClelland group's meaning is Wendell Johnson's familiar concept that diagnosis sometimes occurs before the fact and contributes *ipso facto* toward the actualization of the hitherto non-existent quality. The lack of moral circumspection lies in the degree, perhaps not great, to which fixation in an arbitrarily chosen behavioral dimension can occur through specific experience, as distinct from biological inheritance. What sanction can be found for efforts directed toward increasing the number of engineers over that of poets?

The Educative Process and Aptitude Training

To summarize the argument thus far, the behavioral sciences are not developed to the extent that specific aptitudes can be adequately defined, identified, and measured; therefore, prescriptions for the cultivation of specific aptitudes cannot be devised.

The second phase of the argument against claims that the common school can and should accomplish the training of artists in art and musicians in music is grounded in *educational* theory, as distinct from *psychological*. We must first consider at reasonable length the nature of "general" education, as distinct from "special" education.[31] Educational theory, unless the concept is otherwise qualified (i.e., medical education, teacher education, engineering education, etc.) is developed around the notion of what experiences are constructive for people *in general*, in the conduct of *general affairs*, i.e., common understandings essential to satisfying and constructive participation in the social institutions of their time.

From the beginning of the graded sequence in the American school to the end of the junior high school, as is well known, essentially all formal school experiences are required. At these levels in the child's development, curricular structure prohibits too early specialization, in favor of the progressive development of the child on commonly needed behavioral fronts. The concern for general education continues into the college years; there the issue of when to begin specialization, and in what proportions it should be introduced, becomes so critical that entire institutions emerge on one side or another. Thus the "liberal arts" college exists, as distinct from the "university." In the latter institution there is a typical pattern of approximately half general studies (the first two years) and half specialization (the major and related fields of study) leading toward or accomplishing vocational preparation.

The first point in the argument against the school's assumption of too broad responsibilities is based on a logical interpretation implicit in the concepts involved. *General education involves and is grounded in those*

experiences serviceable in educating and training common higher mental processes
such as are tapped by the general intelligence test, as distinct from the education
and training of idiosyncratic mental processes, as yet undefined and unmeasured,
but hypothetically proposed as existent and discretely operable. The instructional program for general education should basically engage common
intellectual potentials, such as reasoning, judgment, abstraction, and
understanding per se, rather than particular children's aural or visual
sensitivity which contributes to specific aptitude for tonal or graphic
art.

General education enhances the understanding of nature, and of man
and his institutions and ideas, for the sake of what might be termed
in an earlier sense "philosophical" purposes. What things are real?
What things are good? What things work, and why? This cultivation
of understanding contributes pervasively to man's functioning as a
citizen, a member of a family, and a friend or foe of given causes. It
may contribute, and should, to the manner in which a person perceives
his vocation and the use which he makes of his particular talents. But
neither the purposes, nor the processes, nor the products of the vocational training of the artistically talented in art are the same as those
of general education; and the excellent conservatory training of the
talents (identified as best possible) of the musician differs from excellence in the general education of the musically talented person. It is
the wholeness of the talented engineer or architect for which the common school is properly responsible, the education and elaboration of
his pervasive modes of thought and behavior, rather than the cultivation of idiosyncratic particulars, no matter how significant these may
be personally and socially. Miseducation does not occur because vocational training must begin at some point in youth but because general
education *unnecessarily* drops out of primary focus.

Closely related to this point is the problem of the maturation of the
individual within a social context. Before the individual is sufficiently
mature socially and biologically for direct accomplishments within the
area of his particular genius, experiences catering to the special aptitude are different from the pointed, specialized training leading toward
adult competencies. Such experiences contribute toward the *in*direct
nourishment of the specific interests, provide outlets for intrinsic needs,
and allow for the maturation of the personality in accordance with
its own dynamics. But the *deliberate educative process* should not conduce
directly toward the precocious development of special abilities out of

context with concomitant maturational elements or opportunities within the culture. The ten-year-old "astro-physicist" is scarcely yet a responsible, productive figure in the science or technology of outer space. It is plausible conjecture that educational experiences beyond his field of special competency (i.e., in the present illustration, social ethics, logic, semantics, philosophy of science, exceptional pursuits in mathematics, etc.) will serve him better in ultimate accomplishments toward human welfare than would immediate and continuing pressure in the direction of the specific competency.

It may be pertinent to examine several practical features of the school as it has developed in American society. The *structure of the curriculum* that the usual school offers is appropriately consistent with what we term general education. The curriculum samples from the universe of knowledge already attained through various modes of inquiry. It explores into this cumulative heritage but, as can be readily observed, does not attempt to develop the process skills internal to the different branches of knowledge. The general education curriculum, under almost any of the diverse conceptions that have been attached to it, uses knowledge as a means toward other ends, not as a means toward further knowledge in the same vein. The development of future historians through studies in historiography or the development of medical practitioners through laboratory skills both proceed under a rationale that sets them apart from general education for the citizen.[32] Studies in the content of history, however, or in personal health, both belong to general education for all.

School subjects must be handled by school teachers. In the pattern of training for the American school, the prospective teacher pursues some 125 to 140 semester hours of studies all told, approximately 15 to 18 hours each in an eight-semester sequence. Of these studies, approximately 60 hours will be devoted to general or liberal education. In the remaining 60 to 70 hours, the student undertakes such specialization as the institution provides for and pursues elective courses that accomplish for him various purposes. The courses designed to acquaint prospective teachers with the heritage of the school in American society are known as "professional education," and their pursuit typically occupies some 20 to 30 semester hours of the total in a four-year program.

Now in this preparation, concerned as it is with general education and an introduction to the problems of education in a democratic society, there is little experience which brings the prospective teacher insights concerning special aptitudes and their guided development. On the other hand, the claim is more reasonable that such general courses as educational psychology, curriculum theory, and instructional methods and materials, as well as subject matter preparation, equip the teacher with comprehensive, though elementary, understandings of the nature of mind as a whole and its development through experience. These mental processes pervade all the academic behavior of the child and therefore involve all the teachers in his general curriculum, i.e., in courses in language arts, social studies, mathematics, and the natural sciences. The elevation of general experience for the gifted child is possible and practicable in this respect. In a discussion of "the educational problem," McClelland and his colleagues state:

> Suppose we could locate that sleepy boy in the back row, the potential poet; what would we do for him? Would we offer him a liberal scholarship to one of our better private schools? Would we "enrich" his curriculum with special readings in poetry, or in the Greek classics? Or would we perhaps excuse him from school requirements altogether on the ground that he would do better as a self-educated man? Or would we supply him with a vocational counselor who would help him find his real niche in life? These are not silly questions. The plain fact of the matter is that we do not know what we would do; we do not know enough about what goes into the making of a poet. We may know somewhat more about what goes into the making of a scientist or a professor (based on IQ tests and academic training); but we still know far too little to be confident about how to develop talented performance out of talent potential.[33]

This phase of the argument suggests, then, that general education properly bears upon the general qualities of mind possessed by the individual and only *indirectly* upon his specific talent per se. Premature efforts to develop these talents directly are misplaced. The individual's need for total maturation and society's limited tolerance for individual differences suggest the undesirability of contributing to the prodigiousness of children. And it is highly questionable whether the ultimate gains from present educational endeavors bearing upon particular genius add very much to those delicate, unknown processes of creative genius itself. Certainly experimental evidence is lacking that attempts at special education for musical talent in the common school have increased the number of significant artists in this field.

Conclusion of the Argument and Some Positive Considerations

Those school systems which claim to develop educational programs around specific aptitudes do not do so in fact. The reasons for their failure, even in the face of vigorous and earnest endeavors, are evident in psychological theory and in the nature of the educative process. If it is impossible to establish usable definitions for specific traits, isolating each particular quality from the matrix of the total personality so that operable educative processes can be directed exactly toward it, and if neither the structure of the educational curriculum nor the preparation of school teachers is or can be geared realistically toward the implementation of such desirable intentions, then the enterprise is impossible of execution. We have noted further the theoretical inconsistency of the common school's attempting to accomplish the specific artistic training of a Pablo Casals, a Norman Rockwell, or a Frank Lloyd Wright, or the scientific genius of a Robert Oppenheimer or a Norbert Wiener, rather than the excellent general education of such persons.

The foregoing argument is not intended to suggest the abrogation of public responsibility for the priceless gift of genius. There are good and valid means through which the school program can recognize and relate to the specific aptitudes of pupils as the behavioral sciences progress toward more adequate conceptualization and instrumentation. By way of ending this section on a positive note, certain of these methods will now be discussed.

First, it should be recognized that general education for the gifted also serves to enhance their specific talents. Educational literature is replete with injunctions against the too narrow education of scientists and technicians. What is usually proposed as essential to the more complete development of specialists is a grounding in exactly the type of general education which is recommended here and which will be treated further at a later point. Specifically, improved general education is appropriate in that it tends to support the judgmental and inferential properties of behavior in the context of which the specific talent becomes manifest.

Secondly, general education—the education of the whole person— also involves the development of non-intellective dimensions of personality. It is well known that many artists (Callas, Wright), statesmen

(Strauss, Stassen), and scientists (Oppenheimer, Rickover) have suf-
fered unnecessary difficulties in human relations, difficulties which have
tended to hinder the more fruitful pursuits of their particular abilities.
It is a better natural scientist who can perceive the function of science
in culture and a better statesman who can reckon effectively with
motives and skills less idealistically directed than his own. Therefore,
in an indirect manner, through the education of the person with talent
as distinct from the development of the talents per se, the general
education curriculum does contribute to the nurture of great human
abilities.

At the same time, this supportive function can operate in a total
school program that allows for and expects the relatively untrammeled
pursuit of particular interests by way of elective experiences and opportunities for expression. The elective system accommodates individual interests by permitting some choice of courses among a variety
of specialized arts and sciences. It allows the child driven intrinsically
toward a particular area of achievement to follow his spontaneous
bent in that direction. This type of "natural" pursuit of a particular
interest, while the dominant influence is toward general experience,
might well be just enough to afford the specific talent an opportunity
to ripen at its best rate, governed more by biological determination
than by administrative guesswork. This much individualization of the
prescribed curriculum is wholesome on all known grounds.

And last by way of positive considerations, it is suggested that the
educational program serves both the child and society by the mere
process of calling attention to significant exceptional personal characteristics. The school is not necessarily the only social agency that
can contribute to the development of human potential. Society has not
kept pace with the progress of science in devising institutional arrangements which will capitalize upon human genius—financial awards,
temporary and intermittent residential communities of developing
prodigies, and apprenticeships of the potentially able to those already
demonstrably able in the various frontiers of culture. The school can
arrange for the systematic search for talent and call its discoveries to
the attention of children, parents, and the community leadership
(governmental bodies and private benevolent enterprises). Ordinary
guidance procedures allow for this type of home-school-community
co-operation, and parents and community could be urged even more

vigorously to bring supplementary efforts and facilities to bear upon the talented child's promising capacity at appropriate points in his total development.

Among practices specifically involving community efforts to discover and train artistic talent, a continuing program in the New York area approximates closely the type of adjunct service to the educational program of the school which the present work suggests. The ninth annual search for musical talent in the schools, sponsored by the *New York Times* and radio station WQXR, is described in a news account:

> This year young music students will be judged by a panel consisting of Rudolf Serkin and Van Cliburn, pianists; Leonard Rose, 'cellist; Isaac Stern, violinist, and Abram Chasins, music director of WQXR.
>
> As in the past the project is open to gifted young pianists, violinists and 'cellists in the ninth through the twelfth grades who attend public, parochial and private schools in metropolitan New York and neighboring states.
>
> All successful applicants will, after a preliminary screening, be heard by the panel, and the most talented will have the opportunity to make radio and concert appearances. Previous participants in the Musical Talent in Our Schools series have appeared with the youth concerts of the New York Philharmonic and the Little Orchestra Society.[34]

The use of accomplished artists in the identifying process, the provisions for non-school training and experience, and the directing of the efforts to age levels beyond the elementary school where some degree of specialization would properly begin are all commendable features of this enterprise.

In sum, the theory proposed here sanctions full use of reliable knowledge of psychological variables and developmental processes. To the extent that elective offerings in the common school program allow for exploration of the various arts and sciences as a means toward greater understanding, or toward the incidental satisfaction of intrinsic interests, specific courses and activities are justified; to the extent that the graded school curriculum is stretched toward attempts to accomplish the specialized functions of conservatories and graduate schools, the efforts are not justifiable and are not wise.[35]

THE SOCIAL SIGNIFICANCE OF SPECIAL EDUCATION FOR THE GIFTED

A departure from routine and traditional processes requires imagination and a certain willingness to traffic in the ideal and the potential, as opposed to the present reality. Since this work proposes such a departure, imaginative statements concerning the possible effects of improved education for the gifted are appropriate. The possible effects of deliberate efforts to devise suitable educational experiences for such persons are far-reaching indeed, and the social significance of the enterprise is apparent from several points of view.

Historically, American educational practice has first recognized the special needs of deviant groups that were handicapped in various ways. The concentration upon a more adequate program of training for the handicapped is itself a profitable enterprise from the social point of view. The gain in bringing a dependent child to the point of self-sufficiency in an economic sense, or in a psychological, is immeasurably significant to the individual personally. To the society which supports and nourishes him the investment in educational procedures yields a return close to the amount of the investment itself, somewhat more or somewhat less. In the democratic ideology, the personal elevation itself would be worth disproportionate social investment; the additional yield of economic and personal sufficiency adds appreciably to the worth of the undertaking.

Where the exceptionally able are concerned, simple reflection upon the social value of past and continuing contributions in all branches of science and art achieved by men and women of genius suggests immediately a practical value more in the proportion of one thousand-to-one, or ten, or even a hundred thousand-to-one, rather than the more nearly one-to-one return in the education of the handicapped. In proper context shortly, the question will be raised "What could the world afford to pay for the cure of cancer ten years earlier than it will eventuate in the natural course of events?" This particular question suggests the advantage in general of deliberate, radical, and imaginative attempts to reconstruct the educational program for young people who show present signs of great human abilities.

Ligon's practical adaptation of Catherine Cox's studies of historical men of genius (frontispiece) suggests the presence in schools throughout

America today of boys and girls who possess intellectual abilities similar to those of men like Copernicus, Luther, and Jefferson. Such an idea is staggering. And yet, in the absence of reason for believing that the present childhood generation is more devoid of potential for eminence than past generations have been, it can scarcely be denied that youth of the potential of those men mentioned are enrolled in the common schools.

Of the promise that these mentally gifted individuals hold for society many acknowledgments may be found. Two of Hollingworth's dramatic expressions, for instance, are:

> Turning to positive considerations, we know that these pupils—they and no others—will possess as adults those mental powers on which the learned professions depend for conservation and advancement. Also, we know that they will be the literary interpreters of the world of their generation. And they will be the ones who can think deeply and clearly about abstractions like the state, the government, and economics. We know this because we have seen a group like this "grow up" over a period of fifteen years, and we know what "became" of every one of them. . . .[36]

and

> More and more it becomes clear that human welfare on the whole is much more a matter of the activities of *deviates* than it is a matter of what the middle mass of persons does. Those educators who make a joke of the genius and regard the dullard as a mere figment of the imagination of psychologists, or who solve the educational problems which these children present by the simple device of "not believing in" them, fiddle while Rome burns. It is the deviate who takes the initiative and plays the primary part in social determination. . . .[37]

Worthy of special thought are those superbly penetrating points of view expressed by Edward Lee Thorndike with respect to superior ability. His imagination is not centered at this point on the educational process; rather it points to social importance, to characteristic use of high ability, and to the values placed upon it. From a single chapter in his *Human Nature and the Social Order* ("Great Abilities") come these passages selected to represent the essence of his point of view. With respect to the values resulting from an early realization of potential greatness, he writes:

It is probable that a continuous account of the superior abilities that appear at ages 14, 18, and 22, with provision to keep careers open for their talents, would be a useful social investment. Even if nine out of ten of the recipients of such attention and aid achieve only moderately, the investment may yet be profitable provided one in a hundred of those near the top is enabled to do a higher quality of work than he would otherwise have done.

The full argument in support of this conclusion would be long and intricate, but its gist may be realized by considering what the world could afford to pay to develop the ability to cure cancer or make it fashionable for nations to settle their disputes by justice rather than by force, ten years sooner than it would otherwise be developed. Even a slight rise in a very high ability is, roughly speaking, priceless. Even a small chance of such a rise is worth a large expenditure. We should not miss the chance by failure to discover the promising candidates early.[38]

With respect to an ideal utilization of great capacity:

The best function of exceptionally high abilities is to perform valuable services which no lesser ability can perform at all, as in scientific discoveries, inventions, masterpieces of painting, music, literature and other fine arts, difficult problems and decisions, and difficult feats in inspiring, persuading, reconciling and otherwise managing individuals and groups.

From the moment that a man or a woman has demonstrated his possession of such ability, society should, in its own interest, arrange that he does for it what only he and his kind can do. (These statements hold true even when there is not surety that he can do so and so, but only a certain probability higher than that for anybody else and enormously higher than the probabilities for 999 men out of a thousand.) If by a miracle some possible Newton or Dante could shovel as much sand per hour as ten thousand men, so that he could command four thousand dollars an hour as shoveler of sand all over the globe, society should, if possible, persuade him not to take that contract. (As the world is, the possible Newton or Dante would be wise to exercise his shovel magic for a few hours, so as to live thereafter free from financial worries.)[39]

With respect to the unrealized potential especially in the upper levels of ability:

Nobody knows how many of the very high possibilities in the genes of the ten million persons born in this country from 1870 on who survived to age 50 or later, have been realized. To be definite we may consider the fate of the top thousand in the ten million, that is, the top one per ten thousand. If some omniscient guardian angel could have recorded the possibilities of each of the ten million at conception, at birth, at age 5, at age 10, at age 15, at age 20, at age 25, at age 30, and so on, nobody knows how fully the possibilities existing for any thousand at any age were realized in their lives thereafter. But not the most ardent believer in the relative importance of the genes and their tendency to find or create the environment they need, would claim that the possibilities were 100 percent realized.[40]

And finally, with respect to the proportionate value of the gifted when they occupy the apex of a pyramidal organization of talents bent in a common direction:

To make the matter more realistic let us suppose that the services of Mr. Gifford, the president of the American Telephone and Telegraph Company, have in the last ten years added one one hundredth of one percent per year to the cheapness, accuracy, convenience, etc., of telephone use. They probably have done more than that. If every group of persons on the company's payroll for a sum of salaries equal to his salary ($210,000) had done as much, telephone service would have been improved beyond recognition. If by paying him or somebody else $420,000, this addition could have been two hundredths of a percent per year instead of one, it would have been a marvelous bargain. The addition of three hundred switchboard operators to speed up service, or two hundred linemen to reduce breakdowns, which would cost as much or more, would be as one drop to a bucketful of value.[41]

That the distribution and use of great abilities is not so mathematically precise as is implied in these sketches, Thorndike more than many others, was aware. This exercise of imagination, however, is stimulating and enlarges expectations as to superior abilities generally and intellectual superiority specifically. The use of high capacities, and the values placed upon them by any particular society, is of course the function of a more broadly conceived policy than that for which the educator is responsible. At the end of his defense of higher salaries for superior executives, Thorndike expresses uncertainty that pecuniary rewards will accomplish what might be better effected through a system of values altered toward greater appreciation for superior social contributions. Thorndike's observation in this connection, when applied to the jolt the Western World received as Russia's dramatic scientific and technological feats ushered in the space age, testifies to the latent value inherent in his vision.

In view of the convincing nature of such arguments, it seems strange that people are occasionally found who object to special education for the gifted. Until quite recently, one interested in this cause could expect to encounter the argument, for instance, that such provisions violate the democratic process. Adams and Brown took note of this argument some thirty years ago and cited Dewey as having spoken of the "paradox" in democratic thought:

> The leveling tendency of democracy has created a problem in American public education. Of this paradox Dewey has said "Democracy has been unjust to the gifted student." Our political philosophy has announced equality of creation; our educational philosophy has translated this concept into equality of opportunity.[42]

To trace the ramifications of this argument is not so necessary today, in a changing climate of opinion. The counter-argument, however, and an overall point of view with which this book is in harmony, was eloquently expressed in the recent report of the Rockefeller Brothers Fund, Inc. Commenting upon the "tug of war between equality and excellence in a democracy," the report states:

> Every democracy *must* encourage high individual performance. If it does not, it closes itself off from the mainsprings of its dynamism and talent and imagination, and the traditional democratic invitation to the individual to realize his full potentialities becomes meaningless. More, perhaps, than any other form of government, a democracy must maintain what Ralph Barton Perry has called "an express insistence upon quality and distinction."
>
> The eighteenth-century philosophers who made equality a central term in our political vocabulary never meant to imply that men are equal in all respects. Nor do Americans today take such a view. It is possible to state in fairly simple terms the views concerning equality which would receive most widespread endorsement in our country today. The fundamental view is that in the final matters of human existence all men are equally worthy of our care and concern. Further,

we believe that men should be equal in enjoyment of certain familiar legal, civil, and political rights. They should, as the phrase goes, be equal before the law.

But men are unequal in their native capacities and their motivations, and therefore in their attainments. In elaborating our national views of equality, the most widely accepted means of dealing with this problem has been to emphasize *equality of opportunity*. The great advantage of the conception of equality of opportunity is that it candidly recognizes differences in endowment and motivation and accepts the certainty of differences in achievement. By allowing free play to these differences, it preserves the freedom to excel which counts for so much in terms of individual aspirations, and has produced so much of mankind's greatness.[43]

It will be understood, of course, that special education for the intellectually superior does not guarantee notable achievement on the part of each gifted person receiving the education. Scarcely more than common sense is needed to realize the number of variables that pertain to the frtiuion of the promise of youth, variables involving the whole matrix of social and personal circumstance surrounding the developing person. Even within the psychological traits denoting high ability, enough has been said in this study already to indicate that the prediction of notable achievement from the mere presence in childhood of superior potential is a process far from sure. Only when the behavioral sciences have been developed well beyond their status at present will a sufficient reliability of prediction be attained. The argument in this work is predicated upon the *enhanced probability* that youth identified early by the best present techniques, and schooled in a general education program which is the best that imagination can devise, will accomplish more than if they remain unidentified and accomplish routinely a program of education devised for persons of ordinary ability.

Reflection, once more, upon the historical achievements of men and women of genius and upon the contemporary achievements of adults in Terman's gifted group indicates the real promise of special education for the gifted. Intelligent and purposeful educational planning, it is reasonable to expect, will result in (1) the identification and development of more people of superior ability, (2) their improved preparation for productivity because of experiences more appropriate to their learning capacity, personal need, and anticipated social role, and (3) the launching of such persons into socially valuable enterprises earlier than under the present system, where years of schooling encroach even upon the period of normal adult productivity.

The gain would be noted first in the top level of creative genius, in persons who would be launched sooner into the life-versus-laboratory milieu and whose peculiar genius would ripen earlier. It would next be noted in the improved potential of a still larger percentage of able persons, just under these in capacity, who would qualify to assume special vocational roles in an advanced and complicated culture. The need for better educated, more extensively trained persons for mere participation in this complex, diversified economic, political, and industrial world is noted in crescendo from many quarters. Whether in electronics engineering, the practical management of megalopia, or research in the behavioral sciences, there is an increasing need for persons of distinctly superior ability to maintain the technological and social advance for which the twentieth century has become known.

chapter three | *TOWARD AN EDUCATIONAL THEORY*

The radical transformations in human culture that have characterized the past hundred years are frequently remarked upon by social scientists. So great are the changes imposed upon man's social institutions, and therefore upon man himself, that the suggestion has been made that modern man in the modern world is a different reality from ancient man in the ancient world. Sociologists have brought out very clearly the fact that advances in man's discoveries concerning the operations of nature, and the consequent technological reconstruction in his way of controlling nature, affect economic behavior, social customs, and even the beliefs and values derived from an older culture. Students of this process of change predict an increasing pace, rather than a foreseeable decrease. What, then, should be the character of the new-world education for those youth who promise to be the most effective human agents in reckoning with and furthering these changing circumstances? The present chapter offers a framework for thought about this problem composed of three parts: (1) a *setting*, in which certain characteristics of the contemporary world are indicated; (2) a *process*, in which certain underlying principles or operational assumptions of an educational program commensurate with this problem are sketched; and (3) a *product*, in which the results of such educative experience are suggested in terms of the kinds of persons who would be developed through it.

THE SETTING: CHARACTER OF THE MODERN WORLD

The contemporary social order, whether viewed from the American scene alone, that of the Western World, or that of all people, is both changed and changing. This fact contains inescapable implications for the education of persons who will live in and interact with this changing culture; it is even more apparent that the fact of change injects itself critically into educational thought concerning the development of those destined to become responsible agents for continuing such change and for reckoning with problems of human welfare arising within it.

A brief assembly of facts[44] will serve to remind the reader of the dramatic and imposing array of differences that exist between the world of today and that of one or two life spans ago:

Changes among People and Societies of the World

A world population doubled in the past hundred years and quadrupled in the past three hundred

A decline or stability in population growth among Western nations other than America, with increases in fifty years of nearly 60 percent in the Soviet Union, 30 percent in China, and 50 percent in India

In America the number of persons 40 through 65 has tripled in the past fifty years, the number over 65 has quadrupled; proportions of young to old in other world powers favor youth

In our country, the tremendous growth of cities and suburban population centers, with the emergence of urban patterns of thought to replace agrarian; mobility of population, travel, changing residence, business responsibilities interstate and international; the rise of the labor movement and corresponding changes in outlook; welfare of working classes; racial status of minority peoples in flux, great advances on economic, legal, and social fronts for Negroes

Changes in Ideological Realities and the Play of Power

A modern history no longer being written as a story of struggle among predominantly Western powers, but rather the rise to significant power status of China and Russia; the decline of Japan, the division of Germany, the dramatic fall of Fascism; the emergence of new nations in Africa; Arab nationalism

China's massive social experiment, the "Great Leap Forward"; and Russia's "Survey of Potential" as a possible prelude to new economic blueprints

Two attempts at worldwide political organization; the establishment of an international "war crimes commission"

Emergence of the question of domain in outer space, with neither America nor its sister nations of the West exerting effective earliest claims; missile age diplomacy

Changes in Things and Conditions (in America)

Earth satellite: science fiction in 1954; in 1959 realistic plans for landing human beings on the moon and their return

Decreased working hours, 25 percent from 1890 to 1950, but a 450 percent increase in output per man-hour

Vast governmental projects serving to transform regions and to facilitate economic progress—Tennessee Valley Authority, the 60 billion dollar super-highway building program

73 million vehicles anticipated for American highways by 1970

20 billion spent for home furnishings and appliances in 1957; power companies planning 250 percent increased output over next twenty years

one million telephones in 1900; 45 million in 1951

a big boost for the 18 billion dollar travel, resort, and motel business, now growing at the rate of about 3 billion dollars a year

15 million more jobs now than in 1939; nearly half our jobs did not even exist in their present forms just 25 years ago; in all, the needs of America will call for 22 million new jobs in the next 15 years

Judging by past experience, two million more businesses will be established to make and distribute the growing production of American mills and factories during the next 25 years

What is the meaning of these facts to modern man? The following interpretations were offered in the sources from which the facts have been drawn:

We have learned that one basic discovery can create a whole new industry. For example, most of the new "wonder drugs" were not even heard of 10 years ago. The magic of nuclear energy in making our lives more comfortable and convenient has only begun to be revealed. Plastics, the miracle maker that supplies almost every other industry, has expanded 40-fold in just 20 years. In little more than a decade the television industry has sold over 47 million sets. And at least 40 percent of the other electronic products people will be using 10 years from now are still to be invented.

Twenty-five years ago air travel was an adventure. Now, to many, a lurching train seems as slow and uncomfortable compared to air transportation as the old-fashioned buggy seemed compared to an automobile. Radio and television are tending to make the whole country one community, in which vast numbers may listen together to one voice and watch one scene. To an extraordinary extent, experience has been extended directly by increased mobility and less tangibly by the long reach of communication.

American society has been rapidly changing. Marriage is becoming a relationship that is permanent only with mutual continuing assent; the family is a unit of parents with children while they are growing, rather than a lifelong aggregation of grandparents, parents, and children. Each generation largely goes it alone, and the oldest often is lost. Leisure time has grown—and it has become filled haphazardly with diversions often of dubious worth and little suited to the newly numerous middle-aged and old people who are left with empty time. And the "American mind" seems dizzied and dismayed by the swirling changes through which it has moved. . . .

In his longer life and his modern world, the modern man is in total a largely new phenomenon. And he has largely new needs. He lives in a world in crisis . . . most of the changes indicated are proceeding with increasing rapidity; almost everything seems to be moving (the hope must be) to new crescendos of marvelous living—or, conceivably, of explosive disintegration if affairs go awry. . . .

Sociological analysis provides a more generalized and systematic statement of the impact upon modern man himself of these dramatic changes in his physical world and social affairs. George S. Counts makes vivid interpretations in this vein. Certain of his ideas are cited at this point by way of further depicting the social aspects of the "setting" within which the education of the abler youth must proceed.

So swiftly have these material features of our old agrarian civilization passed away that Lincoln, Grant, and even Cleveland would feel bewildered in the America of today. Indeed many members of the older generation now living experience a sense of bewilderment. And for the most part those of younger years who may feel at home in this new world really do not realize what kind of a world it is. They have experienced no other.

The uneven advance of industrial civilization, the swift transformation of the material foundations of life and the lag in institutional, ideological, and moral adjustment, have generated the terrifying crises, the wars and depressions, the revolutions and counterrevolutions, of our time. Our world, in both its domestic and its international aspects, is out-of-joint. Our practical inventiveness, in the words of Stanley Casson, has far outrun our "moral consciousness and social organization." We have one foot in a civilization that is passing away, the other in a civilization that is only beginning to take form. Or to phrase the dilemma more aptly perhaps, as our feet tread the earth of a new period our heads continue to dwell in a world that is gone.[45]

Dramatic testimony to the elevated "common sense" of the natural scientists, who play a significant role in these changing conditions of man, are certain points of view related to these sociological perspectives, emerging from the 1958 Parliament of Science. In consideration of the grand sweep of their accomplishments of the past several decades, this assembly of scientists, invited *pro tempore* to the philosophical role, suggest that "man is breaking with the past, its limitations and its safeguards." Continuing, with constructive and convincing imagination, they observe:

> We are in fact saying that man is on the very edge of a new relation to the atom, to the cell, to himself, and to the universe in which he is set. Many forces have been active, but clearly it is science which has been chiefly instrumental in bringing about this new relation. The new relation will place new demands on all man's resources—especially on his capacity to handle this new power with wisdom, restraint, and decency.
>
> This scientific revolution will totally dwarf the Industrial Revolution and the other historical instances of great social change. It will be more compelling, and will pose more urgent problems, because of both the pace and the magnitude of the changes which now impend.
>
> What faces man is not, in any restricted sense, a scientific problem. The problem is one of the relation of science to public policy. Scientific issues are vitally and almost universally involved. The special knowledge of the scientist is necessary, to be sure; but that knowledge would be powerless or dangerous if it did not include all areas of science and if it were not effectively pooled with the contributions of humanists, statesmen, and philosophers and brought to the service of all segments of society.[46]

More than a decade (and several millions of people) ago, Henry Steele Commager, impressed by a similar review of fermenting culture, raised at length some critical questions facing the American nation, questions the answers to which were also of vital concern to the entire world. Commager was writing prior to the entry of the space age and somewhat before Americans had been forced to realize that their position at the apex of world power was not inherently secure. His questions, which are even more significant today, provide an appropriate conclusion to the present description of the world setting against which the education of the gifted must be viewed.

> Out of an amalgam of inheritance, environment, and historical experience, Americans had fashioned a distinctive character; could

they preserve and develop that character in a changed environment and under the impact of a new set of historical experiences? Adventure, experimentation, and mobility had marked their character; with the frontier gone, immigration dammed up, and resources running low, could they retain their enthusiasm for fresh experience and novel ways, their ingenuity and adventurousness? They were wonderfully inventive in the physical and technological realm; would they prove equally resourceful in the realms of social institutions and of morals? They had achieved the highest standard of living known to history; how would they live? Their society had changed from rural to urban; would they learn to master the city as their forefathers had mastered the country? Immigration had all but ceased; what would be the final product of the interracial melting pot? Fifteen million Negroes confronted one hundred and thirty million whites; would racial conflicts continue to frustrate democracy, or would they find a solution to the racial problem through ultimate amalgamation or through the establishment of such economic and social security as would permit mutual tolerance?

They had created an economy of abundance; could they fashion a political mechanism to assure the equitable distribution of that abundance? They had become the richest people on the globe; would they use their wealth to prosper society or to display power? They were democratic in law; would they be democratic in fact? They were equalitarian by conviction; would they be equalitarian in conduct? They had developed technology to its highest point; would they learn to make technology their servant rather than their master? They were using up their natural resources more rapidly than they were replacing them; would science reverse the process, or would they be forced to a lower standard of living or to economic imperialism? Agreement upon fundamentals had enabled them to maintain a two-party system; would the clashing ideologies of a new age destroy that agreement and fragmentize their politics? They had solved the ancient problem of liberty and order; would they succeed in maintaining order in a war-troubled world without such suppression of liberty as would change the character of their state? They had become increasingly like the peoples of the Old World; could they avoid the clash of doctrine and opinion, the conflict of church and state, of class and party, of race and section, that had for so long rent Europe with dissension and war?

The whole world had an interest in the answers which history would make to these questions.[47]

THE PROCESS

It is a major contention of this study that radical revisions are essential both in the organization of the graded sequences in school and in the conception of the role of knowledge in education. Thus, the immediate discussion will first offer suggestions regarding the organization of the school and then present certain ideas concerning the inadequacy of the present treatment of knowledge in the education of men and women of extraordinary abilities.

A Life-Span Concept of Education

The American practice of devoting the first six of seven grades of the system to "elementary" schooling and the latter five or six to "secondary" schooling is subject to criticism. Henry C. Morrison once suggested another conception which seems to accord better with our knowledge of human development and the nature of experience. He described as "secondary"

> . . . that region in the process of schooling within which there are no essential and critical differences in the nature of the process of learning under instruction. Or, to put it another way, . . . the region throughout which there is some outstanding and controlling characteristic of teaching which is not found and cannot be applied earlier and which is not found, or ought not to be found, later.
>
> Such a comprehensible test can, we think, be found in the school procedure in which the pupil is capable of learning through study and the use of books but is incapable of systematic personal growth, except under the constant tutorial presence and constraint of the teacher. This region is the *secondary school*, at least so far as teaching is concerned.[48]

He suggested that in terms of the organization by grades as then known this span would begin at some point around nine years of age. With respect to the upper limit, he observed:

> The other end of the secondary school is quite as important. It is not the twelfth grade nor the sixteenth, but rather the point at which

the evidence shows that the pupil has matured; that he has attained the intellectual, volitional and conduct responsibility, the fundamental methods of thinking, and the sustaining cultural interests which make him a self-governing intellectual and social being. If he reaches that point at fifteen years of age, he must have his higher opportunity either in his present school or another. If denied and kept within the constraining influence of the secondary classroom, he is more than likely to become intellectually sterile. If, on the other hand, the graduate school finds itself with a student who has never attained intellectual self-dependence, it must choose between letting him go and carrying on for his benefit instruction of secondary grade.[49]

It is this conception that leads us to formulate the principles of general education which follow shortly so as to pertain to that span of grades from the intermediate level through the non-specialized portion of the general college. Any subordinate grade divisions within this total span are properly conceived as segments of general, as distinct from professional or technical, education.

But the concept of general education pertains well beyond the period in which youngsters are formally engaged in full-time schooling. Adult education, as the acquisition of new knowledge and the review of knowledge formerly held, becomes increasingly necessary to the full life. The belief that education should extend through the life-span is characteristically well expressed by Robert M. Hutchins in the introductory volume of a work that is transcendently useful for general education and scarcely excelled in magnificence of conception, *The Great Ideas, A Syntopicon of Great Books of the Western World* (and the keyed volumes of "Great Books"). Hutchins writes:

> The Editors believe that these books should be read by all adults all their lives. They concede that this idea has novel aspects. The education of adults has uniformly been designed either to make up for the deficiencies of their schooling, in which case it might terminate when these gaps had been filled, or it has consisted of vocational training, in which case it might terminate when training adequate to the post in question had been gained.
>
> What is here proposed is interminable liberal education. Even if the individual has had the best possible liberal education in youth, interminable education through great books and the liberal arts remains his obligation; he cannot expect to store up an education in childhood that will last all his life. What he can do in youth is to acquire

the disciplines and habits that will make it possible for him to continue to educate himself all his life. One must agree with John Dewey
in this: that continued growth is essential to intellectual life.[50]

On the factual side, recent figures indicate a tremendous present
expansion in adult education.

> About eight million persons in the United States attend at least
> one formal adult education class each year. . . . The figures exclude
> correspondence courses, individual instruction, private lessons, educa-
> tion by radio and TV, and on-the-job training. Almost 30 percent
> of the students in adult education classes are *over* 45 years of age and
> approximately 70 percent are over 30.[51]

In practical terms, the organizational scheme suggested here provides
for clearly distinctive educational processes in general education extending, say, from approximately grades four or five through grades
fourteen. The end of "junior college" is a practical terminus for general education in the period of youth which must yield at this point
to specialized training and stabilization of the person within a life
calling. It does not mean that vocational and professional training is
not to begin prior to this point; nor does it mean that general education ceases, as has just been indicated. On the other hand, this conception of a "secondary" level of schooling allows for consistent and
manageable educational objectives, curricular content, and teaching
methodology both in the preparatory period of education for youth
and in the continuing general education of adults—a consistency apparently unattainable in our present loose conception of what developmental purposes are proper at given points in the life span.

Education as Cognitive Perspective

But an organizational structure for education, even a life-span conception, is only part of the need. What is learned, why it is deemed
worthy of being learned, and to what ends the products of learning
lend themselves—these are the truly important questions. If it is fair
to think of the gifted individual as a life-long learner, a frontiersman
on the spearhead of cultural advance, what should be the nature of the
knowledge which he pursues? It is contended here that the anticipated
social role, more in the vein of a *reconstructionist* within the culture

than of a mere *participant in the status quo*, dictates unusual conceptions of the very nature of the knowledge and learning processes of most worth. We must now explore into certain of these unusual kinds of knowledge.

The conception of what useful knowledge is and how it should be attained has become extremely narrow in the typical American school. Despite a respectable accumulation of educational theory to disallow the virtue of such processes, the teaching and learning acts are essentially those of *fact-giving* and *fact-getting*. This conception of *fact* as the basis of the educational process is both unnecessary and critically undesirable. The mental processes involved in the acquisition of facts about things as they are, are of a low order in the range of human intellectual potential. Descriptive facts and principles which represent man's accumulating store of reliable knowledge about physical and social realities are properly recorded in encyclopedias, texts, and other sources of reference. So great is the body of existing knowledge that learning grounded in such facts can only be selective; and no selection of facts to be included in the general education of people from kindergarten through general college can be completely defended against the particular bodies of knowledge excluded as a result. The curriculum of the common school represents a pitiable sampling of man's total knowledge, a sample acquired through undisciplined deletions and additions without coherent reasoning with respect to the experience involved, the nature of the human traits related to the experience, or the life conditions for which the knowledge supposedly prepares the youth.

Apart from the impossibility of selecting a range of descriptive facts and principles which adequately anticipate the diverse demands likely to be faced by the youth in the changing conditions through his life career, other significant truths about "facts" serve to disqualify an education centered predominantly in this level of knowledge. Facts differ remarkably in their stability. In view of theories in physics which concern the nature and organization of matter, even the simplest of facts (i.e., "water runs downhill"; "cold contracts while heat expands") sometimes are necessarily viewed as outmoded or incomplete descriptions. Such names as Copernicus and Darwin suggest how at one cataclysmic moment in the history of thought contemporary conceptions of things become displaced by new sets of "facts." And not all facts treated in the educational process, of course, possess the reliability (durability) of these conceptions of nature. How many of the so-called facts of political geography or of the organization of governments studied by school pupils in 1900, or 1915, or 1930, serve those persons efficiently in thinking about the world today. Many readers will have had the experience in the first half of this century of learning a mass of details about the governmental structure and process of countries frighteningly soon to be abolished by new agreements or conquests.

The most serious criticism of an educative process grounded in the pursuit of fact, however, is not that facts change or defy selection. A far more serious criticism is that in the life of the citizen—in his work, his play, his family life, his participation in civic, social, and religious institutions—the critical mental processes in use are not the simple recall and application of learned fact but *thought processes such as judgment, inference, and reasoning*. It is, therefore, the development of the person in terms of increasing precision and appropriateness of thought processes which should form the continuing basis for educational experience, rather than the mere addition of layer upon layer of descriptive fact through successive years of schooling.

It is obvious that thought which leads to constructive results employs reliable and realistic principles and facts pertaining to the situation or idea being deliberated. It is equally true, if not so readily recognized, that a problem of any consequence to an individual or to a group of individuals can seldom be resolved by the use of facts currently known to the deliberating persons. Whitehead, it is said, once observed that "facts, like fish, spoil when kept." Business executives spend a working day seeking for the "statistics" bearing upon the problem in which a decision is to be made; political representatives must keep abreast of the changing economic conditions which give rise to civil law; the consumer must know which refrigerator defrosts in both the freezer and the cooling compartments. But these pertinent and necessary facts are not of the sort that can be "carried in the head." What are so carried, always present with the individual, always used in the conduct of small and large affairs, and always determinative far more than facts of the adequacy with which problems are resolved, are the processes through which the individual realizes his need of such facts. What he *understands of the functional relationships among classes of things, his understanding of the limits of such present knowledge as he does have, and his insight into the need for particular kinds of additional facts* are the truly effective understandings which lead to the successful adjustment of situations to human needs. The development, however, of precision in thought or of insight into the types of knowledge and the modes of thought appropriate to different problems requires the same sustained attention that is presently given to the acquisition of facts. The point here is not to derogate from the direct knowledge of things as they are but rather to indicate the inadequacy of this level of pursuit as the central ingredient in the educative process.

James R. Killian, Jr., then President of the Massachusetts Institute of Technology, made the following pertinent observation with respect to the critical shortage of scientists and engineers:

> . . . the crisis is not a matter of numbers alone. There are many areas of technology that are now closed books to those engineers lacking creative powers or to those whose training or analytical abilities never carried them beyond the superficial methods of handbook engineering. . . . Employers are not just looking for "bodies" with degrees . . . they are pressing the colleges for men with a more fundamental, integrated education in science, engineering and the humanities. . . . They want men . . . with the power to deal with the technologies of tomorrow and not of yesterday.[52]

This capacity to deal with the facts which become real and pertinent tomorrow is the true aim of education. The inevitable cultural lag is prolonged by masses of people in positions of leadership who are equipped only to make the procrustean attempt to fit present situations to the limited structures of their own *outmoded* mentality.

Although the simple internalization of selected facts is not an adequate method of educating the gifted, the vast array of knowledge developed through the ages can be treated so as to form the basis for such an education. This treatment represents an ambitious but possible *pursuit of a perspective upon the whole of knowledge. Not the one-to-one integration of matters of fact but rather the sequential development of knowledge about knowledge which enables the individual to understand the nature, problems, and applications of every major branch of knowledge*—this should be the process around which general education for the intellectually superior revolves. Education for the gifted should embrace graded experiences toward this end, involving abstractions, classifications, generalizations, and complex formulations which lie beyond the individual's own intrinsic reach. It should cease to be the piecemeal assignment of understandings that can be acquired without aid when problems suggest their need.

The insights yielded by this educative process should equip the individual to pursue efficiently any facts within this universe of knowledge that are required for the accomplishment of his immediate ends. As previously indicated, formal continuing general education will be intermittently essential throughout the life span. Only a process of this kind will bring within reach of the intellectually superior individual that knowledge which the changing conditions of the modern world and his own personal circumstances are likely to render essential to this individual welfare and to effective contributions to society.

A basic knowledge of the nature and uses of the mind is either not taught at all in the typical curriculum of today or touched upon indirectly, informally, or as elective experience. Direct instruction is necessary in the modes of inquiry and uses of mind characteristically brought into play by the poet, the philosopher, the theologian, the scientist, the polemicist, and the historian. Thus, recognition of the type of problem before him will put the individual into appropriate intellectual gear for such of these specific roles as the exigencies of life thrust upon him. Instruction is also essential in the fields of knowledge, with the major classifications of problems within each, the types of applications to which these several fields lend themselves, and typical combinations of basic disciplines which occur in the pursuit of all natural and social realities as presently known. Also appropriate to the task are the means for appraising the fitness of given propositions or descriptions for varying types of problems in art or in social theory and practice. All these are the proper ingredients for the educational development of individuals destined on the whole to reckon with the problems of reformation and reconstruction of culture.

To teach the details of the Copernican conception of the universe is less necessary than to teach the theoretical significance of this once radical insight for the properties and functions of all kinds of matter; to learn the limitations upon the view of the world inherent in the Ptolemaic conception of celestial mechanics is to establish a set for seeking limitations and potentials inherent in contemporary conceptions of physical arrangements in nature. To teach the significance of Darwin's theory for the growth, development, and behavior of organisms generally, is to inculcate knowledge of far broader usefulness than merely to describe the present "post-Darwinian" body of fact, especially where such factual presentations are neither presently needed by the student, nor the teaching of them necessary for their learning. Immediately apparent inferences derive from the concept that "classical economic laws" are passing or that "modern mathematics" is emerging, serving to place any particular fact, principle, or process within those fields of knowledge in a structure explicitly understood to be relative to time and concurrent event. Such is the nature of fact; such is the nature of change; and such is the nature of education. For those individuals biologically endowed with ability to reckon with this complex of realities and to assume disproportionate responsibility for the welfare of the human species within this complex, the educator must design experiences appropriate to these grand conditions.

The present conception of education is, then, concerned with the development of understanding to higher and higher levels in all significant areas of reliable knowledge. If, as has been said, the function of science is to "maximize the power of generalization," the function of general education, as described here, is to maximize the student's capacity for internalizing and elaborating upon the generalizations of science and other acceptable modes of inquiry.

Since the intellectual factor is so generic to the whole issue of education for the gifted, certain supporting points of view from educational theorists are offered in further elaboration of the role of cognitive aspects of mind in education. These expressions were conceived without regard to the special intellectual capacity of the gifted. Their pertinence in the latter respect is enhanced in view of the role of intellect in the personality of the highly gifted youngster.

William H. Kilpatrick has stated as one of several philosophic principles this conception of the function of intelligence: "The free play of intelligence stands as our final resource to tell us what to do—intelligence playing freely upon experience in any and all of its content, including the use of intelligence itself." He adds again:

> . . . some have been troubled lest naming the free play of intelligence as our final resort for thought and act means either an effort or a willingness to reduce life solely to the intellectual. Nothing of the sort is meant. Thinking, or the effective use of intelligence, must deal with any and all content of life. Some of this experienced content may

relate to things as material as stone or steel; other content may be as spiritual as a hope, or a fancy, or a sense of duty. Thinking must deal with all.[53]

No further uses for the intellect of gifted children are urged than those demanded in this expression of the role of intelligence in the education of persons in general. The ideal is simply much more readily attainable by virtue of the distinguishing characteristics of the specific group.

Another expression from quite a different source bears striking similarity and helps further to interpret the relationships which are being described here between intellect and the educative process:

> . . . learning is also for the sake of cultivating basic mental abilities; in short, to foster the powers of reason in man. The ability to think in accordance with the facts and with the laws of inference, to choose wisely, to feel with discrimination is what distinguishes man from the animals and endows him with intrinsic worth. Yet reason, while an end, is a means as well—a means to the mastery of life. The union of knowledge and reason in the integrated personality—this is the final test of education. . . .[54]

If this point of view possesses validity for the general education of all students, there is no logic which suggests that the intellectually superior should deny the existence of this superiority and a particular emphasis upon it.

And finally, in this connection, Charles Hubbard Judd's discussion of "transfer" and higher mental processes would almost appear to have been written expressly in reference to the intellectually gifted:

> A review of all that has been written about the transfer of training cannot fail to convince one of the futility of attempting to explain human mental life at its upper levels by simple formulas. Transfer is certainly not characteristic of animal consciousness. Animals below man live in mental worlds which are made up of meager, circumscribed experiences. For them each experience absorbs all the mental energy that is available. There is no overview, no power of generalization. In human mental life there are also narrow experiences consisting in the recognition of particular situations to which direct, routine responses are made. Fortunately, there are in human mental life other and far broader experiences. When the mind analyzes a situation, selects important factors through abstraction, and gen-

eralizes by discovering the same important factors in other situations, something is happening which is wholly different from that which is characteristic of the lower forms of conscious experience. At the higher levels transfer is typical, not exceptional. Indeed, the function of the higher mental processes is to release the mind from particulars and to create a world of general ideas. . . . The psychology of the higher mental processes teaches that the end and goal of all education is the development of systems of ideas which can be carried over from the situations in which they were acquired to other situations. Systems of general ideas illuminate and clarify human experiences by raising them to the level of abstract, generalized, conceptual understanding.[55]

It will be found that several of the principles elaborated in the succeeding parts of this work are designed to aid the bright student to acquire "systems of general ideas" that "illuminate and clarify human experiences."

But this emphasis upon intellect and knowledge is not intended to imply that the development of intellect should be the exclusive burden of education. Sound practices in accord with the broad goals of American education, devoted to the rounded development of personality in its affective and conative dimensions, are presumed rather than excluded. Contemporary interpretation of the dynamics of human or animal nature suggests that these dimensions are "behavioral firsts," essential to practical or moral achievement. It will be noted that Part IV of this work deals with the development of intellectually significant personal and social skills and an effective character structure.

These levels of personality are developed, however, in order to free the intellective aspects of mind for development and to increase the probabilities that the individual's achievements will promote human welfare. *The heart of the educational enterprise, though not the whole, is the intellectualization of experience, the ideational elaboration by the individual of man's cumulative insights into nature, such that continuing perceptions occur within an increasingly comprehensive and meaningful context.* It is through the capacity for intellectualizing upon biological sensations and perception—*raw* experience—that man's control over nature, including his own behavior, advances and is made manifest in the various institutions of civilized societies.

THE PRODUCT

The kind of man that gifted youngsters are able to become, and the kind of man needed to advance the welfare of mankind in the mael-strom of complexities characterizing the new world made by science has been called for in various kinds of treatises. The present discussion of this point will offer the familiar analysis, considering the productive man first as an individual and then as a social personality, in terms of those outlooks which lead to constructive behavior in the community of fellowmen.

In certain respects, perhaps centrally, the classic ideal of the liberally educated man pertains still to the personal development of the able individual in modern society. Neither changing conditions nor the changing pace of change itself appears to have altered the qualities of mind biologically inherent in the human species and appropriate to reckoning with fundamental human problems. Writing in an era on the verge of the present social and technological expansion, Emerson ("The American Scholar," 1837) attempts to define the American counterpart of this classic ideal in his concept of "man thinking." This concept, which unquestionably has too little place in the stars that guide American educational thought today, is especially pertinent to the principles and objectives that govern special education for the gifted.

Within recent years, the American educational philosopher Harold Rugg has described what he calls a major dichotomy in people. Rugg notes that some human beings become "Thing People," and others "Force People." He names certain "Men of the Consensus"—Charles Sanders Peirce, William James, John Dewey, Thorstein Veblen, Walt Whitman, and Oliver W. Holmes, Jr.—claiming that they have con-tacted life in its "non-doctrinaire" modes and have achieved a recon-struction of experience which has lent a new frame of reference to American life in the twentieth century. Although the logic in Rugg's distinction may be open to question, his central conception of "Force People" appears to describe the men who have most significantly understood and affected their contemporary world. Among other char-acteristics of this group, it is noted that they "define the world in terms of function—the relations between things"; that they "accept the concept of change as fact; let their minds conclude what the facts of change conclude"; and that they "express the forces, tensions, push-and-pull in the world . . . in painting, poetry, dance, theatre, education, as well as in science and technology. . . ."[56]

The particular men credited by Rugg as possessing these qualities are suggestive of both the capacities and the characteristic social roles of the gifted. Rugg writes further:

> . . . I saw these men of the consensus as over-view minds, doggedly striving to see life whole, to grasp the totality of industrializing human culture. In the technical sense, because they dealt with the roots, they were the only true "radicals." They were students of the foundations. None was less than a man of talent, and the leaders among them—especially Peirce, James, Dewey, and Veblen—were men of genius; genius, which, as Lowell once said, is something in the grip of which you are—not talent, which is something that you have. They were original men of the frontiers who went forth first where none had trod before.
>
> Men of integrity they were, brave men ignoring danger to their personal fortunes, cutting through to the "dangerous thoughts" of the great areas of controversy that are chronically shunned by timid men. Force men, all—not a Thing man among them—digging beneath the surface pathology of the current of events, searching for deep-running trends, traits, and causes. . . .
>
> Because they were men of encyclopedic ranges of interest and knowledge, they could not be catalogued in any single learned discipline; all strode across scholastic boundaries. They were students of the relationships which can be generalized only in the borderlands between academic fields of knowledge and which frequently throw the greatest light on human affairs.
>
> All were devotees of the philosophy of experience—not an authoritarian among them. Hence they were minds and spirits oriented primarily on the present, concerned with the lives and needs of our people here and now, although they saw them always in the enlightening history of the past.[57]

These Martian doers of deeds in the changed and changing world must be minded for their task. Typical translations of the concepts "adjustment" and "socialization" into educational goals have been too narrow. There is a potential in the biological nature of man that allows him to transcend the limits of learning and behavior imposed upon him accidentally and informally through interaction with particular people in particular regions at particular times. The individual who is to lead his fellow men in adapting to and controlling a miraculously evolving culture must surmount these particulars and embrace a broader and broader understanding of human institutions and values until he becomes essentially *humanized* or *universalized*. The immediate society into which one is born should be but a starting point for this process of ideal and ultimate humanization. The accident of one's birth as an American, a Southerner, an Australian, or an Egyptian, with the consequent inevitable initiation into one of these particular forms of human culture, must be discounted through progressive growth toward the universalized ideal.

As individuals we tend to become arrested somewhere along this course of development at a level less than the full potential of our capacity for growth. In such arrestment, we recognize the fanatical regionalistic, nationalistic, or racistic elements in political and social thinking. Fixation of the individual at a less than possible level of attainment in this life-long developmental task represents a stultification, a perversion, of essential humanity. On the positive side, education which makes the child "bigger" than his home and immediate neighborhood, must not stop making him bigger until he is literally at one with mankind.

Once again, the thought of the assembly of scientists in the 1958 Parliament of Science is relevant. The assembly indicates the only way in which man's greatest collective aspirations can be fulfilled:

> The pursuit of knowledge is an activity of the human race, not an activity of political subdivisions. As citizens we recognize that the hard realities of the present world sometimes require, or at least seem to require, certain restrictions on the complete international freedom of basic research. But we earnestly think that these restrictions are often wrong and futile. Furthermore, we wish to place a special, positive emphasis upon the kinds of scientific problems—the kinds of international cooperation in science—which capitalize upon our universal common interests as members of the human race, such as our common struggle against disease and hunger. Scientists of all nations are engaged in a common enterprise. They are urged to take leadership in international understanding and thus to make progress toward permanent peace.[58]

The gifted must be deliberately educated for participation in, and the advancement of, world culture. This educational aim is both feasible and essential. It is feasible in that superior minds tend to move spontaneously toward such a rational review and reconstruction of experience, and it is essential in view of a world made small by scientific and technological advances in transportation and communication. Though always true of the greatest men, it is still more true today that creative persons are not destined to live and die as benefactors of single places and single societies. A Karl Mannheim may be born and grow to maturity in Germany, but his insights into the social arrangements characteristic of man become equally applicable and useful when he takes a place in English culture; ultimately, his knowledge and his constructive thought, like that of Aristotle and Bacon, transcends all particular times and places and becomes truly *human* in significance.

The maturing youth of today must think clearly about historically emergent notions such as Washington's "entangling foreign alliances" and the issue of state and federal prerogatives in American constitutional history; he must think radically about Arab nationalism, more in terms of human rights than in terms of past political accomplishments and conveniences. Nothing less than these grand aims can provide the "breakthrough" which Lippmann calls for (frontispiece), resolve adequately the social tasks identified by Commager, and begin to measure contemporary educational efforts in terms of Mead's radical inquiries.

This presentation of perspectives toward a theory of education for the most educable has attempted to consider (1) the relationships between general intelligence and general education; (2) the social significance of deliberate educational efforts for gifted persons; and (3) some points of view concerning the *setting* in which education for the gifted must be conceived, the *nature of the process*, and the *type of individual and social being* which the gifted can and must become. This section concludes Part I, "The Superior Student in an Educational Perspective." An attempt has been made in this part of the book to clarify definitions at play in current literature on the gifted and to delineate, through chief recourse to Terman's work, the educationally significant characteristics of the intellectually superior individual. It is hoped that this use of the unfolding data of the *Genetic Studies of Genius* will relate this work to Terman's, and in the spirit which he envisioned.

CONCERNING THE PRINCIPLES WHICH FOLLOW

The educational principles advanced in the succeeding parts of this book are more specific prescriptions within the framework of the various sections of Part I. The principles are designed as guides to the thought of educational administrators, curriculum planners, and classroom teachers. While theoretical in nature, it is hoped that they will be perceived by students as eminently practical in Dewey's sense that nothing is more practical really than sound theory. The principles are stated in the form of proposition and corollary by virtue merely of the convenience of this form. The proposition indicates the generic level of the aspect of the educative process under consideration, and the corollaries, subordinate or related aspects of the same area.

The principles suggested pertain to no single program for the gifted as developed in a given school. Rather, they apply to *all* such programs that truly accomplish the purpose intended; they provide further for the strengthening of practices not so consistently and appropriately conceived. It is only to be expected that in the absence of coherent theory, many *ad hoc* endeavors that have emerged in response to public pressures do not relate satisfactorily either to the capacities of the gifted or to their anticipated social roles. In such instances, these principles may serve as aids in gearing the school practice along more defensible lines.

In similar fashion, as noted in detail earlier, the principles are not intended to apply to one or another age level within the broad span from the intermediate grades through the general college. Only empirical efforts by researchers and teachers can ascertain at what age of the child a particular compounding of ideas suggested by a given principle will apply. Appropriate adaptations of the same principles may pertain equally well to different developmental periods within the broad "secondary" span.

Again, the hypotheses presented are concerned primarily with the educative *process*—classroom instruction and the experience of superior learners. No attempt is made to elaborate upon administrative devices, for it is felt that any of several such arrangements can serve equally well to convey educational and developmental experience; it is even more probable that no administrative device, regardless of how neatly conceived, will suffice toward improved experience in the absence of attendant excellence in the "guidance of learning activities." Further, these ideas concerning instructional content and method are intended to apply to no single subject matter, but rather to that knowledge in general that is or can be used in developing the high potential of the superior learner. Instances involving specific subject matter are almost always used illustratively, with analogous use in other disciplines usually apparent and intended. Experienced and imaginative teachers will perceive in the general principles specific applications according to their own grade and subject responsibilities. Enrichment units at grade levels and in given subject matter may be devised with proper thought and effort.

Finally, the principles advanced here are subject to the limitations of the writer and therefore cannot be exhaustive. Other principles of equal validity may be developed from the observations attendant upon efforts at applying those presently stated. These principles are designed in the manner of the scientific hypothesis: as generalizations depending upon antecedent research, they form the basis for further research designed to test their validity. It is hoped that the contribution of these principles will lie in suggesting the necessity that practical efforts toward enriching the educational program for the gifted be governed by theory, and in exploratory attempts to derive such theory.

FOOTNOTES FOR PART I

[1] National Education Association, *The Identification and Education of the Academically Talented Student in the American Secondary School* (Washington, D. C.: National Education Association, 1958), p. 16.

[2] Margaret Mead, "Thinking Ahead: Why Is Education Obsolete?" *Harvard Business Review*, 36:24–25, November-December, 1958.

[3] Lewis M. Terman *et al.*, *Mental and Physical Traits of a Thousand Gifted Children* (Stanford, California: Stanford University Press, 1926), p. 43.

[4] Paul Witty, "Who Are the Gifted?" *Fifty-seventh Yearbook of the National Society for the Study of Education*, Part II (Chicago: University of Chicago Press, 1958), p. 62. That it is simply majority *practice* which distinguishes this position as newer is indicated by the following early passage from Hollingworth in which a clear realization of the importance of specific aptitudes is manifest.

> This fact, that on the whole abilities cohere in an individual as regards amount, enables us to measure *general intelligence* or intellect. There are, however, certain abilities which show little or no correlation with others. It will be long before we know very much about these specialized aptitudes, but even at present we have identified some of them. Musical ability and ability in representative drawing are two important examples of aptitudes which do not correlate closely with general intelligence. In order to distinguish these special aptitudes from intellect in our discussion, we shall call them *talents*. In studying gifted children we shall wish to notice those who are superior in these special talents as well as those who are of extraordinary intellectual power. (Leta S. Hollingworth, *Gifted Children: Their Nature and Nurture*, New York: The Macmillan Company, 1926, p. 30.)

[5] Educational Policies Commission, *Education of the Gifted* (Washington, D. C.: National Education Association, 1950), p. 43.

[6] Dorothy E. Norris, "Programs in the Elementary Schools," *Fifty-seventh Yearbook of the National Society for the Study of Education*, Part II (Chicago: University of Chicago Press, 1958), p. 223.

[7] Educational Policies Commission, *Education of the Gifted*, p. 43.

[8] Robert F. DeHaan and Robert J. Havighurst recognize the differing educational significance of moderately and extremely superior ability in their designations "first order" and "second order" giftedness. See their *Educating Gifted Children* (Chicago: University of Chicago Press, 1959), pp. 1 and 228–49. Like others, however, they devote most of their volume to practices designed for the less than highly gifted.

[9] In earlier thought, the author followed the Educational Policies Commission recommendation that the criterion for designating the gifted be 120 I.Q. Intervening experience suggests that the theory developed in this work will pertain, as indicated, with increasing appropriateness from approximately this level upwards. It is clearly recognized that accompanying differences in personality—temperament, drive, and other nonintellective factors—may blend in total behavior in such a way as to render the more modest intellectual capacity more completely effective than the higher.

[10] David C. McClelland, Alfred L. Baldwin, Urie Bronfenbrenner, and Fred L. Strodtbeck, *Talent and Society*. Copyright, 1958, D. Van Nostrand Co., Inc., Princeton, New Jersey.

[11] Lewis M. Terman and Melita H. Oden, *The Gifted Child Grows Up*, Vol. IV, *Genetic Studies of Genius* (Stanford, California: Stanford University Press, 1947), pp. 3–4.

[12] Lewis M. Terman and Melita H. Oden, *The Gifted Group at Mid-Life*, Vol. V, *Genetic Studies of Genius* (Stanford, California: Stanford University Press, 1959), p. 3.

[13] Lewis M. Terman and Melita H. Oden, *The Gifted Child Grows Up*, pp. 6–7.

[14] Leta S. Hollingworth, "Problems of Relationship Between Elementary and Secondary Schools in the Case of Highly Intelligent Pupils," *Journal of Educational Sociology*, XIII (October, 1939), 90.

[15] Catherine Cox Miles, "Gifted Children," *Manual of Child Psychology*, ed. Leonard Carmichael (New York: John Wiley and Sons, 1946), pp. 892–94.

[16] Lewis M. Terman and Melita H. Oden, *The Gifted Child Grows Up*, pp. 55–57.

[17] Lewis M. Terman and Melita H. Oden, *The Gifted Group at Mid-Life*, *passim*.

[18] Lewis M. Terman and Melita H. Oden, *The Gifted Child Grows Up*, pp. 353–54.

[19] *Ibid.*, p. 356.

[20] *Ibid.*, pp. 364–67. See further *The Gifted Group at Mid-Life* for a decade of progress by the group: Chs. VII, "The Matter of Career," and XI, "The Fulfillment of Promise."

[21] *Ibid.*, pp. 349–52. Interesting clinical and experimental investigations into parent-child relationships and family structures are apparently adding substantially to knowledge concerning the developmental dynamics which tend toward critical differences in personality and achievement motivation. Fliegler and Bish (Louis A. Fliegler and Charles E. Bish, "The Gifted and Talented," Ch. II, "The Education of Exceptional Children," *Review of Educational Research*, XXIX, 1959) have provided an excellent review of such studies.

[22] Catherine M. Cox, *The Early Mental Traits of Three Hundred Geniuses*, Vol. II, *Genetic Studies of Genius* (Stanford, California: Stanford University Press, 1926), Chart 12A, between pages 60–61.

[23] *Ibid.*, pp. 216–19.

[24] One hopes to be clearly understood that these opinions are not intended as judgments upon men. The works selected to illustrate this point have been accomplished by able men, leaders in this field. It is the status of behavioral science that is in question, rather than the particular thought of given men.

[25] Paul F. Brandwein, *The Gifted Student as Future Scientist*, p. 40. Copyright, 1955, by Harcourt, Brace and Company, Inc.

[26] Robert F. DeHaan, "Social Leadership," *Fifty-Seventh Yearbook of the National Society for the Study of Education*, Part II (Chicago: University of Chicago Press, 1958), *passim.*

[27] Lewis M. Terman, "The Discovery and Encouragement of Exceptional Talent," *The American Psychologist*, IX (June, 1954), 224.

[28] Because the facts known about creativity are still all too few, despite promising work by J. W. Getzels, E. Paul Torrance, and others, and further because it is easy to be misunderstood on such a complex problem, two points in psychological theory are noted by way of delimiting the intended meanings in this presentation. First, it is not intended that high general intelligence be considered dynamic in quality, i.e., that it inherently contains drive toward its own exercise. This might, indeed, be true; but it makes a fairer conception to think correlatively as distinct from causally, suggesting that specific creativity and high general intelligence may both be explained as constituents of an organic biological matrix in which mutually determining sets of factors remain to be discovered. Thus, the total organismic differences between creative persons and those merely productive can be thought of as reflected in and through their intellective behavior, rather than that their intellect itself is dynamic.

Second, though the practical argument is true that intelligence tests as presently conceived and constructed do not measure creativity, this fact does not militate effectively against their use for educational purposes. It can be argued as convincingly that the observational techniques proposed as supplements do not themselves yield the results promised. The concept of creativity is so closely allied to the type of meaning which was originally intended for "intelligence" that if scientists succeed in isolating creativity more definitively, then indices of this trait will, or should, be built into the general intelligence test in the manner that "performance" factors have already been included.

For educational practices in connection with creativity, see Chapter 8.

[29] David C. McClelland, Alfred L. Baldwin, Urie Bronfenbrenner, and Fred L. Strodtbeck, *Talent and Society*, p. 25. Copyright, 1958, D. Van Nostrand Co., Inc., Princeton, New Jersey.

[30] In an unpublished paper, "Traits by Fiat," delivered before the Virginia Psychological Association, Annual Convention, May 1959.

[31] The reader should distinguish between two common meanings of the phrase "special education": (1) specialization of training, leading toward a particular behavioral competence, often defined vocationally; and (2) general educational curricula, modified to meet the particular abilities and needs of homogeneous groups identifiable by significant deviant characteristics, such as the mentally retarded, the physically handicapped, or the intellectually superior. Throughout the present work, unless otherwise indicated, the phrase and idea of "special education for the gifted" is used in the latter sense, i.e., the objectives and processes of general education deliberately reconceived in the light of the identifiable characteristics of gifted individuals. The author is but slightly concerned with the professional controversy as to the prerogative in this problem of one educational specialist, e.g., the special education coordinator or the curriculum supervisor, over another.

[32] In Proposition VII (p. 156), there is an argument for experience in methodology and resources peculiar to the respective academic disciplines as general education for the future scholar. The points of view are compatible when this particular use of knowledge is interpreted as deepening understanding, rather than conducing toward professional skill.

[33] David C. McClelland, Alfred L. Baldwin, Urie Bronfenbrenner, and Fred L. Strodtbeck, *Talent and Society*, pp. 23–24. Copyright, 1958, D. Van Nostrand Co., Inc., Princeton, New Jersey.

[34] *The New York Times*, September 7, 1958.

[35] As previously acknowledged, some splendid efforts have occurred in certain schools to implement the broader concept of giftedness. It would be difficult to maintain that no good at all derives from the application of the best known identification techniques for specific traits and the best known educative devices presently possible within the common school. The program at Portland, Oregon, is widely known for its broadside approach toward the discovery and development of all varieties of promising abilities. Both the Bronx High School of Science and the High School of Music and Art in New York City serve to illustrate the best that science has made possible in this area.

[36] Leta S. Hollingworth, *Children Above 180 I.Q.* (Yonkers-on-Hudson, New York: World Book Co., 1942), p. 289.

[37] Leta S. Hollingworth, "Problems of Relationship Between Elementary and Secondary Schools in the Case of Highly Intelligent Pupils," *Journal of Educational Sociology*, XIII (1939), 102.

[38] Edward L. Thorndike, *Human Nature and the Social Order* (New York: Macmillan, 1940), p. 70.

[39] *Ibid.*, pp. 71–72.

[40] *Ibid.*, p. 81.

[41] *Ibid.*, pp. 94–95.

[42] Fay Adams and Walker Brown, *Teaching the Bright Pupil* (New York: Henry Holt and Company, Inc., 1930), p. 3.

[43] *The Pursuit of Excellence—Education and the Future of America.* Copyright, 1958, Rockefeller Brothers Fund, Inc. Reprinted by permission of Doubleday and Company, Inc.

[44] For most of the following array of factual data and the interpretations immediately following, the author is indebted to two sources: Sidney L. Pressey and Raymond G. Kuhlen, *Psychological Development Through the Life Span* (New York: Harper & Brothers, 1957), Chapter I, *passim;* and The Advertising Council, Inc., *Your Great Future in a Growing America* (New York: The Council, n.d.), *passim.* The material has been adapted and rearranged.

[45] From George S. Counts, *Education and American Civilization* (New York: Bureau of Publications, Teachers College, 1952). Cited in William O. Stanley, B. Othanel Smith, Kenneth D. Benne, and Archibald W. Anderson, eds., *Social Foundations of Education* (New York: Dryden Press, Inc., 1956), pp. 381–82.

[46] American Association for the Advancement of Science, "1958 Parliament of Science," *Science*, CXXVII (1958), 852.

[47] Henry Steele Commager, *The American Mind* (New Haven: Yale University Press, 1950), pp. 441–43.

[48] Henry C. Morrison, *The Practice of Teaching in the Secondary School*, 2nd Ed. (Chicago: University of Chicago Press, 1931), p. 7.

[49] *Ibid.*, pp. 13–14.

[50] Robert M. Hutchins, *The Great Conversation*, Vol. I, *Syntopicon and Great Books of the Western World*, Robert M. Hutchins, ed.; Mortimer J. Adler, assoc. ed. (Chicago: Encyclopaedia Britannica, Inc., 1952), pp. 52–53.

[51] *Better Schools*, September, 1958.

[52] James R. Killian, Jr., Massachusetts Institute of Technology, President's Report, 1955: Part 1, "Meeting the Nation's Scientific Manpower Needs," pp. 3–4.

[53] William H. Kilpatrick, "Philosophy of Education from the Experimentalist Outlook," *Forty-First Yearbook of the National Society for the Study of Education*, Part I, p. 54.

[54] Harvard Committee, *General Education in a Free Society*, pp. 167–68. Cambridge, Massachusetts: Harvard University Press, 1945.

[55] Charles H. Judd, *Education as Cultivation of the Higher Mental Processes*, pp. 200–1. Copyright, 1936, by the Macmillan Company and used with their permission.

[56] Harold Rugg, *Foundations for American Education* (Yonkers-on-Hudson, New York: World Book Company, 1947), p. 69.

[57] *Ibid.*, p. 28.

[58] American Association for the Advancement of Science, *op. cit.*, pp. 852–53.

part two

GENERAL PRINCIPLES
OF THE EDUCATIONAL
DESIGN

It is easy to fall into the habit of regarding the mechanics of school organization and administration as something comparatively external and indifferent to educational purposes and ideals. . . . The school environment and machinery almost compel the more mechanical features of school work to lord it over the more vital aims.

—John Dewey

chapter four

THE LOGIC OF SPECIAL EDUCATION FOR THE GIFTED

Attempts to adapt school programs to the needs of the gifted child have usually taken the form either of administrative provisions, such as regrouping or accelerating the pupils concerned, or of changes in the method and content of the curriculum. Even a cursory examination of the total sweep of special educational programs for the gifted, however, tends to lend credence to Dewey's observation (p. 77). Such programs consist for the most part of disarranging the administrative machinery which has been developed to carry the standard subject matter, rather than re-examining the entire realm of man's knowledge with respect to what new subject matter, and what new modes of handling traditional subject matter, would be possible for the powerful and subtle minds of highly intellectual youngsters. In many instances, acceleration of pupils by one grade, through compacting the subject matter of two or three, is proudly hailed as a "program" of education for the gifted. In essence, advanced placement provisions simply, though commendably, provide for an earlier access to subject matter traditionally placed a year or so ahead in the graded sequence of high school and college. Schools that have made news in the post-World War II era have done so chiefly by virtue of a certain courage to break the educational "lock-step," without, however, showing equal courage and imagination in revolutionizing curricular content. That greater attention to curricular revision is now going on in places here and there does not discredit the observation that it has not gone on throughout this renaissance of thought in behalf of the abler student or that the great mass of schools still have scarcely touched the standard curricular patterns.

There is, however, an inherent *logic of special education for the gifted* which lays the groundwork for bolder and more radical re-conceptions of the total educational process. This logic respects both those biological properties which tend to distinguish intellectually superior persons as a group and the equally distinctive social roles which the group tends to assume as adults—leaders, visionaries, and revisionists, in every aspect of culture. There is a biological principle suggesting that intraspecies variations are in the nature of degree rather than kind. Where differences in educationally critical characteristics, such as intelligence and the processes of learning, are so extreme, however, they amount in practical consequence to differences in kind. Basic capacities which deviate markedly from the mean eventuate in processes themselves so extreme that they can be profitably conceived as different kinds of processes. The experiences of able philosophers and star athletes are markedly different from the experiences of mediocre persons attempting to play either game. The experience is different not only after the acquisition of understandings and skills which differentiate the mature and accomplished performer, but also in the initial and ensuing processes through which maturity is attained. Thus, the characteristic *distinguishing behavioral processes* of intellectually superior people are such as to warrant a *distinctively devised sequence of educational experiences* that takes account of the superior characteristics.

A second aspect of this logic of special education concerns the subsequent use of superior abilities. The adult roles which intellectually superior individuals typically assume involve *advancement of the culture* in all of its dimensions, rather than *mere participation in it.*

The argument for special education for the gifted, then, rests upon these two cornerstones: the biological superiority of the individual (i.e., he *can manage* a different curriculum), *and the particular functions which he is, on the whole, destined to accomplish in the culture* (i.e., he *needs* a different curriculum). It seems unnecessary to belabor the point that such individuals cannot be adequately served by a curriculum developed over the years for persons not so distinguished in capacity or so destined in career. On the other hand, it *is* worth emphasizing that deliberate attempts by qualified educators to review the normal curriculum in light of the needs and capacities of gifted persons can yield substantial results. This is the high and noble purpose which impels all past and present advocates of special education for the gifted. Educational experience, immediate or sustained, which fails to relate to the individual's biological superiority or his probable career does not qualify as special education for the gifted. The curriculum must require such mental processes, and be aimed toward such social function, that it is either impossible or undesirable for children of the generality. To occupy the gifted at lesser levels of experience and in view of lower expectations is to fail both the individual and society.

The propositions in Part II concern the foundations from which the principles of instruction derive and also concern the overall organizational aspects of the school system. The curriculum of the school may be thought of as the entire range of experiences occurring under school sponsorship and designed for the development of the child. It is difficult to differentiate for purposes of discussion the content and materials used in such experiences from the activities, the methods, by which the subject matter is conveyed. The principles which are deduced here embrace both aspects of the curriculum, but no attempt is made in the specific instance to designate a principle as concerning either method or content. The principles, termed "propositions," and the "corollaries," which are more specific ramifications of the primary propositions, will therefore apply to the experiences in their totality which are afforded the child by the school.

The first proposition to be stated is concerned with the very foundations on which the educative design should rest.

(I) That the educational program for intellectually superior individuals should be derived from a balanced consideration of facts, opinions based on experience, and deductions from educational philosophy as these relate to the capacities of the individuals and to the probable social roles which they will fill.

Hardly more than an explicit acknowledgment of the logic of differential education for the gifted, this proposition needs little elaboration. Its general import is to urge a basis in child-centered fact for the educational program, as opposed to traditional curricular concepts and administrative practices. Implications and extensions of this principle are stated as corollary propositions.

As a first corollary, it is urged that the demonstrated capacities of the gifted child be considered in planning his educational program.

(I.A) *That the individual's biological potential as it accords with social reality should establish the limits and the nature of the educational program, rather than facility of operation of established procedures.*

Educational theories derive not only from the possibilities of behavioral adaptation, but also from established cultural modes which represent past and accustomed adaptations. However, it is behavioral potential which should be the crucial and most enduring determinant in educational adaptations. The facts that are known with respect to the nature and capacity of gifted children as a whole should be the points of reference in educational planning for them.

The massive structure of school procedures, of practices already proven administrable, deserves some deference. Experience has shown, however, that this structure is not immutable. Modification is possible in the practices of even the longest tradition. The nine months year, the separate teacher for each year level, the periodic schedule for the school day—such practices as these are so thoroughly accustomed that it is easy to consider them basic to any school procedures. The principle just stated urges that the organization of activities, the selection and rejection of courses, and the concept of what experiences shall enter the school curriculum should be regulated more by behavioral potential than by cultural or social precedent.

It is not suggested, however, that the conventions of society be dismissed from consideration. Habits and expectations deeply embedded within a people become as significant at times as the basic qualities of human nature. The deepest of such expectations might indeed be termed the "social nature" of men in the particular culture to which they pertain. But not all school practices hold quite this place in the minds of people. With insight and energy on the part of educational planners, many practices can be modified. Sex instruction, for instance, can readily be related to the needs of children and youth, the bright as well as others. It should be in the curriculum of the common school, though cautious steps toward such instruction are essential in view of deeply and broadly imbedded social attitudes. However, the practice of requiring "sixteen units" for graduation, or of segregating the dull from the bright for periods of instruction, are not so firmly rooted and do not create the same degree of tension when alterations are proposed.

In an earlier report on the Cleveland program for bright children, this statement is made: "Because of their ability to learn more quickly, they branch out on a richer program of work suitable to their ages and interests *but not encroaching upon the work of grades beyond.*"[1] (Italics added.) This description illustrates thought that is rooted in present practice; it is also an instance in which administrative arrangements precede and influence instructional plans rather than follow from them. Should the interests and the capacities of the child lead vertically within any area of study, it is questionable practice to discourage him from continued pursuit for reasons of program alone.

A further corollary considers the appropriate function of the school within its social framework:

(I.B) *That the values upheld and the skills and understandings taught through the curriculum should reflect the needs of the society of which the school is a part.*

The principle of "social parallelism" is commonly accepted. This principle assumes special significance with respect to the education of the children who will someday exert more than a proportionate share of influence upon local, national, and world affairs. The school must reflect and conserve the best traditions and practices of the society of which it is a part.

At the same time, however, there is philosophical sanction for the idea of progressive reconstruction within the democratic society. Dewey makes much of the idea of change and asks that change become synonymous with progress. In a discussion of what constitutes knowledge, he expresses a view which applies to social phenomena as well as to natural:

> Change becomes significant of new possibilities and ends to be attained; it becomes prophetic of a better future. Change is associated with progress rather than with lapse and fall. Since changes are going on anyway, the great thing is to learn enough about them so that we be able to lay hold of them and turn them in the direction of our

desires. Conditions and events are neither to be fled from nor passively acquiesced in; they are to be utilized and directed.[2]

What directions should social change assume? What values should the school reflect in a society where conservative and radical forces freely interplay? Education for constructive cultural evolution must develop competencies for the task. The limited curriculum of the majority of contemporary schools is designed not to produce *reconstructionists*, but *participants* in the status quo. This is impoverished preparation for the life-span career of individuals whose historical counterparts have changed the world.

But through the ages truly gifted individuals have developed responsibility and concern for universal principles and loyalties that transcend local geographical and political boundaries. In a world contracted by media of transport and communication and possessed of power devices which threaten the survival of nations, a "world view" seems urged upon the gifted. Given his capacity for learning, for acquiring the subtle understanding and flexible responses necessary to reckon with international forces, it follows:

(I.C) *That the curriculum designed for the abler individual should reflect world affairs, especially as they presently bear upon the welfare of the parent society, and look beyond to real possibilities of an adequately founded world order.*

The difficult ambition to preserve the values of the real as movement occurs toward the ideal can be aided by an education appropriately designed. While certain levels of such understandings on the part of the average group can be expected, the education of those who can see the larger perspective, who can perceive wider relations and implications, and who can most clearly realize the significance of changes, is best conceived, it would appear, at different levels of organization and conceptualization. In practical effects upon school programs this means that those studies grounded in Western culture must be accompanied by others exploring the behavioral patterns and the value structures of oriental and slavic peoples. Relationships as significant as those which brought into the American school curriculum reflections of European culture now exist between this country and newer national forces. "Modern languages" as a curricular offering should be expanded to include languages other than the conventional French,

German, and Spanish, for instance. Politics, law, and economic theory; anthropology, psychology, and sociology—concepts from such disciplines adapted functionally to the age level of the child and youth are inexcusably omitted from the curriculum offered the abler child. Only through such upgrading of the curriculum can a true parallelism be effected between the school in any part of the world and the world as it is today.

More than his counterpart of average intellectual capacities, the brighter youth can come to understand and properly promote the ideals of the United Nations, while safeguarding under present necessity the interests of his own national group. He has the capacity to acquire those complex understandings essential to the task, and his schooling, it would seem, should facilitate the acquisition of such understandings.

This proposition and its corollaries indicate that the superior abilities characteristic of the gifted child should be related through the educative process to the probable role of reconstruction which will be thrust upon the gifted individual. Positions of leadership at the local, national, and international level demand insight into the major world societies and skills in the evaluation and maintenance of real values as change occurs. Biological potential on the one hand and the role of responsibility to mankind on the other—these are the poles between which the educational design must be accomplished. Conventional school programs are not geared to this task. Only radical re-formulations of theory and practice hold promise commensurate with the problem. Imaginative, constructive thought, redesigning an education which relates biological potential to the social problem, is necessary to appropriate results.

chapter five | *MEETING INDIVIDUAL DIFFERENCES*

A second area of basic theory concerning the educational design points to the necessity that it be distinctively conceived, apart from that design which best adapts to the capacities of the generality. The formal proposition respecting the school program is:

> (*II*) *That a program of education for the intellectually superior should be relatively unique.*

The philosophy and psychology which urge attention to individual differences imply in their farthest extensions that the educative design for every person be adjusted to that individual's uniqueness. This point of view proposes that any similarly deviant group of people will be best served by an educational program constructed with a view toward their similarities. When the deviant quality is intelligence, so significant in the role of behavior and experience, distinctive variations justify an educational program of special scope, subtlety, complexity, and abstraction. The Educational Policies Commission subscribed to this principle as follows:

> In short, the improvement of education for all will yield improved education for the gifted. But this alone is not enough.

Because their intellectual interests and prospective futures differ from others, and because they can learn more and learn it more rapidly, the educational experiences which gifted students should have in school and college ought not to be identical with the experiences of other students. Some of their education should be the same, but some of it should be different—different as to kind, quality, and level of insight. Every teacher, school, school system, and institution of higher learning should have systematic policies and procedure for the education of their gifted students.[3]

In this work, the position is held that the conjunction of extraordinary learning and thinking capacity with the anticipation of an extraordinary social role demands an educational program whose substance and method are peculiarly adapted to exercising the capacity *and* preparing for the role. The educational experience of gifted youngsters becomes "unique" when these two aims are fulfilled. The qualification "relative" is necessary only in deference to the biological principle concerning intra-species variations which was mentioned in the previous discussion of the logic of special education for the gifted.

In terms of curriculum, this principle suggests a qualitative reorganization of the materials and methods used in teaching, in order that the essential problems of the gifted may be more adequately met. Curricular adaptations suited to the intellectually superior will often be "discouraging to slower intellects." Of the capacities of gifted children, and of the unfortunate use of them in the typical school situation, Hollingworth writes:

> We know from measurements made over a three-year period that a child of 140 IQ can master all the mental work provided in the elementary school, as established, in half the time allowed him. Therefore, one-half the time which he spends at school could be utilized in doing something more than the curriculum calls for. . . .
>
> No exhaustive discussion of time-wasting can be undertaken here, except to say briefly that these exceptional pupils are running errands, idling, engaging in "busy work," or devising childish tasks of their own, such as learning to read backward—since they can already read forward very fluently. Many are the devices invented by busy teachers to "take up" the extra time of these rapid learners, but few of these devices have the appropriate character that can be built only on psychological insight into the nature and the needs of gifted children.[4]

Such activities stand in marked contrast to the proposal that the school experience be organized uniquely in a manner commensurate with the gifted child's superiority.

In a now classic listing, E. J. Swift names a large number of subsequently famous men and women who were awkwardly received by the schools of their day and judged to be failures often in the very fields of their destined fame. The list includes Charles Darwin, Patrick Henry, Jonathan Swift, George Eliot, Sir Walter Scott, Daniel Webster, Schiller, Goethe, and Shelley.[5] It is a reasonable conjecture that many of this number would have been more amenable to formal schooling designed at a level appropriate to their insights and sensitivities. And of course history has not kept a record of the unknown numbers who, unlike those listed, never realized their potential.

If fair, and it is probably that, a further charge made against the schools of three decades ago depicts an even more awkward feature of the school process:

> But there is another side to the question. In the first place, granted that gifted children can learn without help, the fact remains that they are not left to themselves. They are not allowed to remain out of school, as was Lincoln, and educate themselves without a teacher. Worse still, they are not allowed to learn in spite of the teacher. In the ordinary school, the rule for the gifted child is: "This much shall you learn, and no more. If by chance you get through with your lesson before your fellows are through, fold your hands and wait quietly until all have finished studying."[6]

Despite the sound work that some teachers do manage to accomplish with gifted children and the currently favorable disposition toward meeting individual needs which prevails even in the "ordinary" classroom, persons with experience in public schools as presently constituted cannot deny that the attitude expressed by Osburn and Rohan is implicit in many practices existing today.

It is difficult to write of distinctiveness simply in terms of quantity. Writers in the literature of education, without apparent deference to a specific theory of genius, refer to "qualitative" differences between children in the upper and lower reaches of the intelligence continuum, as is witnessed in many of the passages cited in this book. Herbert A. Carroll has described the apparent distinctiveness as being caused by the contrasts in widely spaced levels of ability. It is essentially this idea which has been developed here into a logic of differential education for the superior student and upon which is based the immediate argument for uniqueness of educational experience. Carroll writes:

> Studies of the childhood of eminent men reveal that in the great majority of cases these individuals stood out against the background of average children. They were recognized as being different, as possessing abilities which by comparison seemed almost nonexistent in their playmates. They were already marked for greatness.
>
> A visit to a school which has enrolled children of both high and low intelligence gives one a similar impression. To go from a room containing a group of ten-year-old morons to a room containing a group of ten-year-old gifted children is almost like journeying from one world to another. Even a visitor untrained in psychology or pedagogy could not help but realize that the gifted group was made of finer stuff. In fact this quick transit from a very dull group to a very bright group makes one doubt for a moment the psychological principle that individuals differ not in kind but in degree. However, the illusion of the difference in kind grows out of the contrast of the two extremes. The gifted group would not seem so different if they were being compared with superior children—those with I.Q.'s between 110 and 120 or 130. In the discussion, then, of the mental characteristics of intellectually gifted children it will be kept in mind that they possess characteristics which are common to all, but possess them to such an extreme degree that they frequently appear as being unique traits.[7]

Organization of a different type, generalizations into higher systems of understanding, and greater exploration of the methods and grounds of knowledge—these typical essentials of a relatively unique educational experience would be adapted to the education of children possessing extraordinary capacity for thought and service. The school is meeting the needs of the abler student only when it facilitates the exercise of his special capacities and encourages their development. Too often, great potential, if realized, must of its own initiative thrust through the unstimulating, unfitting routine of a curriculum measured to a lesser potential.

Of corollaries to the principle of relative uniqueness, the first concerns organizational phases of the program itself, it being suggested:

(II.A) *That administrative adaptations of the regular school program, though perhaps incidental to the accomplishment of a largely unique program, must not constitute the uniqueness in themselves.*

Common administrative adaptations allow the gifted student to be accelerated through the grades or offer him as enrichment additional exercises couched at the same levels as those of the regular curriculum. Neither of these devices satisfies the idea of distinctiveness. Rather, a proper organization of the desired school experience must grow out of the nature of the new studies and be as unique in itself as is the derived curriculum. Uniqueness of educational design cannot be accomplished directly through administrative rearrangements of the regular curriculum.

Where administrative shifts such as ability grouping are employed indirectly in the realization of such uniqueness, they should be unheralded changes. Designs to accommodate individual differences do not demand special designations which might serve either to embarrass the recipients of the adaptations or to encourage egotism. Much of the objection to segregating gifted children for instructional purposes centers in the belief that unintended and unjustified value judgments will be caused by the practice. Some practice has involved the use of names for special classes which reveal their purpose and give rise to unnecessary prejudices. A unique education is urged for gifted children not to honor them in a moralistic sense but to meet individual differences more adequately. The logic is the same for the lower deviates on the intelligence continuum as for the upper; hence, as it is inappropriate to label classes for mentally defective children "dishonor" classes, for instance, so is it ill-advised to designate those for the bright as "honor" classes.

To consider a different aspect of the principle of uniqueness, a corollary proposition that acknowledges the peculiar capacity for self-direction that is possessed by the gifted individual is next stated:

(II.B) *That the role of the individual himself should be acknowledged and encouraged in relationships crucial to the educational enterprise.*

Educational planning seems to be centered almost wholly in objective means for engendering attitudes and tendencies toward action and in objective devices for accomplishing the learning phenomenon which are external to the individual. The role of the individual in the process of his own education is by far more ignored than acknowledged. In planning the curriculum, in discussing methods, and in establishing requirements, the governing assumption seems to be that in the individual himself there resides no power and no understanding which can be utilized, but that everything is accomplished through some device struck upon to "cause" the educative experience to become integrated, the understanding or the skill to be acquired. Even the concept of "intrinsic" motivation usually assumes the guise, "How can the teacher conduct the teaching act so that intrinsic motivation will be developed?"

This irony of omitting the individual's capacity for self-determination is crucial enough when the education of the *average* student is accomplished (or attempted) through a pattern of majors, minors, and electives which are independent of the judgment of the person himself. Where the intellectually gifted child is concerned, the irony approaches the magnitude of immorality. Whereas with the average student the motive to learn is perhaps modest and easily frustrated, the tremendous initiative toward the acquisition of further and further understandings is one of the commonplace observations made by students of the gifted. Motive, for them, does not have to be created; it is present and in need only of the most intelligent guidance. The literature on the gifted child acknowledges this strong drive toward intellectual acquisition in numerous ways. The frustration of the drive is also acknowledged, and one of the frequently mentioned causes of the frustration is the inappropriate school regimen to which the child is subjected.

Terman and Oden note among their systematic observations that:

> Nearly half of the gifted children learned to read before starting to school; at least 20 percent before the age of 5 years, 6 percent before 4, and 1.6 percent before 3. Most of these learned to read with little or no formal instruction. One of our gifted girls demonstrated by test that she could read almost as well at the age of 25 months as the average child at the end of the first school grade. (This subject has since taken a Ph.D. degree, and is now teaching in a state university.)
>
> Early indications of superior intelligence most often noted by parents were quick understanding, insatiable curiosity, extensive information, retentive memory, large vocabulary, and unusual interest in such things as number relations, atlases, and encyclopedias.

There is no evidence that these abilities and preoccupations were to any considerable degree the result of artificial stimulation or forced culture.[8]

Yet such students are often "put to their tasks" in the usual school routine, their initiative smothered by external distractions or ignored in the interest of getting on with the program.

The Educational Policies Commission acknowledges at some length the unusual motivation of gifted children and describes how this motivation is sometimes received by the school:

> More than their average classmates, gifted students generally appear to have more desire to learn. Acquisitions of knowledge and intellectual skills, finding answers to questions that spring from their natural curiosity, and receiving the approval of parents and teachers for their intellectual achievements—experiences such as these are highly satisfying to most children and young persons and especially so to those of superior intelligence. Satisfactions so gained stimulate the appetite for more.
>
> The incentive which the typical gifted student normally brings to a learning situation is an asset that can aid the efforts of schools and colleges to develop human talent to the fullest. But too often the asset is wasted or even turned into a liability by the failure to provide educational opportunities with great enough challenge or scope to evoke achievement and subsequent satisfaction. In such a circumstance, the exceptionally able student becomes bored or even hostile to school work.[9]

In view of the testimony and evidence that such important assets to education are the characteristic possessions of gifted children, it is only by gross stretches of the imagination that a school program dominated by the concept of required units, for instance, and of *a* text for American history which will be handled for a few minutes daily throughout a semester or a year, can be conceived as fitting. For individuals whose capacities include in combination exceptional learning ability and exceptional motivation to learn, these concepts are decidedly inadequate. The gifted child, especially if among others of his kind and subject to the stimulation of group enterprise, can more likely handle the gross development of America as a nation, in a functionally conceived presentation, within a period of weeks, while at the same time growing in other subjects at somewhat the same pace. Flexible administrative requirements which permit such adjustments are due the gifted individual.

This concept is sufficiently important to justify a consideration of the content and methods that should follow from its application. It is hardly to be expected that the young person by virtue of his giftedness alone be responsible for determining the pattern of his own education. His drive must be directed and guided by means of appropriate knowledge. Instruction in the nature of human capacities, the nature of development, and the influence of education on these capacities and processes would appear to be essential to his understanding. Without such knowledge, the complex processes of education might never be related meaningfully to the complex processes of the growth and development of behavior.

What specific content would this idea suggest for inclusion within the scheme of education for gifted children? First, the nature of learning as a biological phenomenon might be explored. How does learning occur in which behavior is adapted through experience? To introduce the gifted individual in his secondary school years to facts pertaining to the impressionability and retentivity of the nervous system, to the ideas of sensation, perception, and reaction as psychological concepts, and to the nature of motivation is to instruct him in important processes, a knowledge of which should aid the youngster in self-analysis and self-direction.

Characteristically, the processes of human growth and development are not subjected to systematic study in the regular school curriculum. It would appear from an observation of the curriculum that to study the processes of physics and chemistry, for instance, is more important than to study the processes of mental growth and development in the human being. The child needs to know what sorts of changes are supposed to be occurring in him through the processes of learning and of maturation in order that he can himself encourage the processes and evaluate his progress in them.

Perhaps the most crucial area of knowledge for this purpose, however, is higher mental processes collectively. The gifted child, exceptional in the uses of mind, typically uses it without direct instruction as to the nature of mental operations or of formal disciplines pertaining to their use. Such higher mental processes as reasoning, comparison, evaluation, origination, and abstraction, highlighted as to their nature and as to their pertinence to specific methods of inquiry, would afford sound material to bring into the understanding of the developing child. Instruction embracing the whole of individual psychology with respect to dynamics and processes of mental development, particularly the psychology of learning and thinking, can and should be introduced into the curriculum.

A passage from an autobiographical sketch by Dewey concerning his own intellectual growth serves to suggest more subtle types of personal growth which may occur frequently among the gifted and in which instruction and exploration could be of extreme importance. Dewey says:

> There was, however, one course in the previous year that in retrospect may be called philosophical. That was a rather short course, without laboratory work, in physiology, a book of Huxley's being the text. It is difficult to speak with exactitude about what happened to me intellectually so many years ago, but I have an impression that there was derived from that study a sense of interdependence and interrelated unity that gave form to intellectual stirrings that had been previously inchoate, and created a kind of type or model of a view of things to which material in any field ought to conform. Subconsciously, at least, I was led to desire a world and a life that would have the same properties as had the human organism in the picture of it derived from study of Huxley's treatment. At all events I got great stimulation from the study, more than from anything I had had contact with before; and as no desire was awakened in me to continue that particular branch of learning, I date from this time the awakening of a distinctive philosophic interest.[10]

It is, of course, unnecessary to grant that only infrequently will a new Dewey be subject to public school instruction. His remarks are suggestive, however, of similar patterns in other developing individuals, who, though having less capacity, may still have sufficient ability to make material contributions to society. To teach the gifted child that there may be great potential in such "inchoate stirrings" is to acquaint him with a subtle psychological operation which he has little chance of appreciating without benefit of educational guidance.

More specifically, the nature of the educative process, and of the social institution devised for its promotion, should be brought within the range of systematic instruction. Why the school as an institution has arisen to accomplish certain purposes may be learned by brighter children and the lesson personally applied. Such knowledge is usually acquired incidentally, if at all. If related explicitly to the student's own performance, this knowledge would ensure that each step upward on the educational ladder possesses meaning in terms of expected behavioral modifications.

There is a meaning in the concept of "liberal" education which is appropriate to the needs and uses of people of unusual intellectual capacity and which may have been lost, largely through necessity, with respect to the education of the majority. It is the concept of education as freeing one from the bonds of ignorance and from the necessity of subservient and dependent action and thought. The intellectually superior individual can acquire independent and valid judgments in intellectual and academic issues. He should be encouraged to think this true and to set about gaining such independence. By gaining a perspective in many disciplines and by turning his mind to considerations of practical and social significance which lie beyond the school room, he can progress toward that end. He will thus gain independence from the opinions of others and become able to do his own intellectual searching. Education toward this type of independence should be positively sought, and the experiences of the child in school should develop his capacities toward this end. Liberation from ignorance in matters dependent upon knowledge, from the bonds of expediency in moral actions, and from the appeal to authority for ultimate truths— such a concept, once prevalent in education generally, is still fitting in the education of gifted children.

The application of the principle that the child should contribute to his own education leads further to a consideration of technique and activity as distinguished from content. Among such considerations, one aspect of routine guidance services is especially important. Long-range planning with respect to education and occupation is particularly justified in the case of gifted children. It is apparent that the child of superior intellectual ability can go further in the processes of education than the average child and that if the education represents purposeful adaptation of his capacities, he should continue as far as his capacities warrant. Hence, even the lower levels of school training should give tacit recognition to the probability that the child will continue to college and university work and perhaps to special professional training beyond. The choice of studies, expectations with respect to the development of certain skills, and other general modifications in the educative process ensue from the acceptance of the idea of long-range planning, and such adaptations are to the best interests of the child.

In the classroom, the use sometimes made of gifted children in the aid of those less apt in academic situations would seem particularly appropriate. If the emphasis falls on the gifted individual's growth (as opposed to a primary emphasis upon the service), the practice of using the superior student in tutorial functions would appear to offer several benefits. For instance, the superior individual can profit from the opportunity to perceive that even with effort and interest some people do not learn readily. He can also profit from the opportunity to gain deeper insights for himself through the process of organizing and explaining certain ideas and skills to others. Learning concern for other people through performing them a service; learning greater appreciation for the teacher's efforts and for the undertaking of the school as a social agency; and learning to achieve social acceptance through genuine help in functional situations—all are benefits which would seem to derive from such experience, if carefully guarded with respect to basic purposes.

Encouraging the individual to analyze his own progress is another possible application of this principle. To encourage self-evaluation in terms of consciously achieved and voluntarily accepted goals of development would appear to be a promising antidote to the mass procedures which cannot be avoided. In gifted individuals, critical ability as one of the indices of intelligence is present to an exceptional degree. The present principle would merely bend that capacity for criticism toward the process of education and growth and development.

The education of the gifted individual should also emphasize individual accomplishment and independent thought among those group processes essential to effective interaction among persons in a democracy. Increasingly emphasized under such rubrics as "group dynamics" and "interpersonal relationships" and "learning through interaction" is the idea growing out of organismic psychology that group thinking is more effective than individual, that "two heads are better than one." However, as an appropriate emphasis in the education of the gifted child, it remains to be considered that the individual thinker who is capable of higher levels of synthesis, and of more subtle perception of relationships among variables, has something of value to offer his society. It is traditional that George Washington Carver could use no assistants because he could not communicate his methods. And Einstein made this interesting statement about himself: "I am a horse for single harness, not cut out for tandem or team work."[11] This feeling is implicit in the behavior of a number of gifted individuals. As a "natural" characteristic, it should be respected and used in the optimum development of the person. Optimum development can in no sense imply the negating of such an important tendency toward individuality in performance, and unsuccessful (or even successful) attempts to "socialize" a highly individualistic person (in the usual sense of the term) might result in questionable, if not decisively undesirable, gains.

By way of summary, then, this capacity for self-motivation, when coupled with acquired understandings essential to appropriate choices, will render the intellectually superior child and youth more nearly able to make his way through the school on his own insight than would otherwise be possible. This form of self-guidance would thus represent a step toward, and further practice in, the independence and self-containment which are marks of maturity. The gifted can attain such maturity earlier than the generality, and in a relatively unique educational program, the school would be urged to encourage the unfolding of this potential.

As a third corollary to the principle of relative uniqueness in the educational program for the superior student, consideration is given to the range of individual differences which remain when one has narrowed the group to the upper extremes of IQ. A flexible execution of the design is an essential factor; hence, this corollary to the principle:

(II. C) *That marked extremes in individual differences should be acknowledged through flexibility in planning the program, in its execution, and in the evaluation of outcomes of the processes.*

Flexible evaluation does not necessarily conflict with standards of quality which, in general, may reasonably be held higher for gifted children. Nor does it intend to establish a margin for excusing possible failures. It is a principle emerging from a consideration of the compelling nature of certain interests which sometimes absorb the child of superior intellectual initiative. Such interests may be so engrossing that matters of program interfere with them only at heavy cost. Failure to accomplish less valuable but "required" phases of work during a given term or semester should be weighed fairly against the value of accomplishments achieved beyond those required. Singular achievement in a self-imposed task significant both immediately to the child himself and for his ultimate development warrants credit and evaluation equivalent to that which would have been awarded had the task been required; it does not warrant the vengeance-like marks sometimes applied for simple neglect of accustomed tasks.

Certain of Terman's interpretations of the performance of his "C" group indicate further a need for flexible evaluation especially when a child's performances are so markedly beyond those of the ordinary youth.

> Although many of the C's by the time they reach college show a general deterioration of ambition and interests, others in this group are still riding hard their private intellectual hobbies and are unwilling to adopt those of their instructors. One suspects that later some of these will have to be transferred to the A group.
>
> In this connection I wish to point out that gifted students in general are to a surprising extent self-educated. Learned and Wood find many college seniors untutored in English beyond the high school, who know more English than other college seniors who have majored in the subject. They even find *high-school* seniors who know more science than some college *seniors* who have majored in science preparatory to teaching it in high school. Such facts as these show what the gifted high school student is sometimes up against.[12]

Burks, Jensen, and Terman report an instance of deliberate choice of the mediocre scholastic record in favor of a type of study not credited by the school yet intelligent and purposeful in some ways, a choice which is perhaps more frequent than is commonly recognized:

> The student whose score on the Thorndike Intelligence Examination was by a considerable margin the highest that has been made by anyone entering Stanford since the tests were first instituted, graduated (for the A.B. and J.D. degrees) with a scholastic record that was only a little above average, but with a record for popularity and leadership rarely equaled. On his leaving the University one of us informed him of his Thorndike score and asked what was responsible for his indifferent scholastic record. The answer was that he knew he had a better mind than most men, that in high school he always earned A's, but that when he entered college he decided he ought to study people if he was to make a success as a lawyer. View-

ing the matter retrospectively he said he was entirely satisfied with
the choice he had made; that he had taken care to learn enough law
to know what he was about, and that he knew when the time came
to take the position which had long been promised him in a leading
law firm he would have no difficulty in working up his cases. . . .[13]

It may be noted in passing that this able student's statement that he
knew "what he was about" in law is an informal expression of the
author's notion of education as *cognitive perspective* (p. 102 ff). In the
presence of such intelligent calculation, it is reasonable to question
the view that omniscience may be attributed to the approved comple-
tion of approved tasks in approved ways.

A final corollary in extension of the principle of relative uniqueness
suggests that gifted children properly utilize more highly developed
equipment than the generality of children and youth:

(II. D) *That the education of the gifted individual should involve the use of equipment
and materials beyond that practicable or essential for children in the average range of
intellectual ability.*

More materials will be needed for the appropriate education of the
gifted for the reason that the demonstration of facts and principles at
levels of complexity beyond the reach of average intellectual capacity
often demands different media of demonstration. Laboratory equipment suitable for the exposition of elementary physical laws, for instance, will not in every case permit a demonstration of the more subtle
and complicated principles which the gifted individual will be able to
grasp. And whereas a basic general encyclopedia might suffice for the
ordinary research purposes of average children in the earlier years of
secondary school, the gifted are likely to demand much earlier special
reference works of a technical nature.

The Educational Policies Commission notes this need for more
elaborate equipment:

> Learners should have access to a wide variety of books, pictures,
> realia, and other instructional materials. More materials and a greater
> variety of such materials are needed for students of superior mental
> ability than for others. But superior students need less guidance
> in the selection and use of such materials than do others.[14]

And in another context the Commission notes that the additional materials needed for such purposes will probably lead to more expenses. They feel that the returns would be more than compensatory:

> The improvements in elementary and secondary education that are most needed to carry out effective programs for the education of the gifted vary as to the amount and kind of expenditure required. Some are negligible in comparison with total costs (for example: books, supplies, art materials, sheet music). Others, although expensive in first purchase, may be used over several years, so that the annual cost is not great (for example: science laboratories, shop equipment, musical instruments, and special equipment for audio-visual aids). Still other items would be large absolutely and continuously (for example: more teachers, counselors, significantly better salaries, smaller classes).[15]

It is noted further that the use of tools and aids to solve complex and burdensome tasks at earlier age levels than are customary is feasible with brighter children. The availability of a slide rule or of a calculating machine, with instruction in their use, might, by the very facility which they offer in computation, permit insight into broader mathematical principles. The same reasoning applies to teaching the full operations of electronic data-processing machinery to able students in the upper levels of the secondary school. And it can only be conjectured what leaps of insight into the nature and processes of plant and animal life, for instance, might occur from making available to the intellectually gifted child in the very earliest school years a microscope with which to observe natural specimens.

The use of specialized equipment to accommodate the further reaches of intellect can be extended into the area of mechanical aids and developed systems for facilitating communications. Instruction could be given in systems that minimize mechanical barriers to communication, to the extent that the full acquisition, word by word, of an exceptional lecture, for instance, could be achieved if such full notation were purposeful. To this end, some skill such as speedwriting or shorthand should be taught. And in terms of expression, use of the typewriter should be taught. Occasions demand that the speed, legibility, and general utility of typewriting be substituted for longhand, and the school should prepare the brighter individual for such occasions, on the score that they will occur more frequently in his life span.

Concluding with the suggestion that special equipment is justified, the proposition that the education of the intellectually superior individual should be uniquely conceived has been ramified through previous corollaries emphasizing that administrative rearrangements do not alone comprise uniqueness and that the gifted individual may play an effectual role in his own development.

Such practices as allowing individual plans to substitute for group enterprises; allowing initiative in the pursuit of a project once a perspective is established with respect to purposes and goals; granting freedom to move along the lines of the educative design at any rate of speed commensurate with optimum gain; according permission to vary the depth of exploration with different curricular segments (even allowing haste and superficiality in a given requirement where a broader purpose suggests it); affording a flexible evaluation of total endeavors within a given period; and, perhaps as significant as any practice, allowing some *free time* unstructured by assignments and unfettered even by the design itself, so that the uniqueness of the personality may truly achieve expression—these and other expedients at the level of operation follow upon the proposition of uniqueness and its corollaries.

chapter six | *THE PRINCIPLE OF ECONOMY*

A third major proposal by way of general principles governing the educational design states:

> (*III*) *That the curriculum should consist of economically chosen experiences designed to promote the civic, social, and personal adequacy of the intellectually superior individual.*

To exercise economy in the choice of experiences so that in a reasonable number of years of schooling the behavior potential of the individual may come to include adequate responses to present and future needs requires that experiences be generalized beyond the particular context in which they first occur. It is acknowledged that bright children transfer more readily than do others, and this fact of psychology becomes the source of a principle of education, that the ability of gifted children to utilize the higher mental processes for transfer warrants innovations in the curriculum devised for them.

With respect to school practices, this proposition urges that school time be given to experiences with highest potential for multiple transfer. A curriculum deliberately placed at a high level of generality and abstractness will, under this concept, be practicable and desirable. On the other hand, many experiences couched at a relatively specific or concrete level in order to reach down to the comprehension of the generality misfit the intellectually able and result in the boredom, rebellion, and withdrawal commonly noted. A reaction against formalized intellectualism in education was perhaps right and due; that this reaction extend to the extreme of ignoring or minimizing the capacity which mentally gifted children have for making specific deductions from a valid generalization is a fundamental violation of the principle of individual differences.

Dewey has spoken both of the dangers of "abstractness" as setting experience apart from life and of the value of abstraction for the development of the person. He says:

> It will be apparent that mind is one with intelligent or purposeful activity—with an activity that *means* something and in which the meaning counts as a factor in the development of an activity. There is a sense in which mind is measured by growth of power of abstraction, and a very important sense this is. There is another sense in which it can be truly said that abstractness is the worst evil that infests education. The false sense of abstraction is connected with thinking of mental activity as something that can go on wholly by itself, apart from objects or from the world of persons and things. Real subject-matter being removed, something else has to be supplied in its place for the mind to occupy itself with.[16]

He was in opposition, obviously, not to the legitimate and effective use of intelligence, but to the mechanical usages and routine *memoriter* procedures which had come to characterize much of the school activity in the era of Dewey's initial rebellion.

A practical recognition of the capacity of gifted children to deal meaningfully with abstractions, and thus to economize upon the learning process, was made in an early book on the subject, edited by Helen Cohen and Nancy Coryell. They wrote:

> In discussions of methods of teaching, however, the term "activities" has come to indicate various ways of learning by doing. This interest has resulted from the popularity of the project method and the introduction of large, well-equipped laboratories, stages, and workshops. The values of such physical activities as these devices employ are probably subject to limitations in the case of the intellectually gifted. For example, since superior students can use vivid imaginations, it is more to their advantage to read a substantial book on costumes as these developed from modes of family and court life,

than to expend time and energy in dressing a doll in the style shown in a single picture. The setting of a scene in a Shakespearean play can better be imagined from a well-illustrated book than from a crude cardboard model of the Globe Theatre. Again, laws in physics can very often be perfectly comprehended in terms of equations or statements of supporting facts without individual laboratory rehearsals of known processes. Laboratories and workshops offer valuable opportunities to the superior student, but the purposes and the work could be on much higher experimental levels than are usually encouraged or provided for and directed.[17]

Here is a point of view which urges a re-apportionment of the concrete and abstract elements in educational experience which should characterize all subject-matter presentation. The concept is broad enough to foreshadow the mania for teaching machines.

The proposal that economy govern the choice and organization of experiences in the curriculum for the gifted is meant to emphasize that the intellectual capacities of the educand should be applied to the pursuit of generalizations and abstractions which he demonstrates an ability to handle meaningfully and which will economize upon the time and materials essential to his education.

For those persons who will pursue learning to higher reaches, over a longer portion of the life span, and who by natural bent will search more intensively for unity among variously acquired insights, some simple rubric upon which to structure the content of educative experiences would appear to be helpful. A commonly used category for purposes of organization of materials and courses of study in higher education is four-fold, consisting of (1) the humanities, (2) the social sciences, (3) the natural sciences, and (4) mathematics. The first corollary to the principle of economy employs this division of academic disciplines:

(III. A) *That a four-fold category of the subject matter of the curriculum should be utilized, the areas being the humanities, the social sciences, the natural sciences, and mathematics.*

Not all courses studied would necessarily be so entitled, but the child or youth would be kept in constant reference to this four-fold division as a means toward estimating his progress along important lines of

academic experience and toward facilitating his insight into the processes and goals of his own development. Some of the uses of such a
simple, planning rubric suggest themselves.

The elective system in general school practice is sometimes accused
of permitting students to build the requisite credits or units with
separate studies which do not lend themselves to a comprehensible,
integrated pattern. A four-fold rubric, which is in itself comprehensive,
offers an easily comprehended scheme of organization around which
elective experiences and required ones can be ordered and through
which an ordered estimate of an individual's advancement in knowledge can be obtained.

A glance at the subjects, often only four principal ones, pursued by
a student in a given year of high school frequently reveals patterns
such as: (1) English, U.S. History, World Geography, Algebra; or
(2) English, French, Geometry, Home Economics. In the first of these
patterns analysis by the four-fold rubric suggested here reveals that
for a full year in the developing child's experience no systematic presentations in the natural sciences occur and that one half of his study
load is in social studies. In the second pattern, both social studies and
natural science are missing. So long as school personnel and children
think of school subjects as entities apart from the basic intellectual and
academic disciplines to which they belong, such awkward gaps and
overloads are likely to occur. On the other hand, thought about the
study load of the individual child at a given period, which relates to
the base of four broad areas, easily arranges studies so that all areas
will be represented. Children should advance their understandings on
a fairly even front, in continuous, spiral penetration into the general
range of knowledge. And additions, extensions, and deletions from
the program of offerings in the enriched curriculum or the curriculum
as a whole can occur more intelligently with such a basis in mind.

*Within the areas of knowledge subordinate to the division, only major, com-
prehensive concepts should be explored,* if the idea of economy is to be fulfilled. These comprehensive concepts, of course, may be organized
in a number of ways, but the virtues attributed to the "unit" method
of organization seem to be fitting for the education of the gifted. The
unit method in its richer interpretations allows for an optimum bal-
ancing of intellectual uses with activities involving materials and
concrete processes. Appropriate levels of unit construction can be

found to utilize the extreme capacities of the gifted. A corollary encompassing both the idea of comprehensive concepts for the sake of economy and their organization into units is:

(III. B) *That a curricular organization involving comprehensive, functionally organized teaching-learning situations should be utilized in substantial part in the instruction of the gifted.*

Of course complete distinctiveness in application to the intellectually superior can scarcely be claimed for such an approach to classroom technique. Under several guises some such organization of curricular materials for all children has been evolving for many years. Distinctiveness is more likely to pertain at the level of implementation of the principle than in the theory behind it.

Moreover, this emphasis upon the unit method of instruction does not eliminate the desirability of other methods. Cohen and Coryell have reminded their readers (cf. citation on pp. 103–104) that the gifted child may learn more about costume through reading than through activity of a concrete type; it is equally true with respect to the gifted that a well developed lecture can be as profitable as instruction. The central meaning of a social problem, for instance, and the implications of varying reactions to the problem may be sketched for a group of gifted children through a well organized lecture; and their capacity to generalize and to apply will appropriately be brought into use in making for themselves such specific experiences with the idea as might well have to be part of the *instruction* for the generality. The gifted child in the ordinary milieu of playground and home can make his own laboratory incidentally and in passing, and will tend to do so, for the testing of concepts which have come into his ken. To him the *idea* is the central factor and the crucial point in his instruction. It is not so much a question of developing applications and illustrations for him as of allowing him to develop his own.

In the upper reaches of his secondary instruction, then, looking toward that time when independent pursuit of ideas should become possible, the gifted student should be referred to more and more comprehensive, highly generalized presentations in texts and in lectures — all in the interest of economy—so that as soon as possible he might attain a range of insights commensurate with his unusual interests and learning capacities.

The major proposal of economy and its corollaries hold that with respect to the education of the gifted the exercise of economy will especially pertain. Greater expanses of knowledge can be attained through the use of economically devised, comprehensive concepts, and there is a need for such greater expanses by virtue of the complex civic and personal functions which will be thrust upon the intellectually superior individual. The corollaries have been stated that (1) a four-fold content classification is useful in structuring the experiences of the gifted; and (2) that a functional organization of the curriculum is appropriate, a variety of methods for its implementation being possible. This economy permits a more efficient type of education in accord with the learning capacity of the gifted. It demands an organically conceived educational design promoting the total scheme of values and skills sought, and it establishes disciplines in the process of curricular selection and deletion.

chapter seven | *THE TEACHER OF THE GIFTED*

A final area of consideration respecting the general design of education for the gifted concerns the teacher. It will be maintained that the most able learners should have teachers particularly adept in dealing with the mental and behavioral characteristics which distinguish gifted children. This position is not a denial of any democratic tenet. Rather it is an essential toward realizing the degree of individualization and self-fulfillment required by the democratic ideal. Add the more material concern for the welfare of society (cf. the discussion in Chapter 2 of "The Social Significance of Special Education for the Gifted"), and the position is further substantiated. One can scarcely review the names of historical men and women of genius as studied by Cox, or the contemporary achievements of Terman's children as adults, without acknowledging that the social returns upon investment in the special education of the gifted are most promising, if advances in human welfare through medical discoveries and technological progress can be measured at all. In contrast, the more familiar, expensive, elaborate, and sustained endeavors in behalf of the handicapped, all very essential to the same democratic tenet, on the material side provide only limited returns in the attainment of minimal self-sufficiency and the avoidance of institutional care. Stated as a principle, then, this proposal is made:

(IV) That teachers of intellectually superior children and youth should be among those of the greatest general excellence to be found in the profession.

It is held that this excellence should include deviance in intellectual stature and related personality characteristics similar to that of the gifted children themselves, as a means of facilitating that intimate intellectual and temperamental *rapprochement* without which schooling becomes mere instruction and never education.

What, then, are some of the particular characteristics which should distinguish those best qualified to become mentors to prospective philosophers, scholars, scientists, and statesmen? That the drive toward understanding is one of the more pervasive aspects of the behavior of the gifted child has been indicated. This dynamic quality and related higher mental processes need opportunity for outlet rather than external urging toward expression. It is important that the teacher be able to reckon with the fuller expression of mind at such levels. Yet brilliant reasoning may have aspects of immaturity which can be seasoned by careful guidance. Such guidance requires ability at higher levels than that ordinarily needed for work with average students.

The teacher of bright children will sometimes find himself unequal to some of his students in reasoning potential. Should there be a too great discrepancy, the frequency with which the teacher is compelled to admit error or inadequacy is likely to result in a loss of prestige. Hollingworth notes this point:

> The teacher should be chosen for impersonal interest in educational problems and for ability to maintain an unbiased attitude even toward pupils whose grasp may in some instances exceed her own. The teacher must, in short, be one who can tolerate being beaten occasionally by a child, in intellectual performances.[18]

Somewhat later she makes a similar observation:

> The highly intelligent child will be intellectually capable of self-determination, and his greatest value to society can be realized only if he is truly self-possessed and detached from the influence of both positive and negative suggestion. The more intelligent the child, the truer this statement is. It is especially unfortunate, therefore, that so

many gifted children have in authority over them persons of no special fitness for the task, who cannot gain or keep the respect of these good thinkers. Such unworthy guardians arouse, by the process of "reintegration," contempt for authority wherever it is found, and the inability to yield gracefully to command.[19]

In a description of "what makes the good college teacher," Justman indicates qualities which logically pertain to the needs of the brighter student:

> Watch the master teacher at work! There is little in his performance which is superfluous. Each expressed idea is meaningful and important. A short question may suffice to introduce a whole chain of ideas, a word to redirect a whole trend of thought. Commanding the performance is a recognition that students, too, can read and think and work, that what they need most is stimulating direction. The good teacher is not necessarily exhaustive, "covering" the subject the way a carpet covers the floor; he is selective, revealing the guideposts by which the students can themselves travel more deeply into the subject. His teaching is suggestive, connotative. It leaves the students not overwhelmed by facts, but richer by a few insights and with a growing sense of independence.[20]

It is the gifted students who fit in the richest sense certain of Justman's descriptive phrases—e.g., susceptible to a whole chain of ideas, who "read and think and work," and who "can themselves travel more deeply into the subject." They profit most from suggestion and connotation, as has been noted earlier. At the college level, of course, the differentiation in intelligence is lessened, so that to some degree all college students have moved nearer to that level at which students might be termed "bright" for school purposes. Even at the lower levels, however, qualities such as these of the good college teacher are needed in the instruction of the brighter children.

It is further apparent from experience with intellectually superior students that something of a "philosophical" disposition on the part of the teacher is a necessary personal characteristic. Only a disposition on the part of the teacher to move the concrete facts of history and physiology and mathematics toward their problematic phases parallels a similar intrinsic bent on the part of the pupil. It is this type of mind that will effect relations between issues and disciplines and sense discrepancies and inconsistencies in real situations. The average child in the average learning situation tends to be unaware of such inter-system difficulties and not to be disturbed by them if brought to his attention. And on the positive side, such philosophical behavior is unquestionably requisite to proper conceptions concerning impending changes and proper leadership in such changes.

An able recognition of this dimension in the educative process occurs in the exposition of an educational philosophy of avowed "elitism" which would be suspect today. Independent of his total perspective, however, Michael Demiashkevich appears to see as essential certain qualities of personal disposition in the teacher of the ablest learners. He says:

> Teachers of the elite should in the first place be themselves an elite in the sense of possessing intellectual acumen, character, and general culture. They should, of course, possess knowledge of their special fields and of the fundamentals of the science of education. They should be well-grounded also in the fundamentals of the history of philosophy, irrespective of their specialities.
>
> Again, why philosophy? First, because a teacher of the elite in order to be a competent guide in the matter of character building must himself have a scale of values—moral, scientific, political, aesthetic— as firm and clear as possible. In other words, the teacher of the elite must have a critically worked out general outlook upon life and its fundamental problems. Above all, the teacher has to know how humanity stood in the past and appears to stand in his own time with regard to the fundamental problem of certainty—epistemological, metaphysical, and ethical. Then he will be better prepared to answer their questions and guide the youths in their inherent urge for the ideal.[21]

There are additional reasons why philosophy, as the end of truly advanced study into the nature and behavior of men and material, would seem a fitting pursuit for the teacher of the gifted. That future scientists or scholars in the humanities may possess the insights essential to citizenship at higher levels demands that their thinking be constructively guided in those areas in which they are *not* most adept. Only the teacher who has traveled over such intellectual horizons as those represented by philosophy, theoretical science, and religion; the political and economic ways of man; the manners of his aesthetic expression; and varying value systems as products of cultural growth can possess an adequate perspective upon the total enterprises of man and be able to induce a reasoned and balanced view within the gifted child upon his field of major capacity and interest. Something of education as a way of life and of the idea of its proper continuance through the years are insights which should pervade the spontaneous attitudes and ideals of the teacher of the gifted, in order that subtly and indirectly he may pass them on to those of his charges who can personally realize these processes at their higher levels.

A concept that has lost much of the richness which it once held is that of a student's selecting a place for study "with" a certain man. This idea is prominent in Boring's treatment of the development of thought in experimental psychology. These selected passages are illustrative. Of Franz Brentano, he states:

> He first went to Berlin to study philosophy, and there Trendelenburg taught him to appreciate Aristotle, who came thus to be the dominating influence throughout the rest of his life. A year or so later, in 1856, Brentano went to Munich, where he came under the influence of Döllinger, a Catholic historian and theologian, who was subsequently excommunicated because of his criticism of the Church. This latter fact is interesting in view of Brentano's later difficulties with the Church.[22]

Of Otto Külpe:

> He went in 1881, not to Königsberg, the nearest university, but to Leipzig, in order to study history. At Leipzig, however, he came into contact with Wundt, who diverted him, for the time being, to philosophy and, of course, to experimental psychology, which was still an infant science. . . . He was not, however, entirely weaned from his desire to become an historian. He stayed with Wundt a year, and then went to Berlin for a semester to study history again. Perhaps he was weighing history against psychology in this turning of his back on Wundt and going to the great Berlin historians like Mommsen, Kirchkoff, and Diels. . . . After a single semester he went in 1883, not back to Wundt, but to G. E. Müller at Göttingen. . . .[23]

Of John Dewey and associates:

> In 1894 Dewey went to the University of Chicago for ten years as professor of philosophy. G. H. Mead came with him from Michigan as assistant professor of philosophy. A. W. Moore was assistant in philosophy the next year. . . . In 1894 James R. Angell also came

to Chicago as assistant professor of psychology and director of the psychological laboratory which had been started the year before. In this year, Dewey, the oldest, was thirty-five; Angell, the youngest, was but twenty-five. Dewey was at the time half a psychologist. Mead and Moore were interested in psychology; and Dewey's brilliance was able to exert considerable influence upon the systematic tenets of the others. They were all young. It was just the situation that might lead to a school founded upon a systematic point of view.[24]

Should those most sensitive to behavioral differences not be permitted this classic type of association at earlier age levels? Great figures like the teachers just mentioned are perhaps not the products of any systematic educational enterprise as such, and it is of course not feasible to expect that every public school system have for the convenience of its brighter children a man or two like Brentano or Dewey. But a realistic expectation does arise from the concept. Among the men and women who choose teaching as a profession there are those to whom the ideals of continued growth and of increasing perspective appeal and who are capable of such increasing stature. Perhaps if their professional training encouraged deeper and broader pursuits, more teachers in this vein would be available. Because the sensitive child will be alert to precept, then, his teachers should have conducted themselves in such a manner as to become men and women worthy of a child's *studying* and *studying with*.

Men who think as they talk, rather than recall; who speak from the wealth that they have learned, rather than from what they have been taught; who argue with a clear recognition and sensitive acknowledgment of the positions from which they argue; men who differentiate faith from fact, and label each accordingly; men who in one breath state not only the conviction, but its reasoned base—such are the teachers for youth who are critically and analytically disposed. Subtle indications of attitudes such as the raised eyebrow, a suggestive movement of the hand, or apparent increased tension often pass the average student unnoticed; these form much of the substance of things learned in the case of gifted students. The teacher's language, logic, and general classroom behavior become a part of that total experience of the child which is his curriculum. And only the gifted teacher can lead the gifted child through experiences commensurate with his capacity.

In striking contrast to the level of behavior just described and by way of indicating that teachers do become the subject of the gifted child's concern, this passage from Hollingworth is appropriate:

> The foolish teacher who hates to be corrected by a child is unsuited to these children. Too many children of IQ 170 are being taught by teachers of IQ 120. Into this important matter of the *selection of the teacher* we cannot enter, except to illustrate the difficulty from recent conversation with a ten-year-old boy of IQ 165. This boy was referred to us as a school problem: "Not interested in the school work. Very impudent. A liar!" The following is a fragment of conversation with this boy:
>
> "What seems to be your *main* problem in school?"
>
> "Several of them."
>
> "Name *one*."
>
> "Well, I will name the teachers. Oh, boy! It is bad enough when the *pupils* make mistakes, but when the *teachers* make mistakes, oh, boy!"
>
> "Mention a few mistakes the teachers made."
>
> "For instance I was sitting in 5A and the teacher was teaching 5B. She was telling those children that the Germans discovered printing, that Gutenberg was the first discoverer of it, mind you. After a few minutes I couldn't stand it. I am not supposed to recite in that class, you see, but I got up. I said, 'No; the Chinese *invented*, not discovered, printing, before the time of Gutenberg—while the Germans were still barbarians.' Then the teacher said, 'Sit down. You are entirely too fresh.' Later on she gave me a raking-over before the whole class. Oh, boy! What teaching!"[25]

Under a teacher who could offer him an intellectual diet of larger issues, such mistaken details might not be so violently received. With trivia as the medium, the content, of education, the frustrated mind is likely to grasp at any discrepancies.

The professional training (beyond subject matter and beyond "general" education) of the teacher of gifted children may well begin with that normally administered to teachers. Certainly the historic and present function of the school as an agency of society, the studies in methodology, and those in routine surveys of child psychology and sociology are all important. Certain additional areas would appear justified by virtue of the nature of the task and of the characteristics of the gifted. Particularly studies in personality dynamics and the psychology of adjustment would seem urgent in that, though positively ordered and balanced better than the average, the gifted is nevertheless a difficult child with which to deal. Important also are certain areas of clinical psychology which bear upon positive aspects of development—perhaps psychological diagnosis by means of tests, the ability to interpret behavior in more than its surface aspects, and the ability to interact with the individual or the group in such a way as to contribute to the fuller expression of *their* personality while controlling and understanding one's own.

On the basis of the rationale sketched here, four corollaries to the principle of a specially qualified teacher for the intellectually superior child will be stated:

(IV. A) *That the teacher of gifted children and youth should be deviant with respect to those qualities common to the gifted group.*

(IV. B) *That the personality characteristics of the teacher of the gifted should be adapted to the particular types of stress and demand which arise in dealing with children who have marked initiative, strong and sometimes distinctive interests, and exceptional rational capacity.*

(IV. C) *That the person designated to teach the gifted should, by personal initiative as well as by institutional requirement, have attained a body of insights leading toward a philosophical perspective upon life and extending at some depth into crucial human issues—to the end that the student may study with profit the man, his values, and his behavior.*

(IV. D) *That the professional training of the teacher of the gifted should, in addition to those experiences designed for all teachers, include areas crucial to his task, especially the psychology of personality and selected studies from clinical psychology.*

Three brief appraisals from gifted students themselves will epitomize much that has been said here about the teacher of exceptional children. Elsbeth Kroeber cites these tributes to teachers, made by gifted students in New York City:

> When I went to high school I found in my biology teacher a source of constant revelation. Daily I received from this provocative woman a challenge which prompted me to the most unusual reading for a

girl in her teens: books on a great variety of subjects—on the conflict between religion and science, books on food and adulteration, and books on pure science and social philosophy. This teacher had a most insinuating way of talking about what she had read, or an idea she was entertaining, so that I could not rest until I had followed her into the various realms which she was constantly disclosing.

This teacher illuminates his subject by injecting into it his own personality, and when the factual side of work will have been forgotten the flavor of his teaching will long linger in the memories and influence the actions of those fortunate enough to have learned from him.

The very air is charged with sympathetic enthusiasm. The teacher is active and alert. The pupils are not less so. They see the laws of science in their proper relation to other things. The knowledge of these laws demonstrates the efforts of peoples through the ages. This best teacher, a master, marshals facts. His work is his joy.[26]

It would appear that students upwardly deviant in intelligence have much to gain from those who, like themselves, are intellectually superior, not only through more adequate guidance of intellectual behavior, but also from the influence of other characteristics positively correlated with superior intellect.

No supermen are suggested in these remarks on the desirable characteristics of teachers for gifted children. It is rather that an intelligent, flexible and benign human being should be sought, and his energies directed first toward his own fullest development and then toward the development of gifted children. Such persons are not found in great numbers; nor are they non-existent. Perhaps some larger number than Terman's data show of the gifted themselves might be persuaded to direct their capacities to this end. The mode of life is such as to appeal to many of their inclinations. And no excessive idealism can be fairly charged in this portrayal. The qualities specified are as much economically as extravagantly conceived, in consideration of the fact that the children being guided are those with the most extreme capacities found in the human species and that the tasks which they will tend to undertake are perhaps of unparalleled complexity. Where, if not here, should society designate that its most excellent chosen engineers of human destiny practice their skill?

SUMMARY OF PART II

This section has dealt with issues in the education of the intellectually superior child which are broader than those to be discussed in the following section. They relate to the educational aim, the sources from which such aims derive, the unique nature of the design of education for the gifted, and the personnel who will instruct gifted children and youth. The four major propositions state:

Proposition I: That the educational program should be based on the nature of the child and on the nature of the role he will assume in the social order of which he is a part;

Proposition II: That the program must be conceived uniquely with respect to the capacities which characterize the gifted child;

Proposition III: That economy should govern the designing of the curriculum in order that an appropriate depth and breadth of learning may be acquired within a reasonable period of the individual's young life; and

Proposition IV: That teachers of the intellectually gifted should be the most able that can be summoned to the task.

The two parts following deal respectively with the academic and intellectual phases of the youth's educational program and with his personal, social, and character development. In some instances the principles in these two chapters will reflect points touched upon in the underlying theory of Part I and the principles of design in Part II. In such cases they are specific extensions of the broader principle as it ramifies into the academic or the personal, social, and character phases of the educational program.

FOOTNOTES FOR PART II

[1] Merle R. Sumption, *et al.*, "Special Education for the Gifted Child," *Forty-Ninth Yearbook of the National Society for the Study of Education*, Part II (Chicago: University of Chicago Press, 1950), p. 267.

[2] John Dewey, *Reconstruction in Philosophy* (Boston: Beacon Press, 1957), p. 102.

[3] Educational Policies Commission, *Education of the Gifted* (Washington, D. C.: National Education Association, 1950), pp. 47–48.

[4] Leta S. Hollingworth, *Children Above 180 IQ* (Yonkers-on-Hudson, New York: World Book Company, 1942), pp. 287–88.

[5] E. J. Swift, *Mind in the Making* (New York: Charles Scribner's Sons, 1908), pp. 3–32.

[6] W. J. Osburn and Ben J. Rohan, *Enriching the Curriculum for Gifted Children* (New York: The Macmillan Company, 1931), p. 3.

[7] Herbert A. Carroll, *Genius in the Making* (New York: The McGraw-Hill Book Company, 1940), pp. 114–15.

[8] Lewis M. Terman and Melita H. Oden, *The Gifted Child Grows Up*, Vol. IV, *Genetic Studies of Genius* (Stanford, California: Stanford University Press, 1947), pp. 25–26.

[9] Educational Policies Commission, *Education of the Gifted* (Washington, D. C.: National Education Association, 1950), p. 73.

[10] John Dewey, "The Philosopher-in-the-Making," *Saturday Review of Literature*, XXX (1949), 9.

[11] Albert Einstein (in) *Living Philosophies* (New York: Simon and Schuster, Inc., 1931), p. 4.

[12] Lewis M. Terman, "Educational Suggestions from Follow-up Studies of Gifted Children," *Journal of Educational Sociology*, XIII (1939), 87.

[13] Barbara S. Burks, D. W. Jensen, and Lewis M. Terman, *The Promise of Youth*, Vol. III, *Genetic Studies of Genius* (Stanford, California: Stanford University Press, 1930), pp. 278–79.

[14] Educational Policies Commission, *Education of the Gifted* (Washington, D. C.: National Education Association, 1950), p. 72.

[15] *Ibid.*, pp. 83–84.

[16] John Dewey, *Interest and Effort in Education* (New York: Houghton Mifflin Company, 1913), p. 92.

[17] Helen L. Cohen and Nancy G. Coryell, eds., *Educating Superior Students* (New York: American Book Company, 1935), pp. 323–24.

[18] Leta S. Hollingworth, *Gifted Children: Their Nature and Nurture* (New York: The Macmillan Company, 1926), p. 307.

[19] Leta S. Hollingworth, *Children Above 180 IQ* (Yonkers-on-Hudson, New York: World Book Company, 1942), p. 261.

[20] Joseph Justman, "What Makes the Good College Teacher?" *School and Society*, LXX (1949), 420.

[21] Michael Demiashkevich, *An Introduction to the Philosophy of Education* (New York: American Book Company, 1935), p. 435.

[22] Edwin G. Boring, *A History of Experimental Psychology*, 2nd ed. (New York: Appleton-Century-Crofts, Inc., 1950), p. 356.

[23] *Ibid.*, pp. 397–98.

[24] *Ibid.*, p. 553.

[25] Leta S. Hollingworth, *Children Above 180 IQ* (Yonkers-on-Hudson, New York: World Book Company, 1942), pp. 300–1.

[26] Elsbeth Kroeber, "Biology," in Helen L. Cohen and Nancy G. Coryell (eds.), *Educating Superior Students* (New York: American Book Company, 1935), pp. 323–24.

part three

PRINCIPLES OF INTELLECTUAL AND ACADEMIC DEVELOPMENT

As long as we worship science and are afraid of philosophy we shall have no great science; we shall have a lagging and halting continuation of what is thought and said elsewhere. As far as any plea is implicit in what has been said, it is, then, a plea for the casting off of that intellectual timidity which hampers the wings of imagination, a plea for speculative audacity, for more faith in ideas, sloughing off a cowardly reliance upon those partial ideas to which we are wont to give the name of facts. . . .

—John Dewey

introduction

Part III will be devoted to those phases of the development of the intellectually superior individual which are centered most directly in his greater mental capacity. The academic portions of the school curriculum attempt to transmit to the child essential understandings from the cultural heritage. The processes of knowing, of learning, have traditionally been seen as central to education. This continues to be a proper view, though, as has been seen in part already, the interpretations presented here concerning the role of knowledge in the education of the gifted differ from the usual conceptions of the function of knowledge in the educative process for persons of the generality. Further interpretations along this line will emerge in the propositions that treat of the child's intellectual and academic development.

In recognizing one phase of development, no attempt is being made, of course, to suggest that such development can occur independent of the entire organism. The isolation of this aspect for separate treatment is an academic device only, for the purpose of closer examination and more detailed statements concerning experience in which intellection is predominant.

The emphasis still will be on the organization, structure, and design of the experiences as well as on the content itself, for it is both in the level of organization and in the uses of facts that a distinctive program of education for gifted children is justified, as well as in the sheer nature of the facts chosen for school instruction.

In general, those experiences which are conceived as essential to the gifted represent areas of knowledge and organizations of ideas lying just beyond his independent capacity to formulate at any particular developmental stage. Sheer facts are excluded from the picture very largely. In acquiring facts which pertain to a given issue, as has been noted, the gifted child is his own servant. He needs, characteristically, little supervision at this level. But in those areas beyond mere awareness his problems arise. The putting together of facts in an appropriate organization may comprise one such problem; the synthesis of facts into categories—scientific, religious, sociological, philosophical—may comprise another; and the sheer techniques for correct perceptions within a new field of knowledge may comprise a third. It is with such problems as the following that the principles of the present chapter are concerned: how to help the child who is adequate to the task of perceiving, retaining, recalling, and associating ordinary facts, perform other mental processes with them; how to help him attain those reaches which he cannot attain himself or which he can attain only through unnecessary waste in trial and error.

In this part more than in the following, the principles are immediately relevant to the intellectual superiority of the person. In the life-span development of cognitive perspectives the gifted person is most particularly deviant. What he will know, or be aided to know through devices of the school, determines in considerable measure what social service he will be able to perform. If the development of his higher mental processes is narrowly or haphazardly accomplished, society as well as the individual will be the loser.

This area of the present work may strike some readers as aiming at achievements beyond the capacities even of the intellectually superior youth at the high school and college level. This may be partially true. Only empirical tests by qualified teachers can determine whether or not these principles are attainable with given teachers and given groups of children, and at what particular developmental periods. The present aim might indeed be as high as the present curriculum is low with respect to the capacity for learning which the brighter young person manifests. Some of the understandings called for represent attainments usually acquired, if at all, by men in their maturity. Our principles promise simply to outline an appropriate course and character of experiential development which, if implemented, would appear to launch youth much more effectively onto a life-long career of intellectual behavior on the frontiers of science and human welfare than does the impoverished educational regimen to which they are presently subject.

chapter eight | *THE ROLE OF INTELLECT*

As a first proposition relative to this phase of the educative process, an extension is made of the general proposals in the last chapter that the gifted individual is capable of accomplishing much of his own education and that teaching the gifted child what he can learn for himself is uneconomical. It is therefore maintained:

> (*V*) *That in the education of the gifted individual there should be considerable emphasis upon intellectual activity.*

It seems possible to a degree that experience designed to modify behavior can be achieved ideationally—vicariously, as it were—with brighter children, a fact which should influence the content and method of their instruction.

The literature is replete with evidence that intellectual, theoretical, abstract levels of behavior are the natural modes for gifted individuals. Carroll notes this, for instance, as follows:

> Perhaps the most important mental characteristic of the bright child is that of being able to see relationships, to make logical associations, to adapt abstract principles to concrete situations with identical elements, to generalize. . . .[1]

126

Since a person can possess a capacity and yet have no desire to exercise it, it is important to emphasize that gifted children and youth typically have a strong urge to *use* their superior intellects. Abstracts from Terman's data in Part I, it will be recalled, point to this fact. And with respect to the very highly intelligent of Hollingworth's studies, this is said:

> The intellectual interest and capacity of young children who test from 160 to 200 IQ is incredible to those who have had no experience with the teaching of such children. We have in our classes about a dozen of such extreme deviates. They are the truly *original* thinkers and doers of their generation. A book could be made of the incidents constantly occurring which denote the qualities of their minds. It is these children who suffer from ennui in the ordinary situation.[2]

Again, all of the arguments germane to the significance of theory in science, and to the necessity of understanding and skill in the treatment of theory on the part of students in advanced studies, pertain to the more or less spontaneous capacities and expressions of the superior learner. It is from these persons that criticism and evaluation of the status quo in practices and institutions tend to come, and it is these who note inconsistencies between theory and practice. The generality of students, it is commonly observed, are impatient with theory, and their impatience is in harmony with their inability for adequate reckoning with and among theories. These planes of experience, however, are the best playing fields for the gifted, and the true and proper lines that lead from principle to practice tend to be apparent to them with minimal concrete detail.

Because of their sheer capacity for intellectual activity, their characteristic interest in the use of this capacity, and the undesirable consequences of ignoring such capacity and interest, instructions for the gifted should take the intellectual form. For them, the ratio of abstractions, theories, principles, and generalizations to concrete sensory impact should be distinctively different from that appropriate and possible for the average child.

There are several corollaries to this proposition. The first states:

(V. A) *That, in part, activity held essential to the learning process should be interpreted as mental activity, or implicit rather than overt behavior.*

The idea of "learning by doing" has been worked in many classroom situations to the aggrandizement of overt physical activity, sensory intake and expressive manipulation. The practice has become so widespread as to encourage the misconception that mental activity is not "active." The results of such conceptions have borne most heavily of course upon those children in whom activity of mind is a personal forte. Hence, it is suggested as a principle that the manipulation of concepts be recognized as active educative experience. G. Lester Anderson and Arthur I. Gates treat this point effectively in the following passage:

> Another closely related phase of this problem is one of understanding properly the meaning of activity as it is related to learning. Again, the educator has used this word to modify both "curriculum" and "unit." A learning principle, and a perfectly sound one, is that we learn what we do, or that we learn the responses which we make, or that we learning [sic] by doing. The logical inferences, or at least they seemed logical, derived from this concept that "we learn what we do" seemed to be of this order: We learn by doing, doing means activity, we learn through activity, activity means action, action means overt, physical activity. The misinterpretation which occurred in *this* setting was that activity is always overt, or that physical activity must be present if we are to learn. However, learning activity can be and is implicit; i.e., it can occur without overt manifestations. When children sit quietly listening to music, college students listen to a lecture, or the scientist sits contemplatively at his desk, there need be no overt manifestation of an intellectual or emotional activity that is changing the person involved. These persons are not passive; they are learning, even though externally quiet.[3]

This principle has great significance for school procedures and potentially affects a number of school activities. As the "old" curriculum was deemed unsuited to the majority and had to give way to one better adapted, so it appears the so-called "new" curriculum (in practice, especially) has become unsuited to those not among the majority in intellectual capacity. Some of the activities of the earlier school need to be revived under newer concepts of instructional method as amenable to the capacities of the gifted. There should be, for instance, a renewed emphasis upon debating and other forms of forensic activity; the writing of essays, not as a labored occasional duty, but as an integral part of the continuous activities expected of students; "honors and awards" days which will give more significant place to singular achievement; clubs which avowedly organize for the pursuit of theoretical interests; and "teams" of scholars who travel among schools of similar strength carrying challenges to the best that their competitors can summon in diverse forms of scholarly activity.

As a further corollary to the principle indicating fuller uses of the intellectual capacities of gifted individuals, it appears:

(V. B) *That the instruction of the gifted should be characterized by a pace and a level of complexity which are best suited to their broad.r capacities and that their school achievement shall be evaluated in terms of objectives that are equally advanced.*

Applying both to movement from fact to fact and idea to idea within discussions and to movement from unit to unit within a course, this principle emphasizes that gifted and average children require a different amount of time in which to learn. Ideas structured for presentation to the gifted may and should be differently developed. When functioning at their best, these youngsters feel the *need* for the higher levels of understanding, and this principle urges that their educational program be designed to satisfy that need.

Levels of understanding are implied in this statement by the Educational Policies Commission:

> Teaching for understanding should focus on explanations of the reasons for things. The understandings achieved by all learners will be increased by the teacher's skillful use of "why" and "how" questions; and such questions are especially well-suited to guiding the thinking of gifted students.[4]

And beyond the "why's" and the "how's" lie the "for what purposes" and the "to what consequences," types of thinking which lead toward the theoretical and philosophical frameworks under which the examined disciplines are subsumed.

The texts and references used in the education of the gifted may also be considered from this point of view of paralleling level of instruction with level of mentality. The poor quality in logic, the awkwardnesses in style, which might include the very usages which the serious and able student is trying to eliminate from his own writing, and the unimaginative and unsystematic quality of the development of ideas— all such concomitants to the presentation of subject matter pertain to qualitative levels of instruction. The Harvard Report strikes at "sub-

English" in educational texts, and this attack upon a specific inadequacy can be generalized into support for the entire principle under discussion:

> Great numbers of texts in literature, history, social studies, and science, pored over through interminable classroom hours, are written in forms of English which would be intolerable out of a schoolbook. One gets tired of the refrain that the schools are trying to "teach the clear and simple expression of ideas" when the prose so often used is a string of dead phrases without spring or balance, point or punch, fetid with the author's fatigue and the fog of terminology prematurely introduced. "Art affects us in our unawares," said Bergson. So does lack of art. These pages are not explicitly put before students as models of composition. Their excuse is the subject matter. But they have their effects nonetheless. It is a sound principle that all sentences to be closely studied in the schoolroom should be as well made for their purpose as the best writers can contrive. There will be enough bad models to contend with outside.[5]

Is it not in order to ask that the text possess excellence in more respects than in the presentation of its own particular subject matter? Matters of style in writing, of aptness of expression, of level of thought and discussion, of imagination in the use of incidentals, of subordination of fact to principle—these are important concomitants which, if well ordered, aid the educational enterprise, and if not well-ordered, hinder its effects by that much. The perception of such subtleties may be lost upon the average student; for the gifted, however, these are realities to which responses are made and out of which habits and attitudes are formed.

As instruction at higher levels is urged, so also should concepts and techniques of evaluation recognize qualitative distinctions which best pertain to the activity of the gifted. Recent literature on psychological and educational measurements has emphasized testing for higher mental processes than simple factual recall. Warren G. Findley and Douglas E. Scates have detailed this idea of levels of complexity in the form of questions developed around the person and career of Ulysses S. Grant:

1. Who was the general in command of the victorious Union Army at the end of the Civil War?

2. What generals served under Grant at the Battle of Richmond?

3. During what years was U. S. Grant President of the United States?

4. (True or False?) General U. S. Grant's victories during the Civil War were an important factor in his being elected President.

5. (Multiple-choice) An important factor in General U. S. Grant's election to the Presidency of the United States was
    a) his previous career in politics.
    b) his successful leadership of the Union Army in the Civil War.
    c) the fact that he was a Democrat.
    d) the fact that Abraham Lincoln had expressed a strong desire for Grant to be his successor.

6. Compare Grant's success as a general with his effectiveness as President.

7. In the light of your study of Grant's career, which of the following is the most reasonable inference?
    a) Successful generals are likely to make poor Presidents.
    b) A President who has been a successful general can make considerable use of his military experience in planning to deal with new social problems.
    c) The fact that a man is a good general is no guarantee that he will make a good President.
    d) It is not necessary for a man to be a successful general in order to be a good President.
    e) Success as a general may reduce a man's prospects of being elected President of the United States.

8. What evidence is afforded by United States history concerning the likelihood that a man who has been a great general will later become a successful President?

9. By citing examples from different countries and different periods of history, indicate whether the preponderance of evidence supports or contradicts the claim that successful military leaders make effective political leaders.[6]

The authors analyze the questions thus: The first three are "simple questions of fact"; the fourth requires "understanding of an elementary kind"; the fifth "makes it necessary for the pupil to weigh alternative explanations of cause and effect"; the sixth requires "the summoning

and stating of facts and the pronouncement of a simple judgment";
the seventh asks "the pupil to carry out a process of thinking that
requires a fair amount of knowledge about Grant's career as well as
considerable understanding both of the facts involved and of the logical inferences that may be drawn from them"; the eighth and ninth
"necessitate successively broader knowledge and understanding of military, political, and social history, together with an ability to express
the understanding effectively."[7] Levels represented in questions 7, 8,
and 9 are the natural intellectual provender of the gifted youth; yet
the question may well be raised whether in the program designed for
the average these levels *can* be represented to any considerable extent.
That they usually *are not*, even in upper secondary levels of instruction,
is scarcely debatable.

Further illustrative of appropriate levels of mental performance
through which to appraise the intellectual and educational development of the superior learner are these questions from a sample battery
of the University of Chicago Comprehensive Examinations:

—Which of the following statements would become meaningless or
untrue if the organization or viewpoint of Biological Science
changed, even though the definition of terms remained the same?
  a) The vessels which carry blood from the heart are arteries.
  b) The petals of flowers are modified leaves.
  c) Proteins are absolutely essential in the diet of all animals.
  d) The chromosome number of the cells of the gametophyte
     generation of a fern is half that of the cells of the sporophyte
     generation.
  e) Sodium cyanide poisons by inactivating an enzyme neces-
     sary to respiration in the cell.

—A theoretical physicist conceived a model of the nucleus of a certain atom. He used the laws of physics known to work for large
scale phenomena. He described the workings of the model mathematically. His answers disagree with experimental facts. *Which
of the following should he do first?*
  a) Use the nucleus of a different atom.
  b) Develop new mathematics (such as ab $\neq$ ba, etc.)
  c) Use different fundamental postulates of natural science
     (such as non-uniformity of nature).
  d) Use a different model.

e) Use different laws of physics (such as nonconservation of energy, etc.).

Which should he try last of all?
a) Develop new mathematics (such as ab ≠ ba, etc.)
b) Use different fundamental postulates of natural science (such as non-uniformity of nature).
c) Use a different model.
d) Use different laws of physics (such as nonconservation of energy, etc.).[8]

It is readily observed that such questions as these demand a knowledge of facts, but it is also apparent that processes of mind other than simple association or recall are invoked in reckoning adequately with them. The processes demanded are those in which the gifted child excels. The evaluation of his progress should be made on the basis of growing competency in the management of ideas at these high planes, whereas for his average counterpart, a lower scale of evaluation, closer to the perceptual and the factual, must necessarily be applied.

Improving man's potential for creation is a challenge of primary social importance. Not much is known about procedures in education which foster creativity. This area is so important, however, and it is so commonly agreed that the incidence of creativity is greater in the upper levels of intelligence as now appraised than in the lower, that some deference to the idea of educating for this quality is obligatory in a design of education for gifted children and youth. The present treatment does not directly concern the nature of creativity itself but possible applications of what appear to be reasonably reliable psychological facts known at the present time. A corollary, then, to the principle which urges recognition of intellectual potential in education is:

(V. C) *That the education of the gifted should be designed to promote their tendencies toward creativity.*

First, a position with respect to the nature of "genius" which seems most promising for the practical purposes of education would appear to be essential. Anne Anastasi and John P. Foley, Jr., classify the numerous theories explanatory of genius into four categories:

Theories on the nature and causes of genius are legion. The genius has been credited with a wide variety of attributes, ranging from divine inspiration and a superhuman "spark" to imbecility and insanity. Among these diverse theories it is possible to discern four underlying viewpoints. These will be designated the *pathological, psychoanalytic, qualitative-superiority*, and *quantitative-superiority* theories.[9]

In interpreting the "quantitative-superiority" theories, they write:

The view that genius involves a quantitative superiority regards the genius as the upper extreme of a continuous distribution of ability. The "special gifts" and "creative powers" of genius are attributed, to a lesser degree, to all individuals. Genius is defined in terms of concrete, measurable behavior rather than in terms of unknown entities. To be sure, the accomplishments of genius are not attributed to any single talent, but to an auspicious combination of various intellectual, motivational, and environmental factors.[10]

As this interpretation is generally conceded to be the most dependable from a scientific point of view, the following discussion of education for creativity will depend upon it. Further caution is of course essential in guarding against the assumption that only persons of high intellectual capacity manifest creative behavior. J. P. Guilford has made a sustained attack on this problem. He provides in a fairly early study summary evidence that high IQ and creativity are not one-to-one correlates and indicates that remaining components of the creative act are apparently motivational and temperamental in nature.[11]

Leta Hollingworth analyzed the case studies of twelve highly intelligent children for evidence of creativity, and her conclusions at once subscribe to the absence of a straightforward correlation of creativity and intelligence and offer suggestions which stand as reasonable guides to educational planning in this respect:

If a general statement be attempted on the basis of such data as the descriptions and these summaries afford, it might be to the effect that one-third of these highly intelligent children (A, D, H, L) show notable signs of creativeness. Another third (C, E, I, J) show such indications to a moderate degree. In the remaining third (B, F, G, K) there is at least no indication of marked constructive originality provided by these descriptions.

Certainly these creative dispositions are more conspicuous in these cases than in the general population of children. How these very rare intelligences compare in this respect with those ranging from, say, 130 to 175 IQ we cannot know. Creativeness even at best is infrequent enough. In experiences of daily life of course such creativeness might be more often found in children in the middle range of high intelligences because there are so many more of these in the population.

On the other hand, it may be that creativeness in marked degree appears in these higher ranges only. Under any circumstances it is not an all-or-none phenomenon, and the problem of the correlation of originality with intelligence scores perhaps deserves more careful study than it has received. It seems suggested at least by these few cases that very high intelligence may in some instances become directed along wholly conventional channels, showing itself in the amount of work or the rate of progress, with little or no manifestation of creative originality. If this is the case, it should be important to discover to what extent this is a reflection of the regimentation of the occupation of such children by organized educational projects and close parental supervision, and to what extent it is a characteristic that is native in the individual. If it should be true that creativeness is closely dependent on such a high range of intelligence as that shown by this group of twelve children, a social order that esteems creativeness should give serious thought to the conditions of its cultivation and its development.[12]

For the entire range of mentally superior children and youth, it appears that all the techniques which can be devised offer more promise than the same techniques in use with children who are average in intelligence. It is an admonition typical of Hollingworth that the school not allow potential creativeness to remain undeveloped from general lack of recognition and nurture.

In view of the complex and undetermined nature of creative behavior, it is inevitable that educational procedures in this area be guided more by reasonable and promising suggestion than by obviously valid method. Certain considerations along this line which offer possibility for educational adaptations are to be explored. Any single suggested procedure will, in this area perhaps more than others, demand empirical validation before it can be finally declared useful. It is doubtless true that many apparently promising attempts will turn out to be fruitless, whereas others possessing a minimum of "face validity" will sometimes be proven effective.

Several factors given by Guilford as hypotheses for further investigations in connection with creativity are listed for their suggestiveness with respect to educational practice:

> It is suggested that certain kinds of factors will be found, including sensitivity to problems, ideational fluency, flexibility of set, ideational novelty, synthesizing ability, analyzing ability, reorganizing or redefining ability, span of ideational structure, and evaluating ability.[13]

Developmental exercises designed to elicit such behavior could be profitably integrated with the study of different kinds of subject matter.

Catherine Patrick in a summary of the literature on critical thinking lists certain "conditions which favor creative thought" as they are mentioned in the writings of various students of the problem. The following conditions are given, among others: (1) the time should not be too strictly limited; (2) the problem should be sufficiently difficult; (3) relaxation and the change of activities from those representing the central problem; (4) "periods of idleness in which autistic thinking may promote imaginative ideas"; (5) "spirit of observation and wide-awake attention which isolates and fixates accident"; (6) spirit of optimism; (7) "relaxing the pressure of ordinary routine to allow more free time"; and (8) "close imitative study of good models."[14] Designed primarily from a consideration of the individual thinker in the privacy of his own surroundings and under self-stimulation, certain of these "conditions" nevertheless must pertain to school practices if creativity is to be promoted. These conditions may serve as criteria by which the individual educative device is estimated for its possible influence upon creativity; i.e., where such conditions characterize a school situation, that situation is conducive to creativity.

Ideas as such receive all too little recognition even in the education of the generality. In the education of the gifted, the idea can and should receive central emphasis. Gifted children reach out for ideas; and thought in terms of ideas, as opposed to the material accouterments and implements following from the ideas, appeal to their intellectual interests. Thus the *idea* of psychological measurement is likely to be more attractive than the sheer study and application of an instrument of measurement; the *idea* of electricity as a controlled natural energy, rather than the mechanics of its control; the *idea* of social security; and so on. As ideas "in terms of which life is coming increasingly to be understood," Hugh Hartshorne and his co-workers developed this interesting list which they used to devise measurements of moral understanding and behavior in the "character education inquiry":

The idea of sex	The idea of custom
The idea of God	The idea of design
The idea of right and wrong	The idea of legislation
The idea of natural law	The idea of education
The idea of growth	The idea of work
The idea of evolution	The idea of fun
The idea of co-operation	The idea of the machine
The idea of personality	The idea of self-forgetting service[15]

Direct instruction in ideas like these would contribute to the facility of the superior individual in reckoning with those generic ideas among which creativity is likely to occur.

Brief reference was made in Part I (p. 56) to a work which should long since have been seized upon as a *sine qua non* in the process of general education of brighter youth. Mortimer Adler's accomplishment in *The Great Ideas: A Syntopicon of Great Books of the Western World* would appear to be a ready-made body of thought immediately available for the enrichment of the educational program in the typical American school. And objections that these volumes were executed under a particular philosophical orientation, rendering them unsuitable where this philosophy does not prevail, seem to be pitiably trivial. We concur completely with Robert M. Hutchins' statement that:

> . . . the *Syntopicon* argues no case and presents no point of view. It will not interpret any book to the reader; it will not tell him which author is right and which wrong on any question. It simply supplies him with suggestions as to how he may conveniently pursue the study of any important topic through the range of Western intellectual history. It shows him how to find what great men have had to say about the greatest issues and what is being said about these issues today.[16]

Hutchins rightly adds that "When the history of the intellectual life of this century is written, the *Syntopicon* will be regarded as one of the landmarks in it."[17] In the present author's experience, no more significant single body of textual materials exists for life-span general education. Where sensibly educated teachers, concerned with vital intellectual issues, can be brought to the task of guiding the able youngster through experience with these generic ideas and timeless issues, his general education will proceed in a manner and at a level achievable through no means more convenient and more adequate.

A deliberate attempt to evaluate the magnitude of the specific ideas of certain men as they appear in the perspective of history might be promising. The magnitude and real effects of the ideas of Jesus Christ; the contributions to thought made by Aristotle; the essence of Darwin's theories and their impact upon the science of living things; the ideas of Bacon—studies such as these in the comparison and evaluation of great ideas would appear to encourage a fluency in mental shifting, in the perception of meanings in diverse situations, and in other of the conditions favoring creative thought.

Finally, the educator might well shape a curriculum of ideas out of the selected writings of certain men who originated ideas with which hosts of followers have tinkered. To present the intellectually superior child in the upper reaches of his secondary schooling with a half dozen of John Dewey's titles is to obviate the necessity of his reading several dozens of ordinary textbooks on education which often vitiate the originals. For him to peruse Shakespeare for ideas bearing upon human issues, feelings, and emotions, apart from aesthetic values, is to encounter many live psychological and sociological problems in realistic settings. To read from men of ideas and to revel in their magnificent reaches is to make a close "imitative study of good models" and to promote appreciation for ideas as such. By that much is the facility to manipulate ideas in the act of creative thinking enhanced.

Among the writings of educators who have touched upon this subject, the idea of freedom and of encouragement to pursue the novel thought or the original response appears commonly. Thus Adams and Brown say:

> The teacher who has as her aim in a lesson the appreciation of a piece of literature, a musical composition, a masterpiece of painting, or a worthwhile ideal must be on guard not to standardize the emotional reactions of the pupils. Rather, she should allow the brilliant youngsters to appreciate as they will, and perhaps evolve a new idea or artistic creation of their own.
>
> Those teachers who have worked with this type of adolescent know the remarkable possibilities in creative activities. The imaginations of the bright children are fertile fields into which the teacher may drop suggestions. The term *suggestions*—sometimes involving the

most subtle and artistic touch—is used advisedly. The self-starting minds energized by the initiative of bright children are better directed by suggestion than by dominant teacher control. Hence it is of primary importance, if creative resources are to be tapped, to lead the child to develop his originality rather than to repeat or reproduce without making his own contribution.[18]

Lest the able teacher become fearful of rejecting any form of expressive behavior on the part of individualistic pupils, Carroll reminds us that a touch of common-sense judgment about children's creations may always need to be exercised.

Initiative or independence in thinking is characteristic of the minds of intellectually gifted children. That this is a desirable trait goes without saying. In school it manifests itself through a facility in working out highly individualistic approaches to problems in subject matter. Such creative approaches should be encouraged, but, if the teacher knows of a better method, then she should explain it to the gifted child and recommend that he substitute it for his own. If he can see that it is really a better one, he will make the change.[19]

Though judgment of the novel is difficult, and in many instances the individual teacher might fail to appraise an origination adequately, it does follow that not every creative act is of value. As Carroll implies, guidance through reasoned evaluation of such acts is perhaps a desirable aspect of the creative child's education. On the other hand, it may be quite as important to allow some school experiences of great intrinsic merit to the learner to exist without evaluation.

When the ideas explored in the preceding paragraphs have been applied and the child is encouraged to react in a novel way—actually told that all people react differently and that the unusual reaction is the source of invention—the school has probably done all that it can at the present time to cultivate creativity in its gifted pupils. Beyond such conditions and attitudes, education for origination must await further advances within this important area of behavioral science.

Thus the fifth major principle in this educational design, like the preceding four, is predicated upon biological characteristics which distinguish the gifted group. It has been urged that explicit use be made of the superior intellectual capacities of gifted children and youth. The means for increasing this use include academic presentations with altered proportions between abstract and concrete elements, an appropriate pace of instruction and level of text, properly corrected appraisals of pupil efforts within the medium of higher mental processes, and, finally, unusual procedures and forms of knowledge which promise to nurture creative expression. Instruction of this character simply begins with the perceptual level of cognizance, basic awareness representing nature one-to-one in the human mind, and moves surely beyond to the rarified planes of inference, implication, and generalization upon stuff that is seen and heard.

chapter nine | *THE ROLE OF KNOWLEDGE*

The sixth principle concerns the potential of the brighter child to acquire greater expanses of knowledge and to explore to greater depths the ideas with which he characteristically comes to deal. It may be stated:

> (*VI*) *That the educative experience of the intellectually superior should be consciously designed as generative of further development, extensively and intensively, along similar and related avenues.*

The idea again becomes applicable that it is not the present society to which the growing individual will adjust at the time when he contributes most but to a society in which all manner of change has occurred. Hence, the educative experience that is truly useful is that which prepares him for a progressive readjustment and reinterpretation of the behaviors and understandings learned. Several threads of thought contribute to this idea.

A number of meanings attach to the root *gignesthai*, Greek for "to be born" or "to become," which in English form becomes *gen*. Selected from Webster's *New Collegiate Dictionary* (1949) are the following terms applicable in various ways to the principle just stated:

141

Generalize: v.t. 1. To make general; to reduce to general laws. 2. a. To derive (a general conception or principle) from particulars. b. To derive or induce a general conception, principle, or inference from; to use with a more extensive application. 3. To give general applicability to; as, to *generalize* a law.

Generate: v.t. 2. To originate, esp. by a vital or chemical process; to produce.

Generic: adj. 1. *Biol.* Pertaining to, or having the rank of, a genus;— opp. to *specific.*

-genic: 2. A combining form meaning *eminently suitable for production or reproduction by a* (given) *medium,* as in *radiogenic, telegenic.*

Genius: 4. Inborn mental gift or endowment; talent. . . . 6. Extraordinary power of invention or origination of any kind; as, a man of *genius*; also a person endowed with transcendent ability.

Such meanings fit that type of education which the intellectually gifted child should have. It is he who will generate in the sense of producing changes—new social reforms, new techniques in science, and new advances in practical affairs. He is a person by definition of "transcendent abilities." The proposition just stated emerges from such considerations.

How in detail is this proposition appropriate to the nature of the gifted? From recorded incidents revealing play of mind, such as those reported in individual case studies, it appears that there is a characteristic willingness in the intellectually superior for a movement of the mind toward the levels beyond mere awareness—from fact to principle to implication, for instance—and this principle merely requires the adjustment of school procedure to this aspect of the nature of the gifted child. Evidence of a willingness and ability to make testing movements toward more generic levels of thought lies in these brief samples of classroom discussions by ten-year-old children in one of Leta Hollingworth's special classes:

Is Armor Clothing?

Child Kr (IQ 190). Is armor to be considered clothing?

Child Br (IQ 148). No. Armor is to be considered an instrument of warfare. It is worn *over* clothing.

Child H (IQ 154). Whatever is *worn* is clothing.

Child Do (IQ 188). The knights wore their armor more and more, till finally they wore it when not fighting at all. So it *became* clothing.

Child Kr (IQ 190). They wore the armor as court *dress*. When we went to the museum, we saw armor, which we were told was the court *dress* in Queen Elizabeth's time.

(Class concludes that armor must be regarded as clothing.)

Are Rugs Furniture?

Child Dor (IQ 167). Are rugs furniture or objects of decoration?

Child Th (IQ 171). They may be considered either way. In one way rugs are furniture, because they are *useful*. They keep cold from coming up through the floor. However, they are also decorative, for if we wanted them only to keep out cold, we could buy just *plain* rugs. We buy them to be decorative, so people will want to come to our house.

Teacher. Could we divide all furnishings into useful and decorative? What of chairs, beautifully carved? Are they necessities or luxuries?

Child Do (IQ 156). They cannot be put under either head absolutely correctly, because they are both necessary and luxurious. They are furniture and *necessary*. They are decorative and a *luxury*. . . .

(Class concludes that it is impossible to divide all things arbitrarily into furniture and not furniture, or into necessities and luxuries.)[20]

In contrast to this type of performance, students of average intellectual acumen and interest are caused to move to higher levels of thought (in terms of their own more limited capacity) only with encouragement and through initiative other than their own. Persons of "middling intellect" are likely to be confused and to rely on rote memory at that level of generalization which is most satisfying and meaningful to the brighter student. This is the *method of the mind* of abler individuals, a method which must have its parallel in instruction at higher, more generic levels of idea and its characteristic exercise in the higher mental processes.

Instruction in principle, it may be noted further, instills knowledge which is both generative of further acquisition along related avenues and enduring in value. Instruction in fact is too often tentative and relative. Given a reorganization within a discipline at the theoretical level, as for instance a shift toward widespread acceptance of Gestalt principles in psychology, as distinct from Behavioristic principles, and many of the facts acquired under the original frame of reference must be reoriented or discarded. Persons whose dispositions run toward the specific, and whose instruction has been of the same character, find it difficult to modify their conceptualizations if it becomes necessary. Instruction in principles, on the other hand, conduces less toward intellectual rigidity. That the individual's moral code, for instance, must reflect the major values of the society in which he lives if harmonious adjustment is to be attained is a principle which can hardly ever lose its utility. Instruction in what behaviors are moral, however, may be so little enduring as to become a handicap to understanding between father and son.

Such form and treatment may be given to the text materials in any discipline. With the personal relationship between teacher and child, and with the processes of reading and thinking going on at these calculated levels, the patterns of the child's language and thought will tend to become organized in a manner commensurate with his capacity for thought and discourse. Closely written texts, richly connotative and highly generalized, offer the intellectually gifted educational material adapted both to their needs and desires. To place before those who have the ability to communicate meaningfully at more generic levels printed materials conceived at lower levels is to absorb energy in the process of synthesis and generalization which can begin beyond the immediate and the concrete and proceed further. To adapt educational materials in this way is to afford gifted students the same consideration which is given to students of ordinary ability through vocabulary controls in the text materials designed for their use.

Corollary to this major principle are several subordinate ones. The first states:

(VI. A) *That in the education of the gifted child and youth the scope of the content should extend into the general nature of all the chief branches of knowledge.*

The program should be of broader scope than that for average individuals for the reasons, previously cited, that (1) it *can* be—that the intellectually superior child can learn more than do average children during childhood and youth—and (2) it *must* be—that the demands likely to be made upon him in the advancing of culture render it urgent that he possess such a greater range of knowledge.

Practically, this corollary resolves into the expectation that the gifted child will acquire some knowledge of physics *and* chemistry *and* biology, for instance, instead of some knowledge in any *one* of these that he might elect. Also, the school would expect the brighter child to know something of history in its entirety, as opposed to a knowledge of *any* period, ancient, medieval, or modern. In the communicative arts, he would be expected to study drama *and* journalism *and* debate, rather than any one of the three alone. And, of course, exhaustive elaboration of the usual range of knowledge would add branches not presently represented, e.g., geology and astronomy in natural science.

A greater insight into any one discipline emerges from an appreciation of how that discipline relates to others. Students characteristically come only vaguely to understand what the study of parasitology is, for instance, and perhaps it is months or years later that they accidentally discover that there is a separate field of concentration in animal and in plant parasitology. In like fashion, they muddle through understandings of the relationships which the field of anthropology might have to psychology and to education and perhaps again only by accident learn that physical and cultural anthropology have become separate disciplines. "Classical" economics, as apart from what is to the average student "economics"; ethics apart from religion; philosophy apart from science—these epistemological perspectives, integrated into the education of the gifted child in a systematic manner, will be useful in clarifying crucial problems and in making his independent pursuit of learning easier. It is likely that his interests will be easily directed toward these generic understandings of the relationships between disciplines.

Further corollary to the principle that the curriculum for the gifted be generative in nature is the idea:

(VI. B) *That the curriculum for the gifted individual should but introduce and initially explore the concepts extending over broad expanses of knowledge.*

This principle was stated in essence by Osburn and Rohan, on the basis of their experience decades ago:

> Another principle which has an important bearing upon the education of the capable pupil is that of exploration. The curriculum in the upper grades of the elementary school and to a large extent throughout the high school should be frankly and deliberately superficial. . . . The curriculum question will not be completely answered

until we can offer genuine exploratory courses to capable pupils.
This is true because exploratory courses fit the needs of these pupils.[21]

This statement suggests that only the genesis of a field of study, only the essential nature and structure of a curricular segment, should be presented and that a more thorough knowledge of any field should depend on the child's own motivation to learn or to meet requirements and expectations. In a sense the life-span principle is involved through the assumption that the synthesis of understandings probably will not be complete within the school years, the maturity of the years beyond school being required for the full fruition of the education initiated by the school.

This principle is obviously quite antithetical to proposals that school studies be pursued at lengths which promise mastery of specific skills, as in foreign language, or more nearly complete understanding of all that is presently known in a single science like physics. It is contended here that the enforced selectivity from among particular arts and sciences that these proposals imply involves too great a risk that the knowledge and skills required of the adult will be different from those studied by the youngster. The study of Spanish by hosts of American students is palpably impractical in view of the infrequency with which this language is used in all but the most atypical life careers. As far as language study *must* be centered in one particular language, Russian would have been far and away the more practical study for the past fifteen years. The idea that language study per se is educative justifies Russian as thoroughly as it does Spanish. We have found little reason, however, to heed the unreasoned but impassioned cries for more years of a single language, a single science, etc.

We are proposing a concept which places single studies in a much different perspective and which substitutes the employment of time and effort at more advanced levels of experience and over ranges of knowledge that broaden as the course of general education is run. This is an important issue in educational thought and one on which the reader is likely to be of strong persuasion regardless of the side he favors.

In lieu, for instance, of the school's attempting to teach all significant facts in economics, this principle suggests that it should teach only some of the crucial facts and principles for the sake of the information contained and as illustrative of the *nature* of facts in economics. Adding instruction in the possible uses and interpretations of such facts, the school then *may* stop by virtue of the individual's initiative in pursuing further facts as necessary. The school *should* stop at such a point in order to do justice in limited time to the other areas of knowledge which must be explored in a similar way. *This educational approach will not produce a thoroughly learned individual in selected areas but rather a person who can become thoroughly learned with dispatch in any of many areas.* He will be broadly sensitized to numerous bodies of knowledge and therefore possess greater adaptability than if he were deeply sensitized in fewer. Intensive explorations into details of a discipline, once a perspective upon its principles and methods has been established, will be necessary only when such delving involves difficulties that lie beyond the individual's capacity. Thus, while the school can and should be the stimulus for intensive exploration, the actual exploring will devolve upon the individual himself.

Generally there should be admitted to the curriculum only those experiences that open a substantial field of inquiry and that leave it open to further pursuit. Thus the school would not teach arithmetic through to a certain level, teach algebra to another level, and then dismiss the subject of mathematics as finished. Elementary arithmetic would be taught consciously as leading toward further mathematics in all its branches; and these branches should be brought to the attention of the child, their general nature and function being explained in even the elementary courses. An invitation to further learning is thus left in the mind of the educand, rather than a dismissal. It is to such invitations that the gifted child is peculiarly susceptible, and the idea of exploration over broad ranges of knowledge appeals to this readiness.

As an indication of the feasibility of such organization, these remarks from the preface of a text in mathematics suggest that the authors have consciously worked in that direction:

> This book begins with the first principles of arithmetic and includes algebra, plane geometry, solid geometry, plane trigonometry, and an introduction to spherical trigonometry. The reader is led into algebra as a useful extension of arithmetic and the fundamental operations are explained on the basis of those arithmetic operations which are already familiar. Geometric figures which occur in the various fields of human activity are studied, and the concepts and principles of geometry are developed intuitively or experimentally.

Geometry leads naturally to trigonometry and, in connection with the sphere, to spherical trigonometry. All of these phases of mathematics are considered, not as separate disciplines but as essential parts of a single science, so that all of these phases may be available in solving technical problems.[22]

Thus "general" mathematics supersedes all particular branches of mathematics as the subject is reduced to organization for the school curriculum.

Within the areas to be explored for basic concepts and principles, the gifted individual may be expected to progress rapidly. It is not being suggested, however, that instruction be cursory. Rigorous requirements, adjusted to the level of exploration and to the purposes of the design, may be established under this conception. It is a generative level of experience which is suggested, as opposed to a terminal one. In the instance of the average child this organization and approach to educative experience may not be practicable; in the instance of the intellectually able, such planned contact is likely to be highly effective.

A further corollary to the major proposition being developed suggests:

(VI. C) *That the content of the curriculum should be organized in a manner which reduces to generic areas the concepts undertaken for instruction.*

This principle demands a reorganization of subject matter into forms which respect more than do ordinary courses the intellectual context from which each subject has emerged.

The ordinary school subject usually fits into a larger category of experience or function. Thus grammar is only a partial aspect of communicative behavior. This fact the brighter child can perceive and appreciate. Algebra, in like fashion, is only one way of quantifying the processes of nature. The brighter child's mind functions characteristically at the higher level and in terms of the larger category. Fruitful applications of learned facts and principles arise for the most part when they have been moved in this way to more abstracted planes.

Traditional subject matter designations, such as algebra or American literature, are less fitting than courses generalized in nature, such as mathematics or literature. Rather than teach a specific skill in a particular mathematics division, for instance, a course in mathematics would teach and emphasize the idea of the quantitative apprehension of the facts of nature through mathematics. It would be taught, for example, that the area of a surface may be apprehended in any of several mathematical languages—arithmetic, geometry, or algebra. In reckoning the speed of an object through space, the student would undertake as part of the problem to find which branch of mathematics is best suited for the specific inquiry. The application of techniques in algebra or in geometry would follow the perception of the type of problem under consideration; these two subdivisions of mathematics would not be isolated from their more generic context as devices for study in and of themselves.

In a practical organization of subject matter, the idea looks like this sketch by Adams and Brown:

> *The Mathematics of Science.* A chart, a notebook, an article, or a talk could be directed toward demonstrating the application of mathematics in the various sciences taught in the curriculum. The following are suggestive examples:
>
> (a) Geography. Map scales, isothermic lines, altitudes, latitude and longitude, astronomy of geography, etc.
>
> (b) Biology. Arithmetic and geometric progression in the growth of population and the ability of plant and animal life to support population, ratio as seen in the balanced aquarium, etc.
>
> (c) Chemistry. Measurements of liquids, weight quantities, balancing of chemical equations, use of mathematics to determine the blanks in the table of atomic weights, etc.
>
> (d) Physics. Pulley, lever, gas expansion laws, gravity problems, barometric pressure calculations, Fahrenheit and centigrade equivalents, electric resistance problems, etc.
>
> *Aim:* By the force of the suggestion involved, to show the universality of mathematics.[23]

And, of course, more subtle applications of the idea can be made. The principle would not be best exemplified until an organization were conceived in which the "universality" of mathematics could be taught, not only through "the force of suggestion" and application, but in terms of organized principles involving directly this kind of knowledge.

As with mathematics, a more generic approach to instruction in language suggests itself as suitable in the educational design for the intellectually superior individual. The language curriculum at present is arranged in segments representing the particular language of a given people. Since gifted children and youth will someday pursue many-sided careers in a world that is rapidly becoming smaller, language instruction would be more fruitful if leveled, not at the particular language of German or Arabian people, but at language in general. Acquaintance with the fact that in the study of any language, phenomena and problems fall into sub-groups—phonetics, morphology, semantics, grammar, etc.—is sufficient to clarify in advance a field which might otherwise seem fraught with the confusion of arbitrary forms and rules. The aims and processes of this type of language education are radically different from those characterizing the traditional conception of the role of language in education. Instead of ends, the particular usages in single languages or language families become examples, structural elements that illustrate linguistic principles. A sound understanding of these foundational principles moves the individual well along the path toward mastery of any language.

This principle as adapted in language instruction does not suggest that the youth with superior learning capacity should learn *all* known languages. Estimates indicate the existence of some 2500 of them. Nor does it suggest necessarily that a dozen major languages should be attempted. It does suggest, however, that graded instruction in the universal characteristics of language, with copious illustrations and applications from the major language families of the world, would result in a resourcefulness on the part of the adult such that were he later to be moving with invading armies from France to Germany to Czechoslovakia to Russia, for instance, he could effectively and economically adapt to the linguistic demands of each country. The diplomat could, with a shortwave radio, a quarter's worth of old newspapers, a dictionary, and a grammar, prepare himself for respectable management of the language of the country to which newly assigned, with scarcely more trouble than he takes to brief himself on that country's history and traditions. It appears inappropriate to teach a selected range of specifics when foundations to these particulars can be laid in such a manner that individual initiative is sufficient for the remainder of the learning. The student is deprived unless the most generic level of instruction and learning of which he is capable is used. However unusual this essentially educational argument (as distinct from *linguistic*) may seem, it respects both a world made small by media of communication and transportation and the diverse roles which must be assumed by future leaders in a world of change.

Not only whole fields like language and mathematics but single ideas applicable to several fields should, according to the principle under discussion, be abstracted and generalized in the education of superior students. The single idea of *growth* is integral to biology, physiology, psychology, and even philosophy. Yet the sheer impact of the meaning of growth usually awaits incidental acquisition by the "growing" mind of each individual student who ultimately apprehends it. The nature of growth is put to the student in such specific, "unnatural" forms, through various disciplines, that he fails to see the phenomenon as applicable to many different sciences and studies—indeed, to life itself. A generalized and broadly applicable treatment of the idea of growth is evident in the following passage, which will serve to illustrate how curricular content should be treated according to the principle under discussion.

> One of the peculiar properties of living units is their ability to grow or increase in mass. This increase is one that involves all parts, internal as well as external. Whenever in a living system anabolism exceeds catabolism, growth, or the accumulation of stored reserves, is inevitable, for substances are accumulated faster than they are broken down. Growth is one phase of development, for nearly all kinds of living things start individual life very small and grow larger and larger up to a rather definite size limit. Mere increase in size, however, is only one of the aspects of development and is doubtless incidental, for greater size is useful in providing material for differentiation of numerous parts for special functions.
>
> Growth is responsible, however, for more than mere increase in size; it also determines the form of organisms through differences in rate of growth of different parts. In fact, the differences in size and proportions of parts in different organisms built on the same general plan are due to local differences in growth rate of different groups of cells or different parts of the protoplasms.[24]

Expressions such as "living units" and "anabolism exceeds catabolism" contain ideas that are enriching, in that they focus in the light of higher abstractions, first-order observations. The idea that living units usually begin life small and grow to a larger size may strike the intellectually superior student as a near-obvious observation that is more thought-provoking than he had realized before. His philosophical temperament will probably be sensitive to the hint at purposefulness in nature in that "size is useful in providing material for differentiation." And then, perhaps most enlightening of all, will be the idea that part differentiation derives from differential rates of growth. Such passages, carefully and thoughtfully perused, should contribute to the truer education of the gifted. Intellectually, the ideas are not pabulum, and they are inherent in several disciplines.

Whereas this kind of subject-matter content might register with the average child in much the same memoriter fashion as some of the present more theoretical course work, the brighter child will already be reaching for such a level of thought through a more genuine understanding. Again, this is the level where experience is most meaningful for him.

A final principle, subordinate to the proposition under discussion, may be stated in this manner:

(VI. D) *That the theoretical bases should always be given for the facts, opinions, and principles presented to the gifted individual.*

Thus the entire subject of psychology, for example, should not be introduced to the student by texts or teachers that are partisan to any particular school of thought. Particular theses may certainly be introduced, but the underlying school of thought should be openly declared. In this manner many statements which are made in the form of fact will be correctly couched and perceived as opinion. Their acceptance or rejection may occur with entire respectability, in contrast to the moral obligation to be persuaded personally by "objective" truth. Such a difference is of extreme importance to the gifted student. Careless usage or sheer failures in text or lecture to place declarative statements within a theoretical framework may leave the gifted child critically mis-instructed. His thinking can advance through his own initiative if clear theoretical foundations are structured for him.

In terms of actual curricular content, what kinds of ideas lend perspective to subject matter? A few illustrative suggestions can be offered. In the study of history, a perspective through theories of history should be introduced at some point in the educational design. Have progressive steps in civilization arisen from something in the very nature of the times, social and natural influences combining in such a manner as to evoke in certain persons that leadership which the course of events indicates was present; or conversely, have the persons of select men caused progress through the ages? Such instruction in theory will lend a reflective base to the study of the facts of history, giving exercise to higher mental processes and providing a level of understanding beyond the facts themselves. The gifted student will find it useful to his thinking to be taught that men who write usually reflect subtly or grossly some orientation which characterizes their outlook: one historian will see the hand of God directing the changes in thought and behavior that are recorded, while another will see economic forces alone at play. Such perceptions may be beyond the immediate reach of the gifted child by virtue of his youth. Insights at these levels too often occur by accident and individual trial and error; conscious instruction would speed understanding and facilitate progress toward the ultimate reaches of the individual's learning capacity.

In like manner, the field of religion may be used to illustrate the real and important function of perspectives in instruction. The gifted child will profit from instruction in the fact (as opposed to slow, incidental, and perhaps disillusioning discovery) that while it is the traditional emphasis in the common faiths of his society to see religion as oriented toward the supernatural, there are systems of religious thought centered in the natural alone. And morals and religion should be placed in some sort of perspective for the youth who may be led by his own logic to reject both because of intellectual impossibilities which appear to reside in certain religious concepts.

The perception of such distinctions usually requires a maturity of thought and a lengthy period of relevant experience for which the exceptional general intelligence of the gifted child may not readily compensate unless guided by appropriately designed instruction. Religious dogma presented as such and not couched in the same form as knowledge arising through sense experience would be presented in a fair perspective, with due caution, and with respect for the verb *to be*. That religious experience may be as valid as any other, though of a different nature and of a different origin, that what "is" in religion is dependent upon what faith one has assumed—these concepts will survive later knowledge and experience and thus obviate much bitterness and the unnecessary rejection of an area of experience rich and fruitful in human life.

Again, for the intellectually inquisitive individual to be faced one day in his reading with an analysis of metaphysics into the branches of axiology, etiology, and ontology is for him to have discovered incidentally and later what might have been presented systematically and earlier as a purposeful orientation to the discipline of philosophy. The classification reveals that there are recognizable sub-groups of problems among the total of philosophical inquiries and therefore imparts an immediate *order* to the chaos of specific wonderings that may have flooded a youth's private thought for years. Thereafter, he finds himself, not reading indiscriminately in philosophical literature, but insightfully pursuing those problems of men that concern value or reality according to his momentary interest. Cognitive stress is reduced and understanding, retention, and report facilitated, through this entirely comprehensible perspective.

In the discussion of educational processes in Part I, it was suggested that the end of education might be conceived as the attainment of "a" perspective, broad and comprehensive, extending into all major areas, of the nature and processes of the universe.

The idea of the generic in the curricular content and organization intended for the gifted child, giving rise to the major proposition and to the corollaries just stated, applies with sufficient distinctiveness to the rapid learner to be a principle in his educational scheme. Intelligent children learn more, continue to learn longer, extract more meaning from what they sense, apply and associate more accurately, are interested in ultimates, and learning is a more essential part of their life's need. These principles are laid down as means to develop such functions. The curriculum which explores systematically a wide range of knowledge will give the brighter child a more adequate basis for delving into this range at any given time when there is need. The idea of placing a perspective upon those aspects of knowledge which are passed on to the gifted individual fits into his need for integrating the diverse elements of his knowledge and relates to his sensitive awareness of the incompleteness of present knowledge. Brightness implies this kind of rationalizing force and it should be recognized and utilized in the educative process.

Only when broader generalizations than are possible to its own reach are made available to that inquisitive mind which is reaching for them does stimulation to growth in stature and wisdom occur. Instruction at such levels is appropriate; instruction at lower levels is uneconomical and, to a great extent, unnecessary. Vast issues which the unaided individual cannot handle without greater maturity and experience should be defined for the gifted youth by the school, just as slighter issues are presently defined and clarified for the average individual. Through ability and inclination the gifted person tends to extend his understandings toward that unity of thought which is the finest flower of human attainment. Cannot the school start him on such a road and facilitate his progress in that direction?

chapter ten | *INSTRUCTION IN THE METHODS AND SOURCES OF KNOWLEDGE*

It is reliably observed that the adult often has little occasion to use what the child learned. A large part of school learning appears to be useful only temporarily or in further "artificial" school processes. This fact gives rise to another proposed distinction between the education of the average student and that designed for the gifted. A proposition suggesting that the gifted youngster's activities be directed toward the more enduring learning of methods by which knowledge is derived, and by which it is acquired by the individual, may be stated:

> (*VII*) *That the education of the gifted child and youth should emphasize enduring methods and sources of learning, as opposed to a terminal emphasis upon present states of knowledge.*

This principle suggests that learning should be conceived as the continuous, on-going acquisition of data pertinent to problem situations, not as a set of given facts which, it is hoped, will apply to problems that arise subsequently in the life career. It recommends that the energies of the growing child be put to a different use. The suggested learning is more useful than the traditional, yet feasible in terms of the capacities of the intellectually superior individual.[25]

The data have shown that the gifted individual evidences a propensity for learning in childhood, and it is reasonable to presume that, given opportunity to express itself appropriately, the tendency will remain in adulthood. The immediate proposition suggests that some of the instruction designed for the individual of whom this fact is true ought to recognize this fact in the teaching of understanding that will continue to be useful to the gifted in typical pursuits throughout his life career.

As has been stated, the intellectually superior child can be expected to acquire for himself many of the facts and principles needed and to have these in order when it becomes necessary to report or use what has been learned. Habituation in the ability to acquire such learnings independently in the process of carrying on some important activity would encourage the individual not to amass learning as such, but to acquire whatever learning is essential to accomplishing a given purpose. It would encourage him to adjust flexibly to changes in the structures of existing facts, shifting his previously acquired knowledge forward to the demands of the present situation. On the other hand, to learn facts as they are with no consideration to the methods by which they were discovered, their relativity in time, and their inherent limitations is to build understandings which contribute to rigidity rather than to flexibility. Under this proposition the individual will not be taught to *recall* the facts bearing on a necessary course to faction in adult life; he will be taught to *acquire* them. The laws concerning trespass; the age at which social security benefits are available; the incidence of mental disorders in a nation—these facts change, and only present facts are appropriate to present action. Answers to these questions which might have been correct at some past time are simply misleading as time moves on.

Two aspects of this proposition are developed in separate corollaries. The first states:

(VII. A) *That instruction in methods of inquiry should be included in the education of the intellectually superior child and youth.*

This principle urges that the child be acquainted with the basic methods of inquiry within the various fields. This acquaintance would extend into both understanding of the nature of the several disciplines and practice in their use. The method of historical research, with its logic, values, and controls and its appropriate applications and limitations, should be studied and practiced in the general education of gifted children and youth, not to make them precocious historians but to show them how history is written. In like manner, those disciplines should be taught which employ a rational and logical type of exploration or testing for facts. Scientific modes of inquiry should be introduced, with an exposition of their inherent controls, advantages, and limitations. Understanding the methods by which facts are discovered and evaluated, the individual student is prepared to appreciate more fully the accuracy and the pertinence of what he reads and to pursue his own inquiry into problems. To learn that appeal to authority in one area of human experience is acceptable (i.e., in some religious practice) and that in another only appeal to sensory experience is of value encourages greater appreciation of living in its multiple aspects and permits personality integration through a mental organization in which these varied modes of behavior are appropriately understood and utilized.

This principle adapts easily to instruction, since research of various kinds is, as a rule, easily performed. The abler individual should be encouraged to use knowledge of research techniques to ascertain facts for himself. The discovery and organization of information becomes, then, an educative exercise, over and above the sheer apprehension of facts.

This principle also contains certain implications for the use of text materials. Some practice has moved away from the use of a single textbook even in ordinary school situations, and it is generally recognized that a close dependence upon a textbook robs both instructor and student of the challenging opportunity to organize material themselves. It follows that reference works of a general nature should be used for some of the functions ordinarily performed by a school text, in order that the child may use research practices in selecting pertinent facts and ideas himself. In this sense, encyclopedias, manuals, and source books come into larger play, and the use of multiple texts and references is promoted.

Whatever specific methods of instruction emerge as fitting to the individual situation, the principle would seem to be warranted in that those capacities of the gifted child which will be required in later years are here permitted to function and develop early. And since the learning of facts presents less difficulty for him than it does for the average child, the discovery of facts and the organization of them for learning provide additional activities designed toward bringing the school experience to a level more nearly commensurate with his demonstrated capacities.

The second corollary to the principle that methods of inquiry should constitute a portion of the gifted child's instruction is:

(VII. B) *That existing sources of knowledge should be emphasized as a regular part of instruction in any subject matter area.*

When a problem in an area formerly surveyed as school experience occurs in a new situation apart from school, data pertinent to the problem are examined more pointedly than would be the case if they were exclusively relevant to a school situation. Thus the student of physiology takes on a new interest in diseases of the heart when his own mother becomes subject to such illness. Out of deference to the fact that a reopening of areas once generally perused will be a frequent necessity in the lives of gifted individuals as they practice in the various professions, instruction in the sources of knowledge seems appropriate. Sources within the literature of the several disciplines, authorities in the various fields who have contributed generously to the literature, agencies devoted to the promotion of knowledge and functions deriving from it—instruction in these matters is suggested here. The student of physiology referred to above should carry with him the knowledge that reliable information on heart functions and pathologies is accumulating at the present time at such and such a research center. Such knowledge is likely to be of more enduring value than any set of specific facts, for those persons and agencies whose research or thought has produced the present knowledge are most likely to continue to advance the frontiers in that field.

Instruction in sources should extend also into the types of literature pertaining to different subjects. To teach him to distinguish between essays expounding a theoretical point of view and reports of empirical investigations or between texts that survey the accomplished thought within a field and learned journals in which such material is usually first reported is to equip the gifted student for independent academic pursuit. To evaluate quickly the material he encounters through browsing, or through rapid, purposeful surveys, and to sense accurately the type, quality, and relevance of sources are arts which can be taught to the intellectually superior individual and which should be taught in lieu of less enduring information.

Bibliographies are another important source of knowledge. Already accomplished bibliographies in important areas or units of instruction are valuable curricular content, and an important method is the compiling of such lists of resources. Bibliographies place before the gifted student a vast range of source material, so that the student who is sensitive to possibilities of further research in any area can feel adequate to the task.

These principles, the proposition and the corollaries suggesting instruction in methods and sources of knowledge, follow from several characteristics of intellectually superior people. These people learn from experiences broader than those of the school, and they continue to learn through life at deeper levels and for a longer time than do people of average intellectual capacity. For professional men and women and for social leaders, the continued acquisition of understandings is important. The circles characteristic of their thought processes may be expected to grow larger through the wisdom which attends the reflective turn of mind as experience increases. Writers, lecturers, labor leaders, and ministers spend more of their energy in processes of a cognitive, intellectual nature than do persons given to some other tasks. An awareness of the sources and methods of knowledge enables such people to continue to think clearly and to keep abreast of the changes in their areas of leadership. The educational design for gifted individuals should therefore include deliberate instruction in these sources and methods.

chapter eleven

MEANING AND COMMUNICATION IN THE INSTRUCTION OF THE GIFTED

Of central importance in the educative process is the acquisition of meaning. This centrality of meaning in the process of acquiring ideas, and in their multiple association and manipulation, brings into play characteristics of intellectually superior people, such as their tendency toward verbal and ideational facility, so that a further major proposition with respect to their education might be stated:

> (*VIII*) *That the instruction of intellectually superior individuals should emphasize the central function of meaning in the acquisition of fact and principle, and the varieties of reflections of meaning in the developed communicative devices of man.*

Brownell and Hendrickson depict meaning as a property of concepts:

> It has been suggested above that learning tasks of an ideational character are exceedingly numerous. They are also of infinite variety with regard to the amount of meaning which they involve. Accordingly, it is helpful to think of particular facts, concepts, and generalizations as occupying points on a continuum of meaningfulness, such as that illustrated.

161

(Zero) 0 . . . . - - - - - - - - - - - - . . . . . N (Maximum)

At the left end of the scale, near the 0-point, are ideational learning tasks with a minimum of meaningfulness. Here belong the fact that "2" stands for the word "two," that "d" follows "c" and precedes "e" in the alphabet. . . .

At the upper end of the scale near N (maximum of meaning) and far removed from the arbitrary associations just mentioned are ideational learning tasks which are heavily freighted (or should be heavily freighted) with meaning. Here belong such items as the idea of "two," the concept of "justice," the law of diminishing returns in economics. . . .[26]

It is concentration upon the meaning in concepts as they occur in the instruction of gifted children which the proposition just stated demands. It follows, of course, that concepts having maximum meaning should be sought for their greater educational value.

It is natural for the gifted child to "do something with" ideas, but if integration and reconstruction of learned materials is desirable, such processes must be recognized and dealt with through appropriate means. The repetition in form of ideas has come so largely to be the mark of success in the academic situation that the bright child sometimes attains a level of response which is glib and conforming because he finds that it is acceptable and praiseworthy. Too often teachers confuse the reconstruction of an idea, at reaches other than and perhaps beyond those in which they or the text originally couched it, with a student's having "not quite gotten the point." The original turn of mind must often insist upon recognition, and perfect conformity is highly valued. Yet to repeat may be useless for individuals who understand readily. Therefore, movement toward application and inference should be recognized as tacit evidence that the meaning of an idea is understood, and the more advanced reckoning with the idea accepted as a favorable sign.

Another statement from Brownell and Hendrickson highlights further the function of concepts in education and stresses the importance of language. The latter emphasis looks forward to the corollary to follow:

The most evident characteristic of information, concepts, and generalizations is that they are predominantly verbal: They are learned chiefly through the agency of words, and they are used most commonly through the same agency. In the school we deal with the Mississippi River, not as an immediately sensible object, but with the idea as symbolized in words. We deal with historical events of past centuries, not as happenings which we can witness, but in the form of facts and relationships which are recorded, studied, learned, remembered, and used by means of words. Outside of school we acquire the vocabulary of daily living, of work, and of play, together with the rules under which we must operate and associate with others —all mainly through words.[27]

This passage relates to the entire proposition in its concern with the essential meaning in words as representative of things, ideas, behaviors, and processes. An education for the intellectually gifted child which centers in concepts, or briefly, in meaning and its expression, is thus suggested. Sensitive teachers are aware that the mere verbal expression of a principle in a given subject can be understood, ramified, and applied by students whose general intelligence is high; whereas extended manipulation of the concept through analysis, express application, and illustration may result in even less understanding on the part of the average student. The proposition under discussion merely recognizes this fact.

Studying and discussing ideas requires instructional time and effort which is now being consumed in the presentation of facts. As has been suggested in Proposition VII, the habit of fact-searching can be taught to gifted students and the acquisition of facts at certain levels of information entrusted to their individual initiative. The instructional time and effort thus saved could be expended in studying and discussing ideas.

Meaning can be emphasized in the education of gifted children and youth in a number of ways. For example, discussion and study could educe the latent implications of certain key words. Introduced as an object of study to the upper-level secondary school student, the word *intuition* might at first be laughably recognized as referring to feminine "hunches" or forebodings. Next might come the idea of *tuition* in the sense of teaching and then the common usage referring to the cost of college instruction. The idea contained in the Latin root of the term, "to watch, guard, protect," might be considered next. This meaning would certainly cause a somewhat different reflection by the young person upon the nature and function of the school as a social agency. The term might next be generalized into the question whether knowledge is available to the human being through means other than sense experience. Here, perhaps for the first time, the notion so vital in the study of human behavior, of the possible unlearned reaction, of instinct in higher levels of the animal order, and of the possibility of universal sequences in growth and behavior which need not be explained in terms of learning, would be introduced. Deeper levels of insight could succeed, reaching into philosophical speculations to the limits of the individual's capacity. Instruction like this, centering in concepts rich in meanings for moral behavior, political ideology, and forms of social organization, bids fair to produce a fullness of understanding which is not promised by other devices.

Another method for emphasizing meaning in the education of the gifted is the so-called continental procedure, *explication de textes*. This is a method for penetrating a written passage to the very roots of its meaning by careful, intensive, word-by-word, phrase-by-phrase analysis. Such treatment, for instance, of a highly generalized presentation of the basic schools of thought and the basic divergent points of view in educational philosophy would sensitize an individual to the ideational ranges within the subject of education. This concentration upon a fertile passage, effort being exerted to abstract the fullest meaning contained within it, would appear to offer more educative value for the brighter individual than the reading of hundreds of pages in the cursory fashion essentially demanded by present practices.

Argumentative essays are also appropriate media for instruction. Good essays, powerfully supporting opposite sides of controversies, rather than texts which "present both sides" or which gloss over differences without coming to grips with them, are suggested. The brighter child should be able to profit from the challenge of contradictory emphases, and the very highest of his capacities for understanding, evaluating, and synthesizing would be exercised, depending upon the complexity of the idea. Educative value would reside in the attempt to reconcile opposing points of view or to validate one against the other.

Other methods for the implementation of this principle will suggest themselves to imaginative teachers. Those noted should be sufficient for illustration. Corollaries to the main principle can now be developed.

To ensure the full development and use of the gifted individual's facility with words and ideas, it is proposed:

(VIII. A) *That the nature of language, its structures and functions, its integral relationship to thought and behavior, should be part of the education of the intellectually superior child and youth.*

The study of language prescribed in the usual secondary school curriculum is strange and extremely parsimonious in view of the wealth of possible approaches to it. Years of drilling on "correct" grammar and poring over a few selected pieces of literature for their plot or theme are characteristic of the "English" curriculum. It is the importance of some of the more subtle characteristics of language with which the present principle is concerned. The predominant place of verbal behavior in the measurement of intelligence, as well as its importance in the conduct of affairs, would appear to warrant building into the secondary school curriculum some of the aspects of language study which are presently undertaken as "electives" for major students in language or literature at the university level. A few approaches to the study of man's highly developed communicative systems will be suggested as possible educational matter for children whose mental capacities are adequate to the undertaking.

One such approach to language suggests its function in a kind of epistemological frame of reference. A passage from a text by Harold A. Larrabee, in a general context expository of modes of inquiry, indicates this aspect of the functions of language:

> Nevertheless, it may be objected that the historian, like everyone else in search of reliable knowledge, and even more than most inquirers, is obliged to get most of his data from the past in the form of words; that words are themselves abstract generalizations; and that historical knowledge is therefore only a crude and inexact imitation of the sciences. But this overlooks the way in which general expressions function in historical narrative. There is a difference between their use in what Ernst Cassirer calls "living speech" in direct connection with the proper names of individuals, and their sophisticated entrance as highly abstract symbols into the hypotheses of mechanical science.[28]

Thus the ideas are contrasted that words may serve the end of an approximate re-presentation of past events and that words enter the scientific hypothesis as expressions descriptive of processes independent of time and place. Instruction in these kinds of potential uses of words—in effect an elaboration of types of meaning which may be analyzed—is to acquaint the gifted individual with an idea that may have large effects on both his reading and his speaking or writing.

A classification of "primary forms of discourse" by Charles W. Morris is suggestive of another approach to language which would appear to be fruitful if brought to the acquaintance of the intellectually superior child at the secondary school levels.

> A form of discourse is a specialization of language for the better accomplishment of some specific purpose. The everyday language of people is an amazingly complex sign structure performing a multitude of individual and social functions. Its very protean character is its strength, for it provides the matrix in which and through which all human activities are interlocked in symbolic expression as they are interlocked in practice. This strength, however, involves a fundamental weakness: the very multiplicity of functions performed prevents the adequate performance of any one specialized function. So it is that men have gradually devised certain specializations of their common language for the more adequate performance of various specific tasks. Such specializations are here referred to as forms of discourse.
>
> Forms of discourse can be analyzed in terms of the functions they have been elaborated to perform, and light can be thrown on the characteristic human activities and their interrelations by a study of the nature of the forms of discourse which are the products and the instruments of these activities. . . . The present position is that there are three primary forms of discourse (the scientific, the aesthetic, and the technological), and that all other forms are secondary, that is, are a function of these primary forms. . . . The number of the primary forms of a discourse corresponds to the three dimensions of sign functioning: scientific discourse brings into prominence the relation of signs to objects denoted (the semantical dimension), aesthetic discourse accents in a distinctive way the sign structure itself (the syntactical dimension), technological discourse emphasizes the efficacy of the signs in the practice of the users (the pragmatical dimension). The theory of discourse is thus one development of the general theory of signs (technically called semiotic).[29]

The presentation and study of such a passage is instruction in language as an instrument for the communication of varied meanings, instruction at a level of complexity and potential usefulness more fitting to the capacities of the gifted than what is usually offered to him in his "English" courses or in language instruction. It is feasible and desirable that such levels of insight into the uses of language be taught if instruction is to be measured to the capacity and possible use of the intellectually superior individual.

It is observable in case studies of gifted children that they sometimes reproach themselves for being no better able to embrace an elusive idea and to express it, or to make the next necessary step in the solution of some complicated problem. Some of the ineptness in fit between language and idea may be due to inadequacies in the structure of the language to carry the subtleties which the brilliant person senses as necessary to render a desired connotation. This statement by Rudolf Carnap indicates a limitation which may be taken as typical of others.

> For our common language is well adapted for obtaining the gross agreements necessary in practical affairs; but when employed in theoretical pursuits to formulate and communicate knowledge, it is very often not merely inadequate but even seriously misleading.[30]

A systematic analysis of such limitations would afford the gifted an insight leading to greater mastery of thought and language. This study would teach him that language, as the necessary medium through which knowledge is transmitted, is the possible source of some communicative difficulty and further clarify for him the necessity for special symbolic forms in certain theoretical uses, like the sign for infinity in mathematics. For him to know that inadequacy of expression can reside elsewhere than in the person involved could serve to relieve some of the powerful tensions which accumulate in an individual intensely driven by a compulsion to know, to think through an issue, and to express his understandings. The gifted child may be his own most severe critic, and any knowledge which can fairly reduce the bitterness of his criticism is well acquired.

A final illustration of how instruction in the language arts may be better adapted to the needs and interests of the gifted child centers in the relationship existing between habits of speech and habits of thought. It has been proposed that an analysis of speech may reveal the personality of the speaker through the construction of his expressions and the "rhythm, intensity, and emphasis in the act of speaking." It has also been proposed that thought may be categorized so as to indicate major personality orientations. The "formalistic" type is "anchored in

the abstract" and "characterized by 'distancing' and ordered procedure." The "object-bound" type is "anchored in concrete life,"
"egocentric or immediate," and "associative rather than schematic,
dynamic rather than static, and varied rather than perseverative."[31]
We are not interested in the psychological validity of these analyses
but in the interesting view of the functions of language which they
suggest, a view that could be revealed with profit to the sensitive
student.

To summarize, Proposition VIII urges an educational design that
accords a central place to meaning, and the corollary proposes that
varieties of insights into language as the medium of report be developed,
so that the richness of the art and science of communication may be
more fully appreciated. The idea of variety of report would lend itself
to application in controlled expression according to one or another
mode: in the forms of discourse classified by Morris; or in holding
meaning central while various lengths of exposition are achieved
through low and high levels of generalization. And extending further
than the area of meaning and expression, the possibilities of gaining
insights into modes of behavior, and into the structures of personality,
through analysis of speech and thought would lend itself to many
interesting applications. Sheer facility in literary arts is not the upper-
most consideration here. Facility in the manipulation of concepts, embodied as they are chiefly in words, is commonly cited as a considerable factor in general intelligence. Terman, for instance, states in
this connection:

> At these levels the major intellectual differences between subjects
> reduce largely to differences in the ability to do conceptual thinking,
> and facility in dealing with concepts is most readily sampled by the
> use of verbal tests. Language, essentially, is the shorthand of the
> higher thought processes, and the level at which this shorthand
> functions is one of the most important determinants of the level
> of the processes themselves.[32]

The proposition elaborated here is suggestive of procedures which
will take better account of the capacities which intellectually superior
individuals display for concept manipulation through varieties of verbal
and linguistic adaptations. The types of studies suggested are more
commensurate with both need and capacity and feasible at the secondary levels of schooling for the gifted. Presently such approaches

are reserved for specialized courses at the university level. The understandings and the uses to which this kind of study of language may be put are too important to be offered to only a few on any kind of elective basis.

chapter twelve

THE FOUNDATIONS OF CIVILIZATION AS EDUCATIONAL CONTENT

It is consistent with the capacities and anticipated needs of the superior learner that his education be oriented toward the foundations and historic origins of contemporary social practices and institutions. It may be stated:

> (*IX*) *That the instruction of the intellectually superior should include content pertaining to the foundations of civilization.*

This proposition recommends that the study of the facts and ideas behind contemporary institutions, a study traditionally pursued by inspired and able students and thinkers, be formalized into subject matter for school instruction of the gifted.

Ross L. Finney has noted this idea of foundations and, by way of illustration, sketched the content of certain areas that would implement it. His treatment affords a fair illustration of the present proposal. Finney states:

> The exigencies of our argument suggest some elaboration of the phenomenon of cumulative racial learning; to which end a few illustrations will prove helpful. The technique of so simple and commonplace a thing as making bread harks back through a long series

of inventions and discoveries to the very dawn of human life upon the planet. Modern methods in milling, recent improvements in baking, the method of lightening dough, the original devices for cooking, the first cracking of the kernels, the domestication of wheat, the initial discovery of the plant, are among steps in the long series. . . .

Similarly, all our institutions and cultures have evolved; and there is no intellectual exercise more enlightening than to trace that historic evolution in the various social fields. Political scientists, for example, find the genesis of our Constitution in Colonial and English precedents, which in turn they trace back to their origins in the Roman Empire and in primitive Teutonic life.

. . . .

Even the Christian religion has evolved; and the study of its evolution takes us back not only to the Jahveh cult of ancient Israel, but to the religions of Egypt and Babylonia, with prehistoric savagery in the ultimate background. Science has a history of the utmost fascination, surpassed in interest, if at all, only by the history of art: for the relics of primitive art carry us back to an even remoter past. And so it is in all fields. Little by little the race has learned; and the findings of racial experience have been transmitted and accumulated. Thus do we now possess that vast, mental heritage by the use of which we conduct our social life on the present high level of civilization.[33]

To analyze the foundations of American culture and to treat these systematically contributes to a fertile source of thought about contemporary aspects of the culture. The same type of treatment is due civilizations other than American or, more broadly, Western. The fact of "one world" would urge that the same type of treatment be accorded all the major extant civilizations. To understand the foundations of Russian law and of Japanese concepts of ethics is to enrich the understanding of one's own culture in these respects. This broader view, challenging as it is to the intellectual capacities, can be attained only by those possessing intelligence well within the upper ranges.

Specific points of view which disappear in social evolution often become applicable again when conditions change. Thus, the "rugged individualism" which characterized an earlier phase of economic and political activity in America and which has yielded in some measure to a modified paternalistic economy under the expanded control of the state might be useful again if the trend toward paternalism goes so far as to negate the values which it originally served. How much difference is there between the independence of character implied in the concept of rugged individualism and the quality of "inner direction" the absence of which is bemoaned today. New conditions are such that the older concepts of individual initiative might again be needed for the health of society. When we consider that a single generation may eclipse the memory of past movements, the advantage becomes obvious of studying earlier stages in the development of present forms.

Harold Rugg's concept of "Force Men" as opposed to "Thing Men," which was used in another context (pp. 65–66), is also applicable in this connection. Rugg writes:

> As the years passed I have found that the facts of life *did* conclude if only I would *let* them. I was brought to recognize this by an exciting and profound body of Americans who had succeeded in doing that very thing. These I have called the Men of the Consensus and to their leaders I have dedicated my book. Throughout the story of their work we can marvel at their traits. Certainly they were neither Liberals nor Conservatives. Not one was of any Party. Partisan politics was not their business and they eschewed all soapboxes, those of the die-hard Right or Left or of any straddling Liberal party. They were Radicals in the truest dictionary sense—"from the roots thereof"; that is, *they were students of the foundations of man and his culture.* One by one these men—most of them working alone, most of them afraid yet naively brave—confronted the facts of modern life and, even against the loyalties and taboos of their people, let their minds conclude what the facts of life conclude.[34]

And in the description of the dichotomy which he has perceived among people, he writes further:

> These Men of the Consensus were concerned with the forces which shaped both the superficial conditions and the problems of men, with the *relations between Things*—not with the Things themselves. To drive this point home I have set them apart throughout my book, even giving them the special label of Force People to distinguish them inescapably from the Thing People who have dominated Western culture. . . . The distinction is important because it accounts for the varieties of our educational programs, technologies, and expressive arts. Membership in one group or the other deter-

mines how each of us sees the world. It molds a man's attitude toward social change, his vision of the role of history, his understanding of technology and science, and his expression in the arts. Force People . . . Thing People: one of the great human dichotomies.[35]

Those persons who in large measure resemble Rugg's "Force People" and who have achieved a synthesis of thought from the past and present influences in their prevailing culture are the men whose ideas can be read by the gifted youth. Progress in his own thinking at similar planes may be expected to occur. A transmission of the cultural heritage would thus be effected by means of an organization and integration which is like that subsequently to be effected by some of the present generation of "Force People" and passed on to those following.

The idea of studying the thoughts of men who have synthesized the forces at play in their culture and rendered explicit the foundations upon which their present modes of thought and behavior rest combines well with Hollingworth's emphasis upon the study of biography. She has said:

> For many reasons, the study of biography would seem to be especially appropriate in the education of gifted children. We have said that the child should have brought to his attention whatever knowledge will most help him to adjust himself successfully to his world. From researches in differential psychology, we can now predict that children standing in the best percentile for intellect at the age of eight to ten years, will continue to occupy the same relative position as adults. They will be capable of that extraordinary service of intellect which may result, if other personal traits are favorable, in professional, scientific, and artistic eminence, and in moral leadership. For adjustment to life as they are capable of living it, they need information as to how persons have found adjustment, as to how careers are made and are related serviceably to civilization, and as to all various kinds of intellectual work required by the world in their day. Also, they need ideals of sustained effort against odds, of perfection in work, of altruism, and of self-management which arise from close contemplation of the noble.[36]

To encourage the gifted child to study in detail the lives of men who affected the civilization in which they lived, rather than adjusted expediently to its present, felt demands, is to make possible another "close imitation of good models" in areas of understanding crucial to social and personal effectiveness. What better study for those youth in large number destined to be leaders in social progress than an examination of the lives of men and women who in the past have served society in just such a capacity?

A corollary to this proposition refers specifically to subject matter areas, extending the emphasis upon foundations into the individual academic disciplines. The corollary may be stated:

(IX. A) *That the history of the various fields of knowledge should be taught as foundational to present concepts within each academic discipline.*

This principle suggests that the study of the history of a field creates levels of insight in addition to those created by a study of the field's present state. The principles of sociology, attended by a study of the history of sociology as an area of man's thought and activity; the history of psychology in like manner, and the history of philosophy—such presentations permit a depth in understanding not otherwise attainable. The historical dimension of an academic discipline is traditionally reserved for presentation at the college and university level. This principle would merely reduce this experience to systematic curricular presentation at lower levels for that group able to integrate and to use such instruction.

Educational practice following this principle would encourage the reading of histories which describe the origin and development of the theoretical structures distinguishing the several disciplines. Present school practices require research chiefly as an exploration of the *status quo;* it is here urged that history be in more constant reference and more integrally a part of the educative design for gifted individuals.

It is not inherent in the principle that all such instruction should be direct or couched in the form of assignments with the historical dimension as an immediate aim. Incidental acquisition of understandings with respect to the origins and foundations of present things and ideas may be encouraged through the ready accessibility of references which provide such treatment. Through special libraries or through the encouragement to build a private library relating to the individual's particular needs, such incidental acquisition and spontaneous and continuous pursuit at the ripest psychological moments can be effected.

A second and final corollary to the emphasis upon foundations considers the value of literary classics in the educative design. It may be stated:

(IX. B) *That classics of the world's literary and educational store should be treated as foundational in the development of the thought of man and that the gifted should be instructed in such great works.*

A major difference exists between the educational design of today and that of fifty to a hundred years ago in the emphasis upon "classics." Various reasons may be adduced to account for this difference, and not all educators feel apologetic about the present state. It is generally admissible, however, that such literature appeals more to students above average in intelligence and that those virtues attendant upon a pursuit of the classics are most available and appropriate to them. Hence, the principle is derived that classical works of literature and thought should be utilized in the education of the gifted.

Experience with great books yields more than a knowledge of the ideas in which they traffic. Otherwise, a summary of their ideas might substitute for the works themselves. To follow Descartes through his "discourses" upon method is to experience the working of the mind of the man himself through the phrasing of his ideas, their succession, their inclusions and omissions, and the logic and the overall points of view which dominate. Such experience can be particularly fruitful to the gifted child. His own mind works in channels qualitatively more similar to that of the masters than to that of the generality. And to be able to experience the actual thought of the world's great is to lead the brighter individual to challenges in his own thinking which can scarcely be achieved in any other manner.

Great works of literature, fiction and non-fiction, are commonly conceded to have perennial value, successive readings at intervals yielding new insights. Thus the reading of *Gulliver's Travels* is an experience of a certain character at the earlier school levels, and the reading of the same book in adulthood is an experience of a different character. This type of repetition need not be feared as wasteful, for the ideas treated in the classics are important ideas, and the earlier contact may stimulate growth necessary to a fuller apprehension upon subsequent contact.

Copious reading lists, fairly annotated, are suggested, so that the child may accumulate a store of titles which he com s to value through repeated reference and which he will recall read ' when voluntary reading choices are possible for him.

Part III has been devoted to the recommendation of principles of education bearing directly upon the development of the gifted individual's intellectual capacities. The academic disciplines have been explored and some of the issues directly relating to the complex and subtle uses to which the mind of the gifted may be put. In the person of the intellectually gifted individual the school is dealing with superior capacity for learning, superior interest, initiative, and purpose in intellectual matters, and superior personality factors which promise a wholesome use of these gifts to the ends of both individual and social good. It is proposed that the school may meet these characteristics with curricular experiences designed toward their continued nurture through the levels of experience implied in our principles. The major proposals suggest: that the child's superior intellect be optimally utilized rather than neglected or ignored (Proposition V); that present educative experiences be generative of further learning (Proposition VI); that methods of inquiry and sources of knowledge be taught (Proposition VII); that the meaning of concepts and varieties in language and expression receive central emphasis (Proposition VIII); and that instruction in the foundations of the present order of things, ideas, situations, and institutions be taught (Proposition IX). These principles offer substance through which the superior intellect can grow and develop and from which individually satisfying and socially productive uses may derive.

[1] Herbert A. Carroll, *Genius in the Making* (New York: McGraw-Hill Book Company, Inc. 1940), p. 115.

[2] Leta S. Hollingworth, "An Enrichment Curriculum for Rapid Learners at Public School 500: Speyer School," *Teachers College Record*, XXXIX (1938), 304.

[3] G. Lester Anderson and Arthur I. Gates, "The General Nature of Learning," *Forty-Ninth Yearbook of the National Society for the Study of Education*, Part I (Chicago: University of Chicago Press, 1950), pp. 25–26.

[4] Educational Policies Commission, *Education of the Gifted* (Washington, D. C.: National Education Association, 1950), p. 72.

[5] Harvard Committee, *General Education in a Free Society* (Cambridge, Massachusetts: Harvard University Press, 1945), p. 109.

[6] Warren G. Findley and Douglas E. Scates, "Obtaining Evidence of Understanding," *Forty-Ninth Yearbook of the National Society for the Study of Education*, Part I, pp. 48–49.

[7] *Ibid.*, pp. 49–50.

[8] University of Chicago, Board of Examinations, *Sample Questions from Comprehensive Examinations* (Chicago: The College of the University of Chicago, 1948), *pass*. Copyright, 1948, by the University of Chicago.

[9] Anne Anastasi and John P. Foley, Jr., *Differential Psychology* (New York: The Macmillan Company, 1949), p. 577.

[10] *Ibid.*, p. 58

[11] J. P. Guilford, "Creativity," *The American Psychologist*, V (1950), 444–54.

[12] Leta S. Hollingworth, *Children Above 180 IQ* (Yonkers-on-Hudson, New York: World Book Co., 1942), pp. 240–41.

[13] J. P. Guilford, *op. cit.*, p. 454.

[14] Catherine Patrick, "Creative Thinking," *The Encyclopedia of Psychology*, Philip L. Harriman, ed. (New York: The Philosophical Library, 1946), p. 112.

[15] Hugh Hartshorne, Mark A. May, and Frank M. Shuttleworth, *Studies in the Organization of Character*, Vol. III, *Studies in the Nature of Character*. (New York: The Macmillan Company, 1930), pp. 34–38.

[16] Robert M. Hutchins, Preface to *The Great Conversation*, Vol. 1, *Great Books of the Western World* (Chicago: Encyclopaedia Britannica, Inc., 1952), pp. xxv and xxvi.

[17] *Ibid.*, p. xxvi.

[18] Fay Adams and Walker Brown, *Teaching the Bright Pupil* (New York: Henry Holt and Company, 1930), p. 61.

19 Herbert A. Carroll, *Genius in the Making* (New York: McGraw-Hill Book Co., Inc., 1940), p. 123.

20 Leta S. Hollingworth, *Gifted Children, Their Nature and Nurture* (New York: The Macmillan Company, 1926), pp. 331–32.

21 W. J. Osburn and Ben J. Rohan, *Enriching the Curriculum for Gifted Children* (New York: The Macmillan Company, 1931), p. 44.

22 Edwin B. Allen, Dis Maly, and S. H. Starkey, Jr., *Vital Mathematics* (New York: The Macmillan Company, 1944), p. v.

23 Fay Adams and Walker Brown, *Teaching the Bright Pupil* (New York: Henry Holt and Company, 1930), pp. 125–26.

24 Forest Ray Moulton, ed., *The World and Man, as Science Sees Them* (Chicago: University of Chicago Press, 1937), pp. 200–1. Copyright, 1937, by the University of Chicago.

25 There is an apparent contradiction between this principle, which suggests instruction in the methodology behind the derivation of the various academic and scientific disciplines, and the precepts concerning general education which have been presented in Part I. The contradiction is only apparent, however, because in the present proposal studies and practices in methodology are intended to be experiences which deepen the understanding of the facts and principles within the particular discipline, rather than experiences intended to develop functional skill per se. There are differences in degree and in aim between the experience of the history student at the graduate level engaging in numerous historical research investigations as a means toward becoming an historian, and the experience of a bright student in high school engaging in historical research (or scientific) and studying historical methodology as a means of enriching his understanding of the nature of historical propositions and the sources from which they derive.

26 William A. Brownell and Gordon Hendrickson, "How Children Learn Information, Concepts, and Generalizations," *Forty-Ninth Yearbook of the Society for the Study of Education*, Part I (Chicago: University of Chicago Press, 1950), pp. 94–95.

27 *Ibid.*, p. 93.

28 Harold A. Larrabee, *Reliable Knowledge* (Boston: Houghton Mifflin Company, 1945), p. 515.

29 Charles W. Morris, "Science, Art and Technology," *The Kenyon Review*, I (1939), 410–20. Cited in Irving J. Lee, ed., *The Language of Wisdom and Folly* (New York: Harper & Brothers, 1949), pp. 31–32.

30 Rudolf Carnap, *Factors Determining Human Behavior* (Cambridge, Massachusetts: Harvard University Press, 1937). Cited in Irving J. Lee, ed., *ibid.*, p. 45.

31 Fillmore H. Sanford, "Speech and Personality," *Introduction to Clinical Psy-*

chology, L. A. Pennington and I. A. Berg, eds. (New York: The Ronald Press Company, 1948), pp. 160–61.

[32] Lewis M. Terman and Maud A. Merrill, *Measuring Intelligence* (Boston: Houghton Mifflin Company, 1937), p. 5.

[33] Ross L. Finney, *A Sociological Philosophy of Education* (New York: The Macmillan Company, 1928), pp. 32–34.

[34] Harold Rugg, *Foundations for American Education* (Yonkers-on-Hudson, New York: World Book Company, 1947), pp. xi–xii.

[35] *Ibid.*, pp. xii–xiii.

[36] Leta S. Hollingworth, *Gifted Children: Their Nature and Nurture* (New York: The Macmillan Co., 1926), p. 319.

part four

PRINCIPLES OF PERSONAL, SOCIAL, AND CHARACTER DEVELOPMENT

When the consciousness of science is fully impregnated with the consciousness of human value, the greatest dualism which now weights humanity down, the split between the material, the mechanical, the scientific and the moral and ideal will be destroyed.

—John Dewey

part
four

chapter thirteen

PERSONAL, SOCIAL, AND CHARACTER DEVELOPMENT IN THE GIFTED

The principles in Part IV have as their aim the development of the intellectually superior individual in other than the academic and intellectual areas of personality. The modern American school is concerned with the affective and conative dimensions of personality as well as the cognitive. Educational principles relating to these areas usually are subsumed under classifications like "emotional development," "moral (or character) development," and "social development," in textbooks on human development and educational psychology. Emotional and social adjustments tend to free intelligence for fuller play in the experience of the individual, and intellectual capacity appears to develop optimally only when its development is paralleled by sound growth in these "dynamic" substructures of personality. Therefore certain principles of education pertaining to the development within the gifted of emotion, motive, and value, social understandings and skills, are undertaken in the same manner as those relating to their intellectual and academic development. These principles will differ from those applicable to the generality because of the superior intellect and concomitant behavioral characteristics which distinguish the gifted.

The gifted differ less markedly from the generality in the dynamics of personality than they do in intellect. It follows that special educational processes designed to develop these psychological substrata differentiate the gifted from the hypothetical average less decisively. At such points as possible, however, we have abstracted from the general literature on education for character and personal integrity those approaches which involve most significantly the behavioral qualities which science ascribes to the intellectually superior person.

The principles of this part assume the presence of provisions usually made for pupils of all levels of ability, such as a program of diversified extracurricular activities, opportunity for the expression of initiative in student activities, and a guidance program with its customary services. The stated principles will be conceived as modifying or supplementing these usual provisions in the interest of better serving the gifted.

An important part of education in this vein is the development of character and citizenship. In a limited sense, the end of personal and social development might be considered as developed character with respect to the individual and developed citizenship with respect to society. It is difficult to isolate concepts which apply to the one area of development, personal or social, which are not in some way related both to the personal character and to the civic roles of the individual. As will be observed in some of the quoted material, writers often consider the areas so closely related that they treat them collectively. In the discussion that follows what is cited or expressed with respect to aim and ideal or to developmental technique, as related to character, is intended to be applicable to the development of personal and social adequacy in point of view and behavior.

The importance of personal, social, and character development for the gifted is attested by what is generally acknowledged of the values in this area for *all* persons and by the fact that the gifted characteristically assume positions of leadership and influence.

The first portion of this treatment deals with typical problems of adjustment which appear to arise in the development of gifted individuals under heterogeneous environments and school conditions. This discussion leads to theoretical considerations relating the problem of personal and social adjustments to educational endeavor and to the superior intellectual capacity of the students concerned. Specific proposals for the educational design follow upon these background considerations and comprise the major portion of the final part of the systematic theory.

TYPICAL ADJUSTMENT PROBLEMS
OF GIFTED INDIVIDUALS

By virtue of his distinctive characteristics and interests, there are certain difficulties in the achievement of personal and social adjustment which attend the development of the gifted individual in the usual environment. Several students of the problems of these individuals as children have concentrated upon such difficulties. Leta Hollingworth was perhaps at her best on this subject, and much of her work centers in this problem. In one of her relatively early writings, she designates five "special problems in social adjustment" which are commonplace with the child of very superior intelligence and which in some degree apply to the broader range of intellectual superiority considered in the present work. In (1) *the problem of work*, it is indicated that the child becomes increasingly misfitted to the ordinary school program as the intelligence scale is mounted, idleness and boredom and "positive distaste" reaching considerable proportions in the upper intelligence levels. Under (2) *adjustment to classmates* is treated the problems arising from heterogeneous grouping in which the advanced, under-age child will be in contact with over-age, retarded, "minus" deviates. (3) *The problem of play* involves differences in interests and preferences for psychologically complex games. If the gifted child adjusts at all to the generality in this respect, it involves a "difficult compromise" for him. Hollingworth indicates that many good intentions to "socialize" the child through deliberately planned contacts with others in ordinary play fail because of a psychological unsoundness in the procedures. As (4) *problems of conformity* are listed the gifted child's typical reaction against the drudgery of school routine; his frequent superiority to parents and teachers in intelligence, with the attendant conflicts between love and respect on one hand and disgust and disbelief on the other; his quickness to learn maladjustments such as that feigned illness brings coddling; and his general tendency to argue about routine requirements of school and home. In (5) *problems of origin and destiny* are noted those tendencies of the gifted child to be absorbed at early ages in such ultimate problems of philosophy and religion as the meaning of life and death and the nature of a hereafter. Hollingworth notes that often questions asked by the child out of these areas of interest are met by such answers as "You are too young to understand" or "You unnatural child!" As a basic operating factor in such areas of difficulty, Hollingworth suggests the immaturity and imbalance resulting from having the "intelligence of an adult and the emotions of a child combined in a childish body."[1]

Subsequently, Hollingworth adds other special problems of personality development: (1) the role of physique in social adjustment, highlighting the fact that the gifted individual, usually being younger, is smaller than his group associates and hence has certain difficulties in attaining the leadership for which he is generally qualified; (2) the problem of adjustment to a vocation in view of the many-sided interests and abilities of the individual; and (3) a tendency toward isolation and withdrawal arising from the difficulties of adjusting to the play interests of other children.[2]

Two additional concepts occurring in this same presentation relate further to the dynamics of adjustment. The first concerns an adaptation which the intellectually superior individual must make if he is to interact effectively with his associates. The phrasing used by Hollingworth is "learning to suffer fools gladly." Because the connotation of the phrase might strike some as unfortunate, Hollingworth's own development of the idea will be cited so that the essential fineness of the spirit involved may be realized. She writes:

> A lesson which many gifted persons never learn as long as they live is that human beings in general are inherently very different from themselves in thought, in action, in general intention, and in interests. Many a reformer has died at the hands of a mob which he was trying to improve in the belief that other human beings can and should enjoy what he enjoys. This is one of the most painful and difficult lessons that each gifted child must learn, if personal development is to proceed successfully. It is more necessary that this be learned than that any school subject be mastered. Failure to learn how to tolerate in a reasonable fashion the foolishness of others leads to bitterness, disillusionment, and misanthropy.
>
> What is meant here may be illustrated by the behavior of a seven-year-old boy with an IQ of 178. He was not sent to school until the age of seven because of his advanced interest in reading. At seven, however, the compulsory attendance law took effect and the child was placed in the third grade at school. After about four weeks of attendance, he came home from school weeping bitterly. "Oh,

Grandmother, Grandmother," he cried, "they don't know what's *good!* They just *won't* read!"

The story then came out, how he had taken book after book to school—all his favorites from his grandfather's library—and had tried to show the other third-grade pupils what treasures these were. But the boys and girls only resisted his efforts, made fun of him, threw the treasures on the floor, and finally pulled his hair.

Such struggles as these, if they continue without directing the child's insight, may lead to complete alienation from his contemporaries in childhood, and to misanthropy in adolescence and adulthood. Particularly deplorable are the struggles of these children against dull or otherwise unworthy adults in authority. The very gifted child or adolescent, perceiving the illogical conduct of those in charge of his affairs, may turn rebellious against all authority and fall into a condition of negative suggestibility—a most unfortunate trend of personality, since the person is then unable to take a cooperative attitude toward authority.[3]

Many of the actions and attitudes of gifted individuals may obviously be attributed to the difficulty of this adjustment.

A further idea originated by Hollingworth is that problems of social adjustment increase as the intelligence scale is ascended, so that a certain range is considered optimally suited for easiest and most effective adjustments:

> All things considered, the psychologist who has observed the development of gifted children over a long period of time from early childhood to maturity, evolves the idea that there is a certain restricted portion of the total range of intelligence which is most favorable to the development of successful and well-rounded personality in the world as it now exists. This limited range appears to be somewhere between 125 and 155 IQ. Children and adolescents in this area are enough more intelligent than the average to win the confidence of large numbers of their fellows, which brings leadership, and to manage their lives with superior efficiency. Moreover, there are enough of them to afford mutual esteem and understanding. But those of 170 IQ and beyond are too intelligent to be understood by the general run of persons with whom they make contact. . . .[4]

The relativity of adjustment is indicated in this passage, and the general soundness of Hollingworth's observation is easily agreed upon. In its practical applications, however, there might not be enough companions even in the optimum range of intelligence for "mutual esteem and understanding," nor might this range be optimum in an environment where the normative position was lower than the average for the standardization population of the Stanford-Binet Intelligence Scale.

The educator must be sensitive to areas of potential difficulty like these indicated by Hollingworth if the development of the gifted individual is to proceed optimally in all major phases of personality.

Ruth Strang adds other considerations relative to personal and social adjustment, pointing up the difficulties which come to the gifted partly and sometimes exclusively by virtue of their giftedness. She lists among others the following "normal problems and perplexities of growing up":

Feelings of Inferiority and Inadequacy
Unsatisfying Human Relations
Failure to Realize Intellectual Potentialities
Difficulty in Choosing, Preparing for, and Entering a Vocation.

Under "special problems intensified by high intelligence" and "conditions that contribute to maladjustment," she lists these additional adjustive difficulties:

Parental Pressure and Exploitation; Overemphasis on the Child's
     Intellectual Development
Parental Indifference and Neglect
Lack of Opportunity to Develop a Philosophy of Life
Financial Limitations
Poor Instruction in Thinking and Study Methods
A Dull and Meager Curriculum.[5]

Harvey Zorbaugh offers an analytical description of some of the problems listed above:

Furthermore, the highly gifted child's developmental disharmonies are likely to create stresses within his personality, for instance between his intellectual conception of performance and his physical ability to realize it. A preschool child whose development we followed was being taught by his father to skate. He asked for and was given a book on figure skating. The next time he was on the ice he attempted to execute a figure eight. Having failed repeatedly, he took off his skates in frustration and attempted to execute a figure eight crawling about the ice while holding his skates in his hands.

Again, conflict may be created within the highly gifted child's personality by the discrepancy between his intellectual and his emotional maturity. . . .

As the adolescent's world expands, he seeks increasingly for security within widening relationships; he feels the need of orienting his life in accord with social values which will give him satisfaction. But our culture is exceedingly heterogeneous, characterized by innumerable inconsistencies and conflicts among values, standards, conceptions of behavior, and ways of life. The need to work through and resolve these inconsistencies and conflicts is one of the major sources of adolescent stress in America.[6]

It might appear from these dangers to the personal and social adjustment of the gifted that the general finding of upward deviation for them in all significant, measurable traits does not imply a similar deviation in dynamic traits. To Terman's data on this point, however, may be added these findings from the Character Education Inquiry, reported in the three-volume *Studies in the Organization of Character*. A positive correlation between intelligence and moral adjustments is noted in these statistical generalizations: (1) a correlation of .344 (average) between intelligence and honesty, and (2) a "best estimate of the relation between intelligence and a theoretical combination of all our deception tests," a correlation of $-.50$ to $-.60$.[7] Though not sufficiently high to indicate that no direct attention to the development of character is necessary, these correlations do indicate that under the conditions pertaining to the development of the children who were the subjects of this investigation intelligence and character are positively associated. The areas of potential breakdown in personal and social adjustments and in moral behavior, then, despite this extensive treatment of the nature of such difficulties, represent only those areas in which the smaller proportion of adjustment problems fall when they do occur.

THEORETICAL CONSIDERATIONS RELATING PERSONAL DEVELOPMENT TO EDUCATION AND INTELLIGENCE

Can the school cause adaptations in personality and character which are measurable improvements over those which derive through uncontrolled and informal social situations? Vernon Jones has subjected this question to experimental test in a project in which several methods of teaching for character adjustment were tried and the results measured by tests. One of his conclusions points out that under proper methodology behavior can be adjusted towards the moral. He says:

> One of the most important results of the study is the evidence that demonstrable improvement in character and citizenship of children can be made through planned instruction in school. We should hasten to add, however, that the smallness of the improvement, on the average, and the failure to get any consistent gains in some of the trained classes emphasize the difficulty of bringing about improvement in this field, at least by group instruction in school.[8]

Considering that the school does play a role, even if a small one, in the development of the child in these areas and that under studied methods its role might even be enlarged, it is important to know the nature of the developmental processes which are apparently subject to school experience. The Character Education Inquiry yielded suggestions as to the course of development which occurs in the child whose behavior changes toward integrated, consistent, moral performances. One of the notable findings of the Inquiry concerns the relativity and the specificity of the moral response as presently measured in children like those of the study:

> It seems to be a fair conclusion from our data that honest and deceptive tendencies represent not general traits nor action guided by general ideals but specific habits learned in relation to specific situations which have made the one or the other mode of response successful.
>
> Whatever behavior is studied, the general picture holds true. Conduct represents an achieved association between a certain type of situation and a certain type of response. Such terms as *honesty*

and *self-control* are names which the observer may, for convenience, apply to this or that group of conducts which show specified resemblances, but there is no evidence that in grades 5 to 8 the children themselves have developed any great sensitiveness to such general terms either as motives or as cues to action.[9]

This specificity of response and its relativity to the situation points to the fact of behavior as it is, and as it tends to result from the collective influence of environments (including routine school procedures) as they are. We prefer, however, not to consider this set of conditions to be necessary and inevitable. It seems reasonable that if facts as they stand are undesirable, reasoned attempts to alter the conditions which determine these facts would promise different results. We see a power in deliberately constructed educative experiences for developing levels of character which transcend and negate these time-bound experimental findings.

The same authors indicate a reasonable basis for such attempts at character education. Their concept of integration as movement from specificity to generalized behavioral patterns is again best stated in their own terms:

> From what has so far been said, it can readily be seen that integration in the full sense is essential to the most complete use of human powers in the control of natural and human resources. Its *complete* achievement is inconceivable. But growth in integration is necessary for the advancement of life and takes place in proportion as situations, on the one hand, are properly classified in terms of their potentialities, which may be scientifically determined, and, on the other hand, in proportion as systems of response are attached to principles, laws, and ideals, as well as to the concrete demands of immediately perceived situations.[10]

The "attachment of systems of response to principles, laws, and ideals" is therefore the key conceptual basis underlying education for character and social and personal adjustment. Many characteristics of intellectually gifted individuals appear to relate to this concept. Their behavior can come to be dominated by ideals, as opposed to "the concrete demands of immediately perceived situations."

Vernon Jones indicates the peculiar fitness of the gifted child for increasingly consistent and integrative behavioral adaptations. He writes:

The relation of intelligence to character development is probably most readily seen in the role which intellect plays in orienting the individual in his environment. The dull and the bright intellectually are not alike in their ability to foresee the consequences of their acts; neither are they alike in their capacity to sense when greater advantages inhere in remote goals than in immediate gratifications. The more able the individual, the better can he select his environment and mold it in accordance with the ends he would achieve. Moreover, the same environment does not produce the same total organization of learned behavior and values in the bright and in the dull. Indeed, differences in intellect make of identical physical environments different psychological environments. Of course, this does not mean that superior intellect can so alter inferior environments as to guarantee good character under any circumstances. Good intelligence, however, should enable one to achieve the skills, knowledge, and orientation that will help him to make the most of a superior environment, on the one hand, or to resist most efficiently the restricting effects of a poor environment, on the other.[11]

As indicated here, where the capacity to generalize, to foresee, and to anticipate exists, there is the potential at least for this state of performance in which consistency is maintained between the ethical ideal and the practical act. By virtue of their greater capacity for generalization, the "doctrine of specificity" would appear to apply less rigorously to the gifted than to the average or dull among children. This is an important consideration in planning education for personal, social, and moral adjustments of the exceptional group.

Robert Havighurst and Hilda Taba make the following observation concerning an ideal state of character development:

> Character develops through reflective thinking. Moral behavior may also be learned through thinking about moral situations, tracing various kinds of behavior through to their probable consequences, and reaching conclusions which may govern future behavior. If this process is practiced often enough, with guidance which safeguards accuracy of reasoning, it results in a number of general moral principles which may be applied in future situations. In a changing society which constantly poses new moral problems for the individual, it is obviously of great importance that a person have generalized moral principles and that he be able to apply these wisely in specific instances.[12]

The qualities critical to the development of ideal behavior would appear to be, once more, those accounting most directly for the distinctiveness of the intellectually superior individual.

Against this general background relating the problem of education for character and personal and social adjustment to the learning process and to the qualities of demonstrated superiority found in the gifted individuals, certain propositions which serve to implement and to further the purposes of education in these realms have been developed.

chapter fourteen | *APPLYING THE SCIENTIFIC METHOD*

If the question were asked of the principals of typical American schools, "What theory and what plan do you have in your school for the character development of children?" it is questionable that more than a scattered few would state a theory that would bear analysis by the educational philosopher and a plan of action that would bear analysis by behavioral scientists as a specific set of co-ordinated procedures which pertain validly to the purpose. True, moral dicta abound; these depend, however, more upon the accidental personal orientation of individual teachers than upon a defensible program with clear objectives and coherent procedures. These heterogeneous imperatives concerning the "oughts" of behavior are likely to represent contradictory conceptions of the nature of morals and a medley of sanctions for acts involving values, not to mention chaotic practices affecting the psychological substrata that conduce toward constructive attitudes within the person toward himself and society. It is perhaps truer in these areas than in any other significant undertaking by the school that the theoretical bases are not understood, the goals are not clarified, and the methodology is not explicitly developed. Unquestionably more complicated than ordinary academic processes, the development of character in children urges *more* systematic and intelligent concentration, rather than *less*.

As the first of the propositions designed to guide the personal, social, and character development of the intellectually superior, it is suggested that the problem be undertaken in the manner of science. The effectiveness of that body of thought and techniques termed "scientific" for the management of problem after problem in human affairs has been patently demonstrated. It is observed then:

> (X) *That scientific methods should be applied in the conception and in the execution of the education for personal, social, and character adjustments of the intellectually superior individual.*

Certain recognition of the chaos that characterizes practical efforts toward the development of children in these areas has brought this suggestion previously to the fore. Laurance F. Shaffer and Edward J. Shoben, Jr., treating positive principles of mental hygiene, suggest that the most broadly effective single technique which can be brought to the problem of psychological adjustments is the scientific method. They recommend that the same techniques of analysis and attack be applied to these problem areas that are used in the natural sciences.[13]

The same type of approach to the development of character has been suggested and can be used as a guide to both teachers and moral philosophers, as well as to gifted youths themselves who characteristically grope for a stabilizing personal philosophy. Ernest M. Ligon, director of the Union College Character Research Project, has expressed the spirit which characterizes his endeavor:

> *It is certain that there are laws of character development which are just as inviolable and powerful as the laws of nature.* No one will question the fact that many of these laws are probably even more complex and intricate than those that govern our natural phenomena. *We shall certainly not discover them with less painstaking research than that which has characterized physics and chemistry.*[14]

A willingness to supplant arbitrary dogma with experientially based, objectively examined values and to utilize scientific techniques in the conception of the educational design and in its execution is a first and a most important step in the direction of education for character. Not only are the philosophy and method of science fruitful epistemologically, but they are likely to be found personally satisfying by highly intelligent youth, interested in ultimates and sensitive to contradictions that inhere in the use of varying points of view in reckoning with the problems of living.

Ligon elaborated upon Union College methodology, listing in his book *A Greater Generation* seven "minimum essentials" comprising "The Role of Science in the Problem of Character." These minimum essentials are:

(1) *In teaching children* [*character*], *the laws of learning must be obeyed if they are to learn.* [Exposure, repetition, understanding, conviction, application are the five steps in the learning process, according to Ligon.]

(2) *The second basic essential, therefore, which objective evidence has convinced us is necessary for effective character education is that we must have very definite aims to be achieved.*

(3) The evidence seems to prove conclusively that *it is impossible to teach a concept before the maturity of the child makes it possible for him to understand it.*

(4) One of the most important of the basic minimum essentials is in applying the principle of individual differences. *One can no more solve the problems of the personal equation without knowing the factors in that equation than he can solve a mathematics problem without knowing the factors involved. A character trait has no meaning apart from the individual of whom it is characteristic.*

(5) The fifth basic minimum essential for effective character education carries its own conviction when stated, but is probably the least observed as far as traditional methods are concerned. It is that *our curricular materials must be so organized as to constitute a psychologically valid approach to the attitude being taught.*

(6) Now we come to the sixth of our basic minimum essentials. It is that *effective character education is a seven-day-a-week undertaking . . . effective character education probably requires the actively integrated cooperation of all the major influences affecting the child.*

(7) . . . *we must set up reliable and valid measuring devices to evaluate our methods and materials.*[15]

Abstracted from the context of several chapters, these statements miss the rationale which Ligon offers for each. In their substance, however, they represent a practicable adaptation of scientific method to the problem of character development and, by extension, the problems of personal and social adjustment. An educational program designed to effect these ends in children of high ability must involve a methodological concept thus vigorously and clearly identified.

Percival M. Symonds offers a point of view in an earlier work than Ligon's which is just as scientific and just as practical. Symonds calls for the same degree of analysis and "codification" of behavior in these spheres as has been granted the more objective and academic aspects of the curriculum which are passed on to the child as his cultural heritage. He says:

> If conduct is to take its place in school with other subjects of instruction, it must receive the same consideration as other subjects. All other subjects are carefully planned for; courses of study are constructed, and the goals or objectives for each year of instruction are laid down. Arithmetic has of late been receiving exhaustive analysis, until today we know definitely that 100 addition combinations, 100 subtraction combinations, 100 multiplication combinations, and 450 division combinations must be learned, and we are ready tentatively to state when they must be learned. We know definitely the most important words that a child should know how to spell and to read, and we will soon know what important English constructions he should know, both for use in his written composition and for comprehension in his reading. We are apprised of the errors that a child makes most frequently in language. Conduct, if it is to become an objective of education, must receive a similar codification, otherwise it will remain incidental and casual. Conduct, most ancient objective of education, is the most recent acquisition as one of the objectives of formal education.[16]

Such a definite description of the ends and means of character development is obviously needed.

With respect to the observation and measurement of development along the line of personal, social, and moral adjustments, the same idea of analysis into perceivable and manageable components applies, in order that remedial measures may be brought to bear upon those areas in which diagnostic measures reveal inadequacy. Jones has outlined eleven techniques for the measurement of social and moral behavior, which include tests of knowledge, rating scales, tests of judgment in moral situations, tests of actual conduct, long-period observations and ratings as recorded in cumulative records, observation of attitudes as revealed in discussions with peers, and sociometric techniques.[17] The systematic use of such a variety of instruments of evaluation and a follow-up with appropriate instructional measures in areas where weaknesses are revealed would be called for in the proposition being developed, as a further application of scientific method to the area of personal development.

The same manner of approach would appear applicable to the subtle and complex emotional reactions which play such an effective role in behavior. To specify clearly what forms of behavior fall within the categories of love and of hate; to specify and to instruct in the attitudes which resolve into various desirable social responses; and to ramify into their psychological and behavioral bases such simple dicta as "Do unto others as you would have them to do unto you"—such methods promise to increase sound personal, social, and character adjustments.

An essential corollary to the proposition that scientific methods should characterize the identification of and instruction in ethical behaviors and positive personal and social adjustments urges the importance of effective attention to the individual case which, despite the positive program, reveals tendencies toward unwholesome deviation from the acceptable behavior patterns. The remediation of personality disorders while they are in the incipient stage is a logical supplement to intelligently planned procedures for the promotion of wholesome and effective adjustments. The corollary is:

(X. A) *That when incipient disturbances appear, systematic and extraordinary individual psychological services should be afforded the gifted individual as a part of the educational process.*

Remedial efforts in academic areas are customary; testing in subject matter to discover deficiencies and re-teaching to develop areas in which failure is revealed is an established routine. To offer psychological diagnosis and remediation for behavioral tendencies which deviate is to parallel this technique in phases of development where the promise is as great. The principles of learning, discovered through scientific methods in psychology, are utilized in academic instruction, positive and remedial; the principles of personality, also discovered through scientific methods, should be similarly utilized in the remediation of non-constructive psychological adjustments in children whose optimal personal development promises such great social returns.

The combination of adjustment-wise classroom procedures with the services of a team of practicing behavior specialists, trained to recognize and reckon with deviant behavioral tendencies, would serve as a broad base to those procedures of the school which approach personality and character formation through scientific methods.

In summary, then, Proposition X urges that the techniques of science be brought to bear upon the development in gifted children and youth of personal and social adjustments which will free them for their most effective social interactions and for the attainment of greatest personal happiness. In educational applications the scientific method takes such forms as: the systematic working out of desired behavior; the clarification of goals; the discovery of effective methods of promotion and development through experimentation and measurement; and diagnosis and remedial endeavor when the original processes appear to have failed with certain individuals. This extension of the scientific method into the realm of adjustive behavior logically promises the same measure of effectiveness that has been achieved by these means in other areas of child development.

chapter fifteen | *INSTRUCTION IN THE PRINCIPLES OF BEHAVIOR*

It is unreasonable to expect behavior consistent with principles to emerge in the absence of instruction in the principles themselves. Yet in the area of ethical behavior, and in the sphere of personal and social adjustments, this expectation exists. There is no systematic provision in the ordinary school curriculum for instruction in philosophy and ethics and little for the psychological foundations of behavior and adjustment. William M. Alexander and J. Galen Saylor list the subject matter courses which are required in all the curricula of a fairly large and representative high school:

English: Business English, Journalism, Speech, Dramatics, Debate.
Social Studies: World History, American History, Economics, Sociology, Advanced Civics, Economic Geography, Commercial Law.
Mathematics: Advanced Algebra, Trigonometry, Geometry, Business Arithmetic, General Mathematics.
Science: Biology, Chemistry, Physics.
Home Economics: Foods, Clothing, Consumer Education, Interior Decorating, Nutrition, Household Care, Cafeteria.
Foreign Languages: Latin, French, Spanish.
Commercial: Typewriting, Shorthand, Office Practice, Bookkeeping, Retailing.

Industrial Arts: Mechanical Drawing, Woodwork, Machine Shop,
    Printing, General Metals, Auto Mechanics.
Music: Orchestra, Band, Chorus.
Art: I, II, and III.
Physical Education: Boys, I, II, and III; Girls, I, II, and III.[18]

This outline of a typical curriculum of a modern high school appears
to have little place where the philosophical bases for moral behavior
and adjustment could be systematically taught. Apparently what instruction is offered through the personal interest and knowledge of
teachers is offered incidentally and without programmatic sanction.
The generality of students could profit from appropriately adapted
instruction in ethics and philosophy. In the case of intellectually
superior children and youth, the failure to offer such matter in the
curriculum represents a gross and crucial neglect of one of their more
vital expressed interests and needs.

A proposition urging provision for such instruction is:

> (*XI*) *That instruction in the theoretical bases of ideal moral
> behavior and of personal and social adjustments should be an
> integral part of the education of intellectually gifted indi-
> viduals.*

Of this need as expressed by the children in her early experiments,
Hollingworth stated:

> Discipline by self-government is possible to a greater extent in such
> classes [special classes for the gifted] than among unselected children,
> age for age, because they more readily learn what conduct will bring
> comfort and other satisfactions and more readily perceive how and
> when to act upon what they have learned. Intelligence is an indispen-
> sable part of the foundation upon which to build self-government.
>
> *Valid reasons* for behaving in one way rather than another may be
> used much more effectively with the gifted than with children gen-
> erally, because they more readily comprehend reasons and learn to
> act in accordance with them. Appeals to respect for the rights of
> others are with them particularly effective, too, because intelligence
> enables the child to put himself in another's place. . . .[19]

These remarks indicate that attempts to build generalized responses
in accordance with ethical principles relate to certain natural char-

acteristics of the gifted. They also highlight the fact that dictum and dogma are insufficient appeals to the intellectually superior for the positive construction of their attitudes and ideals. An acceptable rationale for moral behavior is therefore an indispensable part of any curriculum purporting to reckon adequately with the personal, social, and moral behavior of gifted individuals.

A corollary to this proposition specifying more definitely the content which would serve to fulfill such needs may be worded as follows:

(XI. A) *That instruction in the problems of philosophy and ethics should be adapted to the secondary levels of education.*

An understanding of the history and nature of moral and speculative problems is as necessary to the intelligent judgment of behavior and belief as an understanding of the laws and problems of physics is to the intelligent observation of physical processes. Only through such study can an individual gain a perspective which will permit him to see the single act in its proper relationship to other acts and to theoretical principle. The uses of human energy in the interest of science, of religion, of philosophy itself, and in political and economic pursuits, can be perceived in their proper relationship to man's collective potential only when the nature and purposes of such partial behaviors are philosophically examined. And behavior conforming to the dictates of the one discipline can violate principles basic to another unless a clear idea of the mutual involvements among human purposes and endeavors is attained.

Finally, the knowledge gained through philosophy that certainty in some realms of human experience is impossible may reduce psychological tensions, affording some security to troubled, inquisitive minds unable to fathom this fact without instruction. Intellectual security that stems from an understanding of epistemology would seem to satisfy a vital part of the gifted individual's personal need. Unfulfilled and inadequately acknowledged in the school program, this need may affect social adjustments and aggravate deviant behavior. Students of the problems of gifted individuals often note their interest in ultimates. Demiashkevich expresses this need as he has sensed it:

> The curriculum for the general preliminary training of the future
> Periclean leaders should, therefore, give also an adequate place to

philosophizing on the part of the more mature elite students about the general ultimate meaning of the facts of life in their entirety, about the "general hang of things," and, in particular, about the problem of ultimate reality. Such students should be assisted by properly qualified instructors toward the acquisition of as much certainty as is humanly possible relative to the ultimate goal of human existence. Similar provision should, of course, be made for the rank and file adolescent pupils, but the elite need it all the more because it is in the nature of the elite to be more acutely stimulated by, or suffer more from, anxiety relative to the final and ultimate meaning of things.[20]

If an attainment in full of such a specific philosophical perspective should seem to lie beyond even the capacities of gifted individuals at the secondary school level, it is suggested that as much be accomplished in this direction as is possible. Thus, subsequent development of the person will be in the nature of increased maturity within a framework of valid initial understandings.

Ethics, as that branch of philosophy concerned with the moral dimensions of behavior, needs little exposition beyond the basic meaning of the term to justify its inclusion in this scheme of education. It is in a sense the intellectual heart of behavior that affects others than oneself. Behavior can only be expedient, situationally determined, immediate and personal, unless some understanding prevails with respect to the nature, sanctions, and consequences of ideal moral behavior. The gifted person's life career in the modern world will bring him into a variety of complex social situations in which the simpler morality of yesterday, informally transmitted and by authority rather than reason, will not suffice to guide action. Consistent moral behavior in such situations can be maintained only by those capable of referring possible choices of action to the broadest rational bases for what we call morality.

By way of illustration, the democratic and Christian ethics would be understood more adequately if compared with the demands upon individual behavior made by other political and religious theories. To explore the "democratic ethic" and to perceive how and by what reasons *any* adjective can be made to modify that noun is to understand more fully the meaning of our form of social and political organization and our predominant religious mandates. The intellectually superior student at the secondary level can move around in the universe of ideas like these, start his growth early with their help, and through growing insight finally attain a more adequate self-realization. Knowledge of this nature is obviously needed for those whose actions are likely to have far-reaching significance for the human family.

A further corollary abstracting from the philosophical context the concept of value might be framed thus:

(XI. B) *That dominant contemporary values should be clarified at the secondary levels of education in order to enhance personal, social, and moral adjustments.*

Enlightenment in the nature of value and an ability to relate it to the psychology of motivation in the human being and to the various systems of philosophical thought would appear to be essential to a defensible choice of values for one's personal allegiance. An analytical description and classification of the values which prevail in present civilization and which have prevailed in the past is in keeping with the reasoned instruction suited to gifted individuals.

Many writers, representing rather widely diverging approaches to the problem of character and personality development, indicate the negative influence upon personal integration of contradictory value systems in the individual's environment. Thus Hartshorne and May say:

> In this analysis we come upon the problem of individual functioning and growth within existing social situations which make contradictory demands upon one and which are incapable of external organization. No matter what may be a child's notion of an ideal family and an ideal school, his own family and his own school may hold to contrasted standards, and he must live in both. It is not surprising, therefore, that our present generation of children shows little integration of character.[21]

And Harold Rugg lends a personal note to the idea, writing of the emphatic and contradictory notions of competition and conformity under which he himself was reared:

> Growing up in this climate as a ninth-generation Massachusetts Nordic during the very years which have been under discussion, I have never been able to see how these conflicting values could possibly produce the personal integrity which is the goal of moral life. The pressures of home, neighborhood, and community life as-

sailed my contemporaries and me hour by hour; unbridled liberty and subservience to community opinion were preached at us and practiced around us in utter cultural confusion. Of the effects, the least evil one was personal confusion, drift, opportunism; the worst and more common one was sheer hypocrisy. I am convinced that our condition was typical of the whole country. The two world wars and the two decades of artificial prosperity and stark depression between them merely accentuated it. The consequence is that today, as we confront history's most devastating economic and political problems, a deep hiatus exists between what we profess and what we are. Our culture is honeycombed with this dishonest pretense; in many parts of it a veneer of respectability covers an inner life of racketeering—in business and finance, in the press and the pulpit, in agencies of communication, even in the school.[22]

These observations urge that the school bring the direct study of values into the curriculum and into the daily experience of the gifted child, who is naturally impelled to analyze concrete acts in terms of abstract concepts and principles.

Few would propose that the school write a synthesis of values and actively propagate it. However, one feasible approach which would seem long overdue is that the school analyze and render explicit such systems of value as seem to prevail and that it encourage the development by each child of his own reasoned synthesis. Each clarification, each correct classification of an overt act of expression of belief, would be an aid toward rendering the individual's own thinking and behaving the more ideal.

It is not universally agreed, however, that there is *dis*agreement among contemporary Americans as to values essential to the democratic way of life. The Educational Policies Commission has suggested that there are certain moral and spiritual values upon which American people are agreed. They list these as:

1) Human Personality—the Basic Value
2) Moral Responsibility
3) Institutions as the Servants of Men
4) Common Consent
5) Devotion to Truth
6) Respect for Excellence
7) Moral Equality
8) Brotherhood

9) The Pursuit of Happiness
10) Spiritual Enrichment[23]

The Commission would have such commonly accepted values brought into the schools for direct instruction, as overriding any particular religious dogma. To explore the values listed and to afford every opportunity for their rationalization and internalization by intellectually superior youth would be education consonant with the principle under discussion.

The concern over the status of religion in the American school is somewhat general. The Educational Policies Commission statement is in essence an attempt to abstract certain concepts which preserve the values traditionally allied with religion and to render them in such a form that they may come within the purview of the school without violating the hard-earned separation of church and state. And Albert Outler, an eminent Professor of Theology, reporting upon a study of the status of religion in higher institutions draws this conclusion:

> One conclusion about the educational revolution, therefore, is clear. Education is by way of being reformed with little or no regard for the possible contribution of *religion* to its reformation. For a very tangled skein of reasons, it has come to pass that, in the name of tolerance and the democratic spirit, American educators (whatever their private religious beliefs and convictions) have in fact suppressed the consideration of the problems of the religious interpretation of reality and human existence in the educational process. Such matters, so the student is told by precept and example, are private affairs, which are entitled to mutual respect, but about which there ought to be no unseemly disputing, such as would be involved if they were to be submitted to critical examination and discussion. Even so, it is not at all uncommon to hear religion sneered at and dispraised—*without* critical examination and discussion—by professors hostile to it. Academic men do have convictions and they do not shrink from controversy; but when religious questions are called, only the secularists, it would seem in the present instance, are prepared to cast their vote with full clarity and assurance. Thus it has come about that, in the practical outcome, religion and the religious life-view have been effectually discounted and made to appear at the very most an accessory, but not an essential, component of the good life.[24]

Any attempt to instill the moral point of view into developing youth must be supported by an appropriate acknowledgment within the school of the values that are objectively attributed to religion.

That all thought be placed in a fair perspective by identifying the theoretical bases of specific ideas has already been urged. The position that the school should acknowledge the values of religion is in harmony with this view. Direct instruction in defensible ideas concerning the nature of religious experience and how it relates to morality appears due to intellectually superior children and youth who sometimes discover for themselves the inadequacy and the sheer falsity of some of the concepts in the disorganized array of opinions and attitudes that pass under the guise of religion. Points of view toward religion which would appear to fit this idea of instruction in values may be found at large in the literature on philosophy and morality. Because of the importance of the area, two such views will be given. Harold S. Tuttle writes as follows:

> The clear inference is that if religion is to engender harmony rather than bitterness, the religious tenets must be taught, as all intellectual truths should be taught, on the basis of evidence and reason. They should not be implanted by conditioning. . . .[25]

The intellectually gifted find religion more attractive when it becomes the subject of scientific inquiry, for then, as the following quotation indicates, it promises to bear a lifetime of study that will gradually yield greater understanding and appreciation. The following is from a textbook in epistemology.

> The very richness and complexities of religious experience have postponed the acquisition of adequate ideas concerning it. Some persons have failed to emerge from primitive fog because they have falsely assumed that there exists some magical short cut to the knowledge of divine things. The search for a spiritual organ, religious instinct, supernatural sense, or other special faculty for directly apprehending God without the aid of ordinary processes of thought has signally failed. A valid theology is to be won by the same sort of hard intellectual labor as a valid esthetics, politics, or metaphysics. Only the beginnings of a scientific study of religion have been made, however, and efficient methods of investigating it are still in the making.[26]

William J. Hutchins has written a "Children's Code of Morals" which appears to appeal, on other than religious grounds, to moral behavior. The code is cited here to indicate that values can be reduced to an appropriate form for systematic instruction in the curriculum of the grade school. Though containing the germs of ideas sufficient to the intellectual capacity of youth and adults, the concepts are couched at such a level that they could be treated during the early years of the secondary school.

1) The Laws of Health: The Good American Tries to Gain and Keep Perfect Health.
2) The Law of Self-Control: The Good American Controls Himself.
3) The Law of Self-Reliance: The Good American Is Self-Reliant.
4) The Law of Reliability: The Good American Is Reliable.
5) The Law of Clean Play: The Good American Plays Fair.
6) The Law of Duty: The Good American Does His Duty.
7) The Law of Good Workmanship: The Good American Tries to Do the Right Thing in the Right Way.
8) The Law of Team Work: The Good American Works in Friendly Cooperation with His Fellow-Workers.
9) The Law of Kindness: The Good American Is Kind.
10) The Law of Loyalty: The Good American Is Loyal.[27]

Sanctions other than the necessity of being a "good American" are likely to be demanded by gifted children. Like the ideas themselves, however, the sanctions can be couched at the children's level and yet contain the essence of ideas which will sustain mature thought.

In order that their behavior might be intelligently guided in accordance with principles, it has been urged that gifted individuals be given a general knowledge of philosophy, a more specific knowledge of ethics, and a facility in recognizing and clarifying the values reflected in actions. But philosophy and theory and ideals are abstractions from the actualities of the behavior of men in the life situation. The realities of behavior, the *actual* as opposed to the *ideal*, must also be reckoned with in the interest of fuller educational development and of preparation for leadership in the real world of human affairs. It is therefore proposed:

(XI. C) *That the gifted individual should be instructed in the processes of social action and in the characteristic behavior of men, as opposed to their ideal behavior, in social situations.*

Society is the loser when a man of vision withdraws into his own private world because of failure to accomplish in the real world plans and interests which, though good, fail through ineffective human strategy. The degree to which the social leader can use his superior abilities depends upon his skill in dealing with the generality of men under normal social influences and psychological motivation. And such skill depends in large part upon an understanding of the dynamics of social processes as they involve the characteristic behavior of normal people. "Advise and Consent" may be deplorable moral philosophy, but recognition of these real conditions is absolutely necessary to effective movement toward ideal political operations. Much of Leta Hollingworth's writing, it has been noted, stresses that it is difficult for the gifted individual to perceive that others are not like him in their insights and abilities. The realization of the huge differences between his level of perception and impulse and that of the generality occurs incidentally in the usual situation and is often attended by unfortunate consequences which might have been obviated through adequate instruction. Instruction in man's fundamental motives and in the less-than-ideal behavior patterns evolved in a social context to satisfy these motives would enhance the leader's effectiveness by teaching him the need for strategy in actualizing the ideal.

The principles of social psychology contain a wealth of understandings which contribute to the end proposed. Such ideas relating to behavioral dynamics as sociogenic motive, the functional selectivity of perception and retention, the origin and function in behavior of attitudes, beliefs, and prejudices, and the socialization of personality in the process of normal development are of first importance in the technical body of knowledge from which can be developed an efficient understanding of the real behavior of men. Failure to accord these areas of knowledge a place in the education of the gifted can hardly be justified. Nor is it adequate that such understandings be available only in elective courses at the university level. These principles of social dynamics are so essential to the intellectually superior individual's effective interaction with others that they should form an integral part of the curriculum at successive levels.

The brilliant and noble reform may die incompletely realized unless the leader initiating it understands the importance of a careful proposal and appeal. Often the cost of learning this reality has been defeat and bitterness for the individual and the loss to society of a promising development. The question is fair what might have been the subsequent course of history had Woodrow Wilson anticipated the probable behavior of Henry Cabot Lodge.

Adams and Brown, in a context praising the opportunities for various kinds of wholesome development through extra-curricular activities, write:

> Closely connected with the development of ethical character will be the effect of extra-curricular activities upon the other social traits which make life more pleasant and efficient. The bright student will find that "the facts," the clear understanding he has of situations, or the glib tongue do not always move others. Either the other pupils may not understand him or they may lack appreciation to the point of being offended. He will find that it is how others feel about a matter that is important. His world will no longer be ruled by logic alone. He will come to appraise others in a new way if he is allowed to see the force of the ego in all individuals regardless of mental status.[28]

The principle under discussion suggests systematic instruction and experience, in addition to the "extra" curricular opportunities for the skills to be developed.

Another method of applying the present principle is to use community resources for the study of institutional dynamics, to visit, as many classrooms do, governmental bodies, civic agencies, and community institutions and observe them in operation. Further insight into institutional behavior could be gained by studying the reasons for the rise and fall of present and past leaders and staff members in such agencies and institutions. What *real* causes lie behind a dean's "request" to return to the classroom, an executive's "promotion" to a nominal position from one in which his actions were of consequence, or the appointment to a judgeship of a minor legislator? The more real, though often uglier, aspects of man's behavior deserve acknowledgment in the instruction of the gifted individual, in a balanced and objective manner, toward the end of his appreciating the differences which exist between the ideal and the real in man's activities. The gifted, idealistic individual may labor under the idea that all men are struggling toward the fullest expression of the ideal in their individual and social efforts. Years of gradual disillusionment may be obviated through fair, positively toned, instruction that recognizes the real as distinct from the ideal and the characteristically limited approach of the one to the other in the ordinary affairs of men.

These insights into the real conduct of men in the agencies and institutions through which civic and social affairs are managed are urged because of the consequences that may follow from their not being taught. It is simple truth which is being suggested, fairly and objectively presented, in the interest of avoiding personal and social failures, bitterness, and anti-social dispositions. Obvious tragedies of major scale, like Wilson's failure, are only part of the ill; on a lesser scale, the instances are more numerous in which the faulty execution of worthy aims has resulted in failure and personal disintegration. This portion of the educational design purports to aid in minimizing the frequency of such disasters and to allow by that much the fuller influence of the gifted individual's potential for advancing both his personal welfare and that of society.

Proposition XI argues that the theoretical bases for ideal moral behavior should be taught to intellectually superior students; the corollaries specify a study of philosophy and ethics at secondary levels, a clarification of current values, and instruction in the dynamics of social interaction. The principles proposed are intended to put adjustment and understanding in these areas on a level with habituation and understanding in other areas of learning. Perhaps it is only through such systematic instruction that the individual can be prepared for consistent, principled action in the complex, ever-changing situations which face the citizen and leader in a democracy in modern times. A knowledge of relevant facts and concepts is essential to the development of generalized ideals of conduct and balanced personal and social adjustments; it is unreasonable to expect subtlety in discernment and straightforwardness of action from persons who are, through absence of instruction, lacking in the knowledge necessary for such responsible and disciplined behavior. High levels of understanding along these lines can be attained by the intellectually superior individual; these principles propose that the school afford the guidance essential to these levels of attainment.

chapter sixteen

TOTAL PLANNING FOR PERSONAL INTEGRITY

Especially in the area of personal, social, and moral adjustments, there are elements in the heterogeneous environments of the child which tend to counteract the positive influence provided by school instruction. Insofar as some of these negative influences reside in the community at large and lie beyond the control of the school, a certain amount of contradictory and destructive influence may always be expected. The principles which have just been considered recommend direct and systematic examination of these ideational and behavioral realities. Within the relatively controlled environment of the school, however, some ordering of influences can be accomplished. The next proposition urges that such influences be controlled by the school as crucial concomitants to the central aims of education. It states:

> *(XII) That the concomitant factors under control of the school should be positively controlled so that they contribute to sound personal, social, and character development.*

This principle is even more appropriate to the education of the gifted than to the education of the generality because the gifted are more sensitive to such factors and to the inconsistencies which they often involve. The teacher of literature who reads light novels in his free time; the teacher of civics who does not vote; a student council with no prerogatives; immorality in athletics under the guise of good sport; lip service to democratic and Christian ideals in schools which segregate according to race or religion—such divergencies between the real and the ideal are seldom lost on the gifted child. Certainly such inconsistencies are undesirable in the education of the generality, but for the reason given they are more undesirable in the education of the gifted.

This principle, by implication, takes note of the remedial nature of much social and moral instruction. Symonds writes:

> It is a thesis of this book that conduct must be planned far in advance. One must not wait until it becomes a problem. Genetic psychology has yet to trace for us the history of conduct development. But the parent needs to have listed the course of development of the habits of conduct so that he may plan for them before they arise as problems. It is easier to go about systematically arranging for the proper and orderly development of habits than to wait until the wrong habits have been formed and then to try to change them.[29]

Though this passage is written for the parent, the same thought applies to the school and its provisions. The point is that, in addition to giving instruction in the nature of behavior which can be called moral and pro-social, the school should arrange its environment so as to lend situational influence to the development of the moral response. Such a procedure would prevent the problems which usually occasion much of the instruction that does occur.

Hartshorne, May, and Shuttleworth were conscious of the possibilities in the idea of a controlled environment, but at the same time aware of its impossibility of attainment under normal conditions and dubious of its effects when the life situation must finally be faced. They write:

> Integration may be achieved if unified demands are made by the child's environment. This implies a *controlled* environment, which, in turn looks toward a twenty-four hour school. Experience with such an environment would lead naturally to a corresponding unity of character if we conceive of unity as external consistency. If such integration, however, were conditioned solely by external circumstances,

it could hardly serve for guidance when the child was removed from the shelter of the school.[30]

It would appear that a recognizable consistency among school practices would strengthen personal ideals and allow for more effective resistance to improper persuasions in the subsequent life situation. That portion of the totality of effective influences which the school's environment comprises is a major share of the developmental stimuli to which the child is subject. The positive ordering of these influences accomplishes certain of the effects promised from total control. It may be that an appropriate experiential balance can be obtained for the constructive in-building of character, through a judicious compounding of elements in the controlled school environment and the inevitable intermittent contact with actual human behavior in the real community.

It is not implied in what precedes or in what follows that all the aims suggested or the techniques through which they can be effected must be bluntly and directly executed. Much of the success of guidance toward sound adjustment, especially where the sensitive, intellectually superior child is concerned, might well lie in the subtlety with which the attempts are made. This is suggested through one of the results of the experimental study conducted by Vernon Jones, who writes:

> Judging by our experience in this study, it appears that from the learner's viewpoint instruction should be indirect. It should concern itself with the solution of specific character and citizenship problems which seem to arise naturally in his environment, centering his attention outwardly upon these problems and not inwardly upon his own improvement in character. But from the viewpoint of supervisors, curriculum-builders, and teachers, the work in character and citizenship, far from being incidental or unplanned, should be systematic and definitely planned.[31]

Of first importance in the attempted ordering of the multiple influences of a school environment is a consistency in the theory from which all the practices of the school derive and to which they can all be related. A synthesis of values commonly agreed upon, such as that offered by the Educational Policies Commission and previously cited (pp. 205–6), could serve this purpose. Adapted to the understanding of different age groups, this code would regulate all the individual undertakings of the students which assumed moral significance. Athletic codes, student government regulations, and the codes of ethics devised for the professional guidance of teachers could be related to these commonly accepted values, which would embody the "moral climate" of the school.

This idea of a synthesis of values is perhaps closely related to what Hartshorne and his co-workers have termed the development of a "functioning ideal for society," here adapted to the smaller society of the school. The idea is stated as one of their major conclusions:

> This [the idea of a controlled environment] relates to the building of a functioning ideal for society which may serve at once as a principle of unified or consistent response and as a principle of satisfactory social adjustment. Such a policy or principle must, therefore, be derived from the inherent nature of social life and growth as experienced by the child himself. It must not only be scientifically sound in the sense that it presents a workable theory of life; it must also emerge in the minds of the children through their own guided experiments in living.[32]

After suggesting this possibility of a synthesis of values which can become a "workable theory of life," the authors go on to indicate how this synthesis can be used to enhance personal development. They then write:

> Two corollaries follow: the corollary of graduated opportunity and the corollary of graduated temptation. The first implies that situations faced by children shall become more and more complex and make constantly heavier demands upon their power of adjustment. If situations change too rapidly, the pupil is confused and resorts to some inadequate system of behavior already learned. If the situations do not change fast enough, they offer no challenge to thought or the intelligent reconstruction of past experience to meet new demands in the light of what has already been learned. So the educator will have available a series of graded opportunities.
>
> In a similar way the second corollary implies that situations which prompt to action already found inappropriate or destructive (and which are unlike those previously experienced) shall be *gradually* introduced in order that resistance to novel appeals may be built up through increasing ability properly to classify each new situation. So the educator will have available a series of graded temptations.[33]

And the following point is made in further recognition that the generalized ideal must be formed in order for the disposition toward moral and social response to carry into the uncontrolled life situation.

> In order that growing consistency in a world of conflicting standards may be achieved, the ideals issuing from experience must become prepotent factors in the stimulation of further conduct and must also assist in the achievement of satisfactory modes of adjustment to aspects of the situation which are as yet uncontrolled by these ideals and standards—they must be tools rather than objects of esthetic appreciation.
>
> Hence the type of experience which brings "satisfaction" must include not only creature comforts and ambitions, but also and primarily the more permanent expanding interests which lead to mental and social growth.[34]

This process of learning is well attested in the literature on "transfer of training" in the academic materials of the curriculum. The same theory of learning is involved in this acquisition of ideal moral principles.

But co-ordination and coherence among the external aspects of the school situation are not enough. Jones found that behavior in the desired direction could be more dependably realized if *supporting experience included appropriate emotional components*. He notes three techniques for providing the needed emotional tone: (1) designing every unit in the character and citizenship training to be "enjoyable"; (2) directing attention toward building "in each classroom a class spirit which would throw the weight of group loyalty in favor of desirable behavior"; and (3) supplying emotional appeal in connection with character training through material in drama, literature, music, and art.[35] If consciously planned and appropriately executed, these techniques would appear to contribute significantly to the type of development being discussed, a predisposition toward *wanting* to behave morally, *wanting* to act in the social interest, and *caring* for others.

A further important concomitant which influences the personal and social adjustments of the gifted child is *the methods by which he is taught*. Through the teacher's methods of instruction it is possible to incorporate some of the most important aspects of education for social adjustment. Much of the theory of "progressive" classroom methods makes explicit acknowledgment of this fact by emphasizing co-operative planning and execution of projects, group discussion, and general capitalization upon the subtle and powerful motivational factors arising in group relationships.

The Hartshorne, May, and Shuttleworth study again offers support for the idea that teaching methods which utilize group dynamics are essential to the best results in the area of personal, social, and character development.

> It can hardly be expected that most children can be taught to be responsible to social ideals unsupported by group code and morale. When the individual is made the unit of educational effort, he is so abstracted from life situations as to become more and more of a prig in proportion as his teachers succeed with him and more and more the victim of a disorganized and detached mind in proportion as they fail. The normal unit for character education is the group or small community, which provides through cooperative discussion and effort the moral support required for the adventurous discovery and effective use of ideals in the conduct of affairs.[36]

The small-group experiences of gifted children and youth should occur, of course, in company with like-minded peers. Those with experience in teaching selected groups of bright youngsters can sense immediately how the probing, questioning, hypothesizing which characterizes their free behavior in the classroom can be turned toward inquiries into the nature of behavior that reflects character.

A fourth important aspect of such a total environment would emphasize *the importance of activities and opportunities for the optimum release of emotional urges to action and self-expression.* The expression of personality through drama, art, and literature; the expression of political and social aptitudes through student government and organizations developed and maintained largely by student initiative; the expression of physical vigor through play and physical recreation—all are appropriate concomitants to the development of personal and social adjustments through the wholesome release of emotional energies and consequent freeing of the personality for its fairest expression. All concomitants could hardly be considered as organized toward the furtherance of social and character development unless a broad and sound program of activities providing these opportunities for self-expression, development of initiative in relatively life-like situations, and peer level associations were part of the school's program.

Reminiscent of the previous discussion of contradictory elements among the various values in the community, a final point in connection with Proposition XII considers *the necessary co-operation of all community agencies bearing significantly upon the child's development.* Through educational councils and committees composed of representatives from these different agencies, a common understanding of the problem may be obtained and some clarification and harmony of objectives for youth achieved. Of home and school co-operation much has been written. The co-operative contribution toward the development of gifted children which can be made by business and industrial groups, by civic clubs and churches, has not been so well explored. In an all-out concentration upon the optimum development of our most socially promising children, however, *special* education should be paralleled by equally *special* part-time jobs and the special class in the public day school should be paralleled by the special class in Sunday School (i.e., comparative religion, sociology of religion, etc.). The need for such all-out concentration and for community co-operation is what Ernest Ligon implies in his assertion that character education is a "seven-day-a-week" undertaking.

The proposition that education for personal, social, and character development should involve a constructive ordering of the concomitant phases of the school's program which bear upon such development has been stated as the third major proposal toward education of the gifted in personal integrity and the final proposal of this book. Important relative considerations are (1) that the school should operate under a relatively consistent "functioning ideal"; (2) that emotional toning should be added to the instruction designed for intellectual and rational appeal; (3) that the teacher's methods should aid in engendering the ideals sought; (4) that student activities should be soundly planned for the release of emotional energies and the practice of peer contacts in relatively life-like situations; and (5) that co-operation among significant community agencies should be effected.

In Part IV the following ideas have been developed with respect to education for personal, social, and character development: that scientific methodology should be basic to the conception and execution of such education (Proposition X); that instruction should be given in the theoretical principles by which the adequacy of adjustments and the morality of behavior are judged (Proposition XI); and that the program for social and character development should involve a positive ordering of all crucial concomitants. These propositions and the attendant corollaries are offered as means for developing the gifted individual in areas of his personality other than the intellectual and hence for broadening educational endeavor toward the aim of a full development of personality.

Of all the concepts that have been drawn upon in the development of the principles in this area, two emerge as singularly important. The first, which forms the theoretical basis for Ernest M. Ligon's work in character education, urges the analysis of Christian philosophy in terms of the specific behaviors implied. The principle of love, which is predominant in this philosophy, is of particular importance as a force in human interactions. To consider the power of love for orienting the total person toward the objects of its application is to realize that through this emotional avenue exists what may well be the most powerful approach to the organization and direction of human behavior. Constant in its sustaining power, totally integrative with respect to the various capacities of the organism, and conducive to the finest behavior of which man is capable, love in the Christian sense would seem to be essential to individual happiness and beneficent social interaction.

The second concept, a somewhat strange ideational partner to the first, but entirely compatible, is that of the applicability of the scientific method of problem-solving to the solution of personal problems, specifically the problem of behaving in a manner at once socially acceptable and personally satisfying. Generally acknowledged, this concept has been distinctively interpreted and applied by Laurance Shaffer and Joseph Shoben, who call it a "positive principle of mental hygiene." Their view of the concept has been used in this work (Proposition X).

Of the effectiveness of a combination of these two concepts, Ligon asserts:

> It follows that *the methods are now available making it possible to bring up a greater generation* of men of good will with strong character sufficient for the task of world leadership so needed today to save our civilization from the destruction toward which it seems so obviously headed,

finer men and women capable of living happy useful lives. It is the thesis of this book that *this can be accomplished through the application of the scientific method and the concepts of the Christian religion.*[37]

Taken together, these two concepts appear to provide the best assurance of behavior which represents a high conception of morality, provides a large measure of personal satisfaction, and advances the general welfare of mankind.

FOOTNOTES FOR PART IV

1 Leta S. Hollingworth, "The Child of Very Superior Intelligence as a Special Problem in Social Adjustment," *Mental Hygiene*, XV (1931), pp. 13–14.

2 Leta S. Hollingworth, "The Development of Personality in Highly Intelligent Children," *Fifteenth Yearbook of the Department of Elementary School Principals* (Washington, D. C.: National Education Association, 1936), pp. 274–78.

3 *Ibid.*, pp. 277–78.

4 *Ibid.*, p. 280.

5 Ruth Strang, "Mental Hygiene of Gifted Children," Paul Witty, ed., *The Gifted Child* (Boston: D. C. Heath and Company, 1951), p. 134 ff.

6 Harvey Zorbaugh, R. K. Boardman, and Paul Sheldon, "Some Observations of Highly Gifted Children." Paul Witty, ed., *op. cit.*, p. 103.

7 Hugh Hartshorne, Mark A. May, and Frank K. Shuttleworth, *Studies in the Organization of Character*, Vol. III, *Studies in the Nature of Character* (New York: The Macmillan Company, 1930), p. 336.

8 Vernon Jones, *Character and Citizenship Training in the Public School, An Experimental Study of Three Specific Methods* (Chicago: University of Chicago Press, 1936), pp. 381–82.

9 Hugh Hartshorne, *et al.*, *op. cit.*, 372–73.

10 *Ibid.*, pp. 355–58.

11 Vernon Jones, "Character Development in Children—An Objective Approach," Leonard Carmichael, ed., *Manual of Child Psychology* (New York: John Wiley and Sons, Inc., 1946), pp. 714–15.

12 Robert J. Havighurst and Hilda Taba, *Adolescent Character and Personality* (New York: John Wiley and Sons, Inc., 1949), p. 7.

13 Laurance F. Shaffer and Edward J. Shoben, Jr., *The Psychology of Adjustment*, (Boston: Houghton Mifflin Company, 1956, 2nd ed. pp. 589–90.

14 Ernest M. Ligon, *A Greater Generation* (New York: The Macmillan Company, 1948), p. 8. Used with permission of The Macmillan Company.

15 *Ibid.*, *passim.*

16 Percival M. Symonds, *The Nature of Conduct* (New York: The Macmillan Company, 1928), pp. 50–51.

17 Vernon Jones, *Character and Citizenship Training*, pp. 132–33.

18 William M. Alexander and J. Galen Saylor, *Secondary Education* (New York: Holt, Rinehart, and Winston, Inc., 1950), pp. 257–58.

19 Leta S. Hollingworth, *Gifted Children, Their Nature and Nurture* (New York: The Macmillan Company, 1926), pp. 144–46.

20 Michael Demiashkevich, *An Introduction to the Philosophy of Education* (New York: American Book Company, 1935), p. 430.

21 Hugh Hartshorne, *et al.*, *op. cit.*, pp. 375–76.

[22] Harold Rugg, *Foundations for American Education* (New York: World Book Company, 1947), p. 490.

[23] Educational Policies Commission, *Moral and Spiritual Values in the Public Schools* (Washington, D. C.: National Education Association, 1951), pp. 17–30.

[24] Albert C. Outler, "Colleges, Faculties, and Religion." *Educational Record*, XXX (1949), 49.

[25] Harold S. Tuttle, *Dynamic Psychology and Conduct* (New York: Harper & Brothers, 1949), pp. 419–20.

[26] Raymond F. Piper and Paul W. Ward, *Fields and Methods of Knowledge* (New York: F. S. Crofts and Company, 1929), p. 336. By permission of Appleton-Century-Crofts, Inc.

[27] William J. Hutchins, "Children's Code of Morals." Cited in Harold S. Tuttle, *op. cit.*, pp. 424–27.

[28] Fay Adams and Walker Brown, *Teaching the Bright Pupil* (New York: Henry Holt and Company, 1930), p. 225.

[29] Percival M. Symonds, *op. cit.*, p. 323.

[30] Hugh Hartshorne, *et al.*, *op. cit.*, pp. 377–78.

[31] Vernon Jones, *Character and Citizenship Training in the Public School, An Experimental Study of Three Specific Methods* (Chicago: University of Chicago Press, 1936), p. 383. Copyright, 1936, by the University of Chicago.

[32] Hugh Hartshorne, *et al.*, *op. cit.*, p. 378.

[33] *Loc. cit.*

[34] *Ibid.*, p. 379.

[35] Vernon Jones, *Character and Citizenship Training in the Public School, An Experimental Study of Three Specific Methods* (Chicago: University of Chicago Press, 1936), pp. 385–86. Copyright, 1936, by the University of Chicago.

[36] Hugh Hartshorne, *et al.*, *op. cit.*, p. 379.

[37] Ernest M. Ligon, *op. cit.*, p. 5.

bibliography

Abraham, Willard. *Common Sense about Gifted Children*. New York: Harper & Brothers, 1958.

Adams, Fay. *Educating America's Children*. New York: Ronald Press Company, 1946.

————, and Walker Brown. *Teaching the Bright Pupil*. New York: Holt, Rinehart, and Winston, 1930.

The Advertising Council, Inc. *Your Great Future in a Growing America*. New York: The Council, n.d.

Alexander, William M., and J. Galen Saylor. *Secondary Education*. New York: Holt, Rinehart, and Winston, 1950.

Allen, Edwin B., Dis Maly, and S. Herbert Starkey, Jr. *Vital Mathematics*. New York: The Macmillan Company, 1944.

American Association for the Advancement of Science. "1958 Parliament of Science," *Science*, CXXVII (April, 1958), 852.

American Psychological Association, Division 16, Subcommittee on Needed Research on Gifted Children. "Needed Research on Gifted," *American Psychologist*, IX (February, 1954), 77–78.

Anastasi, Anne, and John P. Foley, Jr. *Differential Psychology* (Revised edition). New York: The Macmillan Company, 1949.

Anderson, G. Lester, and Arthur I. Gates. "The General Nature of Learning," *Forty-Ninth Yearbook of the National Society for the Study of Education*, Part I. Chicago: University of Chicago Press, 1950. Pp. 12–35.

Anderson, Harold H. (Ed.). *Creativity and Its Cultivation.* New York: Harper & Brothers, 1959.

Baker, Harry J. *Characteristic Differences in Bright and Dull Pupils.* Bloomington, Illinois: Public School Publishing Company, 1927.

Barbe, Walter B. "Evaluation of Special Classes for Gifted Children," *Exceptional Children,* XXII (November, 1955), 60–62.

Bentley, John E. *Superior Children.* New York: W. W. Norton and Company, 1937.

Better Schools, September, 1958.

Birch, Jack W., and Earl M. McWilliams. *Challenging Gifted Children.* Public School Publishing Company, 1955.

Bish, Charles E. "Teaching the Upper 15 Per Cent," *Clearing House,* XXXIII (May, 1959), 515–18.

Boring, Edwin G. *A History of Experimental Psychology.* New York: Appleton-Century-Crofts, Inc., 1929.

Brameld, Theodore. *Patterns of Educational Philosophy.* Yonkers-on-Hudson, New York: World Book Company, 1950.

Brandwein, Paul F. *The Gifted Student as Future Scientist: The High School Student and His Commitment to Science.* New York: Harcourt, Brace and Co., 1955.

Bray, D. W. *Issues in the Study of Talent.* Kings Crown Press, 1954.

Brown, J. F., "Genius." P. L. Harriman (Ed.), *Encyclopedia of Psychology.* New York: Philosophical Library, 1946.

Brownell, William A., and Gordon Hendrickson. "How Children Learn Information, Concepts, and Generalizations," *Forty-Ninth Yearbook of the National Society for the Study of Education,* Part I. Chicago: University of Chicago Press, 1942. Pp. 92–128.

Brumbaugh, Florence M. "Our Youngest Intellectuals Thirteen Years Later," *Exceptional Children,* XXI (February, 1955), 168–70, 195.

Burks, Barbara S., D. W. Jensen, and Lewis M. Terman. *The Promise of Youth.* Vol. III, *Genetic Studies of Genius.* Stanford, California: Stanford University Press, 1930.

Carnap, Rudolf. "Logic," *Factors Determining Human Behavior.* Cambridge, Massachusetts: Harvard University Press, 1937. Reprinted in Irving J. Lee (Ed.), *The Language of Wisdom and Folly.* New York: Harper & Brothers, 1949.

Carroll, Herbert A. *Genius in the Making.* New York: The McGraw Hill Book Company, 1940.

Cohen, H. L., and N. G. Coryell (Eds.). *Educating Superior Students.* New York: American Book Company, 1935.

Cole, Charles C., Jr. *Encouraging Scientific Talent.* New York: College Entrance Examination Board, 1956.

Commager, Henry Steele. *The American Mind.* New Haven: Yale University Press, 1950.

Counts, George S. *Education and American Civilization.* New York: Bureau of Publications, Teachers College, 1952.

Cox, Catherine M. *The Early Mental Traits of Three Hundred Geniuses.* Vol. II, *Genetic Studies of Genius.* Stanford, California: Stanford University Press, 1926.

Cutts, Norma E., and Nicholas Moseley. *Teaching the Bright and Gifted.* Englewood Cliffs, New Jersey; Prentice-Hall, 1957.

DeHaan, Robert F., and Robert J. Havighurst. *Educating Gifted Children.* Chicago: University of Chicago Press, 1957.

————, and Jack Kough. *Identifying Students with Special Needs. Teacher's Guidance Handbook* (Secondary School Edition), Vol. 1. Chicago: Science Research Associates, 1956.

Demiashkevich, Michael J. *An Introduction to the Philosophy of Education.* New York: American Book Company, 1935.

Dewey, John. *Democracy and Education.* New York: The Macmillan Company, 1916.

————. *Interest and Effort in Education.* Boston: Houghton Mifflin Company, 1913.

————. *Reconstruction in Philosophy* (Reprint edition). New York: The New American Library of World Literature, Inc., 1950 (Original edition 1920, Holt).

————. "The Philosopher-in-the-Making," *Saturday Review of Literature,* XXX (October, 1949), 9, 10, 39–44.

Dransfield, J. Edgar. *Administration of Enrichment to Superior Children in the Typical Classroom.* Teachers College Contributions to Education, No. 558. New York: Bureau of Publications, Teachers College, Columbia University, 1933.

Drews, Elizabeth M., and John E. Teahan. "Parental Attitudes and Academic Achievement," *Journal of Clinical Psychology,* October, 1957.

Dunlap, James M. "Gifted Child in an Enriched Program," *Exceptional Children,* XXI (January, 1955), 135–37.

Educational Policies Commission. *Education of the Gifted.* Washington, D. C.: National Education Association, 1950.

————. *Manpower and Education.* Washington, D. C.: National Education Association, 1956.

————. *Moral and Spiritual Values in the Public Schools.* Washington, D. C.: National Education Association, 1951.

Einstein, Albert, (in) *Living Philosophies.* New York: Simon and Schuster, Inc., 1931.

Finney, Ross L. *A Sociological Philosophy of Education*. New York: The Macmillan Company, 1928.

Fliegler, Louis A., "Levels of Creativity," *Educational Theory*, IX (April, 1959), 105–8, 115.

——, and Charles E. Bish. *Summary of Research on the Academically Talented* (1959). National Education Association (Originally published in American Education of Research Association) Review of Educational Research. *Education of Exceptional Children*, XXIX, No. 5. 1959.

Frampton, Merle E., and Elena D. Gall (Eds.). *The Intellectually Gifted* (Reprint from Vol. III, *Special Education for the Exceptional*). Porter Sargent, 1956.

Freehill, Maurice F. *Gifted Children*. New York: The Macmillan Company, 1960.

French, Joseph L. (Ed.). *Educating the Gifted: A Book of Readings*. New York: Holt, Rinehart, and Winston, Inc., 1959.

Gallagher, James J. *Analysis of Research on the Education of Gifted Children*. Springfield, Illinois: Office of Superintendent of Instruction, 1960.

Garrett, Henry E. "Traits by Fiat," Unpublished paper read before the Virginia Psychological Association, Annual Convention, May 1959.

Gavian, Ruth W. (Ed.). *The Social Education of the Academically Talented* (Curriculum Series No. 10). Washington, D. C.: National Council for the Social Studies, a department of the National Education Association, 1958.

Getzels, Jacob W., and Philip W. Jackson. "The Meaning of Giftedness: An Examination of an Expanding Concept," *Phi Delta Kappan*, XL (November, 1958), 75–77.

Ghiselin, Brewster (Ed.). *The Creative Process*. Berkeley: University of California Press, 1952.

Goddard, Henry Herbert. *School Training of Gifted Children*. Yonkers-on-Hudson, New York: World Book Company, 1928.

Goldberg, Miriam L. "Recent Research on the Talented," *Teachers College Record*, LX (December, 1958), 150–63.

Gowan, John C. "Dynamics of the Under-achievement of Gifted Students," *Exceptional Children*, XXIV (November, 1957), 98–101, 122.

Guilford, J. P. "Creativity," *The American Psychologist*, V (September, 1950), 444–54.

——. "The Structure of Intellect," *Psychological Bulletin*, LIII (July, 1956), 267–93.

Hall, Theodore. *Gifted Children—The Cleveland Story*. Yonkers-on-Hudson, New York: World Book Company, 1956.

Hartshorne, Hugh, Mark A. May, and Frank K. Shuttleworth. *Studies in the Organization of Character*. Vol. III, *Studies in the Nature of Character*. New York: The Macmillan Company, 1930.

Harvard Committee. *General Education in a Free Society*. Cambridge, Massachusetts: Harvard University Press, 1945.

Havighurst, Robert J., and Hilda Taba. *Adolescent Character and Personality*. New York: John Wiley and Sons, Inc., 1949.

———, Eugene Stivers, and Robert F. DeHaan. *A Survey of the Education of Gifted Children*. Supplementary Educational Monograph No. 83. Chicago: University of Chicago Press, 1955.

Heck, Arch O. *The Education of Exceptional Children*. New York: McGraw-Hill Publishing Company, 1940.

Henry, Theodore S. "Methods of Teaching as Adapted to the Instruction of Gifted Children," *Nineteenth Yearbook of the National Society for the Study of Education*, Part II. Bloomington, Illinois: Public School Publishing Company, 1920. Pp. 96–111.

Hildreth, Gertrude H. "Characteristics of Young Gifted Children," *Pedagogical Seminary and Journal of Genetic Psychology*, LIII (December, 1938), 287–311.

———, F. N. Brumbaugh, and F. T. Wilson. *Educating Gifted Children*. New York: Harper & Brothers, 1952.

Holland, John L., and Ruth C. Stalnaker. "A Descriptive Study of Talented High School Seniors; National Merit Scholars." *Bulletin of the National Association of Secondary-School Principals*, XL (March, 1958), 9–21.

Hollingworth, Leta S. *Special Talents and Defects: Their Significance for Education*. New York: The Macmillan Company, 1923.

———. *Gifted Children: Their Nature and Nurture*. New York: The Macmillan Company, 1926.

———. "The Child of Very Superior Intelligence as a Special Problem in Social Adjustment," *Mental Hygiene*, XV (January, 1931), 3–16.

———. "The Development of Personality in Highly Intelligent Children," *Fifteenth Yearbook of the Department of Elementary School Principals*. Washington, D. C.: National Education Association, 1936. Pp. 272–81.

———. "An Enriched Curriculum for Rapid Learners at Public School 500: Speyer School," *Teachers College Record*, XXXI (January, 1938), 296–306.

———. "Problems of Relationship between Elementary and Secondary Schools in the Case of Highly Intelligent Pupils," *Journal of Educational Sociology*, XIII (October, 1939), 90–102.

———. *Children Above 180 IQ*. Yonkers-on-Hudson, New York: World Book Company, 1942.

———, and M. V. Cobb. "Children Clustering at 165 IQ and Children Clustering at 145 IQ Compared for Three Years in Achievement," *Twenty-Seventh Yearbook of the National Society for the Study of Education*, Part II. Bloomington, Illinois: Public School Publishing Company, 1928. Pp. 3–33.

Hutchins, Robert M., and Mortimer J. Adler. *Great Books of the Western World* (*A Syntopicon*). Chicago: Encyclopaedia Britannica, Inc., 1952.

Hutchins, William J. "Children's Code of Morals," in Harold S. Tuttle, *Dynamic Psychology and Conduct*. New York: Harper & Brothers, 1949.

Jones, Vernon. *Character and Citizenship Training in the Public School, An Experiment in Three Specific Methods*. Chicago: The University of Chicago Press, 1936.

———. "Character Development in Children—an Objective Approach," Leonard Carmichael (Ed.), *Manual of Child Psychology*. New York: John Wiley and Sons, Inc., 1946. Pp. 707–51.

———. *Character and Citizenship Education, A Syllabus for Use in Teacher Training*. Washington, D. C.: National Education Association, 1950.

Judd, Charles H. *Education as Cultivation of the Higher Mental Processes*. New York: The Macmillan Company.

Justman, Joseph. "What Makes the Good College Teacher?" *School and Society*, LXX (December, 1949), 417–21.

Keliher, Alice V. *A Critical Study of Homogeneous Grouping*. Teacher's College Contributions to Education, No. 452. New York: Bureau of Publications, Teachers College, Columbia University, 1931.

Killian, James R. *Massachusetts Institute of Technology, President's Report, 1955:* Part 1, "Meeting the Nation's Scientific Manpower Needs."

Kilpatrick, William H. "Philosophy of Education from the Experimentalist Outlook," *Forty-First Yearbook of the National Society for the Study of Education*, Part I. Chicago: University of Chicago Press, 1942. Pp. 39–86.

Kirk, Samuel A. "Needed Projects and Research in Special Education," *Forty-Ninth Yearbook of the National Society for the Study of Education*, Part II. Chicago: University of Chicago Press, 1950. Pp. 320–34.

Kone, Elliott H. (Ed.). *Language Laboratories: Modern Techniques in Teaching Foreign Languages*. New Haven, Connecticut: Yale University Audio-Visual Center, 1960. Annual Bulletin No. 19 of the Connecticut Audio-Visual Education Association.

Kotschnig, Walter M. "Educating the Elite in Europe," *Journal of Educational Sociology*, XIII (October, 1939), 70–81.

Kough, Jack. *Practical Programs for the Gifted*. Chicago: Science Research Associates, 1960.

———, and Robert F. DeHaan. *Identifying Students with Special Needs. Teacher's Guidance Handbook, Elementary School Edition*, Vol. 1. Chicago: Science Research Associates, 1955.

Kroeber, Elsbeth. "Biology." Helen L. Cohen and Nancy G. Coryell (Eds.). *Educating Superior Students*. New York: American Book Company, 1935. Pp. 14–32.

Lamson, Edna E. *A Study of Young Gifted Children in Senior High School*. Teachers College Contributions to Education, No. 424. New York: Bureau of Publications, Teachers College, Columbia University, 1930.

Larrabee, Harold A. *Reliable Knowledge*. Boston: Houghton Mifflin Company, 1945.

Laycock, Samuel R. *Gifted Children*. Copp Clark (Canada), 1957.

Lee, Irving J. (Ed.). *The Language of Wisdom and Folly*. New York: Harper & Brothers, 1949.

Lehman, Harvey C. *Age and Achievement*. American Philosophical Society Memoirs, Vol. 33. Princeton, N. J.: Princeton University Press, 1953.

Lewis, W. Drayton. "A Comparative Study of the Personalities, Interests, and Home Backgrounds of Gifted Children of Superior and Inferior Achievement," *Pedagogical Seminary and Journal of Genetic Psychology*, LIX (September, 1941), 207–18.

————. "Some Characteristics of Very Superior Children," *Pedagogical Seminary and Journal of Genetic Psychology*, LXII (June, 1943), 301–9.

Ligon, Ernest M. *A Greater Generation*. New York: The Macmillan Company, 1948.

McClelland, David C., *et al. Talent and Society*. New York: Van Nostrand, 1958.

Martens, Elise H. *Curriculum Adjustments for Gifted Children*. United States Office of Education Bulletin, No. 1, 1946. Washington, D. C.: United States Government Printing Office, 1946.

Mead, Margaret. "Thinking Ahead: Why Is Education Obsolete?" *Harvard Business Review*, XXXVI (November-December, 1958), 24–25.

Miles, Catherine Cox. "Gifted Children," Leonard Carmichael (Ed.), *Manual of Child Psychology*. New York: John Wiley and Sons, Inc., 1946.

Morris, Charles W. "Science, Art and Technology," *The Kenyon Review*, I (1939), 410–20. Reprinted in Irving J. Lee (Ed.), *The Language of Wisdom and Folly*. New York: Harper & Brothers, 1949.

Morrison, Henry C. *The Practice of Teaching in the Secondary School* (Second edition). Chicago: University of Chicago Press, 1931.

Moulton, Forest Ray (Ed.). *The World and Man, as Science Sees Them*. Chicago: University of Chicago Press, 1937.

Murphy, Gardner. *Human Potentialities*. New York: Basic Books, Inc., 1958.

National Education Association. *High-School Methods with Superior Students*. Research Bulletin, Vol. 19, No. 4; September 1941. Washington, D. C.: Research Division, National Education Association, 1941.

National Education Association, Educational Policies Commission. *Manpower and Education*. Washington, D. C.: The Commission, 1956.

National Education Association. *The Identification and Education of the Academically Talented Student in the American Secondary School*. Washington, D. C.: National Education Association, 1958. Conference Report, James B. Conant, Chairman.

————. *Administration Procedures and School Practices of the Academically Talented Student*. Washington, D. C.: National Education Association, 1960.

————. *Modern Foreign Languages and the Academically Talented Student.* Washington, D. C.: National Education Association, 1960.

National Manpower Council. *A Policy for Scientific and Professional Manpower.* New York: Columbia Press, 1953.

————. *Womanpower.* New York: Columbia University Press, 1957.

National Society for the Study of Education. *Forty-Ninth Yearbook*, Part I, *Learning and Instruction.* Chicago: University of Chicago Press, 1950.

————. *Education for the Gifted. Fifty-Seventh Yearbook*, Part II. Chicago: University of Chicago Press, 1958.

Newland, T. Ernest. "The Gifted," *Review of Educational Research*, 1953.

————. "Essential Research Directions on the Gifted," *Exceptional Children*, XXI (May, 1955), 292–96, 310.

————. "Implications of Research in the Area of the Gifted," *Exceptional Children*, XXV (January, 1959), 195–98.

New York State Education Department, Bureau of Secondary Curriculum Development. *Fifty-Six Practices for the Gifted from Secondary Schools of New York State.* University of the State of New York, 1958.

The New York Times, September 7, 1958.

Osburn, W. J., and Ben J. Rohan. *Enriching the Curriculum for Gifted Children: A Book of Guidance for Educational Administrators and Classroom Teachers.* New York: The Macmillan Company, 1931.

Otto, Henry J. (Ed.). *Curriculum Enrichment for Gifted Elementary School Children in Regular Classes.* Publication No. 6, Austin: University of Texas, Bureau of Laboratory Schools, 1955.

Outler, Albert C. "Colleges, Faculties and Religion," *Educational Record*, XXX (January, 1949), 45–80.

Passow, A. Harry, *et al. Planning for Talented Youth.* Bureau of Publications, Teachers College, 1955.

————, Jane E. Beasley, and Deton J. Brooks, Jr. "Adapting the Curriculum to the Needs, Capabilities, and Talents of Individual Students," *Review of Educational Research*, XXVII (June, 1957).

Patrick, Catherine. "Creative Thinking," Philip L. Harriman (Ed.). *Encyclopedia of Psychology.* New York: The Philosophical Library, Inc., 1946. Pp. 110–13.

Pegnato, Carl W., and Jack W. Birch. "Locating Gifted Children in Junior High Schools; A Comparison of Methods," *Exceptional Children*, XXV (March, 1959), 300–4.

Pintner, Rudolph. "Superior Ability," *Teachers College Record*, XLII (February, 1941), 407–19.

Piper, Raymond F., and Paul W. Ward. *The Fields and Methods of Knowledge.* New York: F. S. Crofts and Company, 1929.

Plaut, Richard L. *Blueprint for Talent Searching: America's Hidden Manpower*. New York: National Scholarship Service and Fund for Negro Students, 1957.

Portland Public Schools. *The Gifted Child in Portland*. Portland, Oregon: Portland Public Schools, 1959.

Pregler, Hedwig. "The Colfax Plan," *Exceptional Children*, XX (February, 1954), 198–201.

Pressey, Sidney L. *Educational Acceleration, Appraisals and Basic Problems*. Bureau of Educational Research Monographs Number 31. Columbus, Ohio: The Ohio State University, 1949.

————, and Raymond G. Kuhlen. *Psychological Development through the Life Span*. New York: Harper & Brothers, 1957.

Raup, R. Bruce. "Some Philosophical Aspects of Grouping," *Thirty-Fifth Yearbook of the National Society for the Study of Education*, Part I. Bloomington, Illinois: Public School Publishing Company, 1936. Pp. 43–56.

Robinson, Helen M. (Ed.). *Promoting Maximal Reading Growth among Able Learners*. Supplementary Educational Monographs No. 81. Chicago: University of Chicago Press, 1954.

Rockefeller Brothers Fund, Inc. "The Pursuit of Excellence," *Special Studies Project Report V*, America at Mid-Century Series. Garden City, New York: Doubleday & Company, Inc., 1958.

Roe, Anne. *A Psychological Study of Eminent Psychologists and Anthropologists, and a Comparison with Biological and Physical Scientists*. Psychological Monographs, General and Applied, Vol. 67, No. 2, Whole Number 352. Washington, D. C.: American Psychological Association, 1953.

Rogers, Carl R. "Toward a Theory of Creativity," *ETC.: A Review of General Semantics*, XI (1954), 249–60.

Rugg, Harold. *Foundations for American Education*. Yonkers-on-Hudson, New York: World Book Company, 1947.

Sanford, Fillmore H. "Speech and Personality," L. A. Pennington and I. A. Berg (Eds.), *Introduction to Clinical Psychology*. New York: The Ronald Press Company, 1948.

Scheifele, Marian. *The Gifted Child in the Regular Classroom*. Bureau of Publications, Teachers College, 1953. No. 12, *Practical Suggestions for Teaching*.

Schrader, Beunah Vesta. "A Critical Examination of Principles and Proposals Related to the Teaching of Superior Children," Unpublished Master's thesis, University of Colorado, Boulder, Colorado, 1939.

Shaffer, Laurance F., and Edward J. Shoben, Jr. *The Psychology of Adjustment* (Second edition). Boston: Houghton Mifflin Company, 1956.

Shertzer, Bruce (Ed.). *Working with Superior Students: Theories and Practices*. Chicago: Science Research Associates, Inc., 1960.

Stanley, William O., B. Othanel Smith, Kenneth D. Benne, and Archibald W. Anderson (Eds.). *Social Foundations of Education.* New York: Holt, Rinehart, and Winston, Inc., 1956.

Stedman, Lulu M. *Education of Gifted Children.* Yonkers-on-Hudson, New York: World Book Company, 1924.

Strang, Ruth. "Mental Hygiene of Gifted Children," Paul Witty (Ed.), *The Gifted Child.* Boston: D. C. Heath and Company, 1951.

Sumption, Merle R., *et al.* "Special Education for the Gifted Child," *Forty-Ninth Yearbook of the National Society for the Study of Education*, Part II. Chicago: University of Chicago Press, 1950. Pp. 259–280.

———, and Evelyn M. Luecking. *Education of the Gifted.* New York: The Ronald Press Co., 1960.

Swift, Edgar J. *Mind in the Making.* New York: Charles Scribner's Sons, 1908.

Symonds, Percival M. *The Nature of Conduct.* New York: The Macmillan Company, 1928.

Taylor, Calvin W. *The 1955 Research Conference on the Identification of Creative Scientific Talent.* Salt Lake City: University of Utah Press, 1956.

———. *The Second (1957) Research Conference on the Identification of Creative Scientific Talent.* Salt Lake City: University of Utah Press, 1958.

———. *The Third (1959) Research Conference on the Identification of Creative Scientific Talent.* Salt Lake City: University of Utah Press, 1959.

Terman, Lewis M. "Educational Suggestions from Follow-Up Studies of Intellectually Gifted Children," *Journal of Educational Sociology*, XIII (October, 1939), 82–89.

———. "The Discovery and Encouragement of Exceptional Talent," *The American Psychologist 9.* June, 1954.

———, *et al. Mental and Physical Traits of a Thousand Gifted Children.* Vol. I, *Genetic Studies of Genius* (Second edition). Stanford, California: Stanford University Press, 1926.

———, and Maud A. Merrill. *Measuring Intelligence.* Boston: Houghton Mifflin Company, 1937.

———, and Melita H. Oden. "The Significance of Deviates: II. Status of the California Gifted Group at the End of Sixteen Years," *Thirty-Ninth Yearbook of the National Society for the Study of Education*, Part I. Bloomington, Illinois: Public School Publishing Company, 1940. Pp. 67–74.

———, ———. "The Significance of Deviates: III. Correlates of Adult Achievement in the California Gifted Group," *Thirty-Ninth Yearbook of the National Society for the Study of Education*, Part I. Bloomington, Illinois: Public School Publishing Company, 1940. Pp. 74–89.

———, ———. *The Gifted Child Grows Up.* Vol. IV, *Genetic Studies of Genius.* Stanford, California: Stanford University Press, 1947.

————, ————. *The Gifted Group at Mid-Life.* Vol. V, *Genetic Studies of Genius.* Stanford, California: Stanford University Press, 1959.

Thorndike, Edward L. *Human Nature and the Social Order.* New York: The Macmillan Company, 1940.

————. "Gifted Children in Small Cities," *Teachers College Record,* XLII (February, 1941), 420–27.

Tryon, Carolyn, and William E. Henry. "How Children Learn Personal and Social Adjustment," *Forty-Ninth Yearbook of the National Society for the Study of Education,* Part I. Chicago: University of Chicago Press, 1950.

Turney, Austin H. "The Psychological Basis of Grouping," *Thirty-Fifth Yearbook of the National Society for the Study of Education,* Part I. Bloomington, Illinois: Public School Publishing Company, 1936. Pp. 81–116.

Tuttle, Harold S. *Dynamic Psychology and Conduct.* New York: Harper & Brothers, 1949.

Tyler, Leona E. "Studies on Motivation and Identification of Gifted Pupils," *Review of Educational Research,* XXVII (October, 1957), 391–99.

University of Chicago, Board of Examinations. *Sample Questions from Comprehensive Examinations.* Chicago: The College of the University of Chicago, 1948.

Walsh, Ann M. *Self Concepts of Bright Boys with Learning Difficulties.* New York: Teachers College, Columbia University, 1956.

Whipple, Guy M. *Classes for Gifted Children: An Experimental Study of Method of Selection and Introduction.* Bloomington, Illinois: Public School Publishing Company, 1919.

Wilson, Frank T. "A Survey of Educational Provisions for Young Gifted Children in the United States, and of Studies and Problems Related Thereto," *Pedagogical Seminary and Journal of Genetic Psychology,* LXXV (September, 1949), 3–19.

Witty, Paul. "A Genetic Study of Fifty Gifted Children," *Thirty-Ninth Yearbook of the National Society for the Study of Education,* Part II. Bloomington, Illinois: Public School Publishing Company, 1940.

———— (Ed.). *The Gifted Child.* Boston: D. C. Heath and Company, 1951.

————. "Who Are the Gifted?" *Fifty-Seventh Yearbook of the National Society for the Study of Education,* Part II. Chicago: University of Chicago Press, 1958.

Wolfle, Dael. *America's Resources of Specialized Talent.* New York: Harper & Brothers, 1954.

Woodrow, Herbert. *Brightness and Dullness in Children* (Second edition). Philadelphia: J. B. Lippincott Company, 1923.

Worcester, Dean A. *The Education of Children of Above-Average Mentality.* Lincoln: University of Nebraska Press, 1956.

Wrenn, C. Gilbert. "Potential Research Talent in the Sciences Based on Intelligence Quotients of Ph.D.'s," *Educational Record*, XXX (January, 1949), 5–22.

Zorbaugh, Harvey W. (Ed.). "Gifted and Talented Children," *Journal of Educational Sociology*, XX (October, 1936), 65–108.

———. "The Education of Gifted Children in Secondary Schools," *Journal of Educational Sociology*, XIII (October, 1939), 65–128.

———, R. K. Boardman, and Paul Sheldon. "Some Observations of Highly Gifted Children," Paul Witty (Ed.). *The Gifted Child*. Boston: D. C. Heath and Company, 1951.

INDEX

index

Ability grouping, 90
Abstractions
    use by gifted children, 103–
    104
Adler, Mortimer
    *The Great Ideas: A Syntopicon of
    Great Books of the Western
    World*, 56, 137
Adult education, 56–57
Age distribution
    U.S.A. population, 49
Aptitude training, 34

Behavior problems
    gifted individual, 185–189
Biological potential
    education planning, 82
Brandwein, Paul F.
    natural science program, 30–
    31
"Busy Work" fallacy, 87

Carroll, Herbert A.
    differences in levels of ability,
    88–89
Character development
    in the gifted, 183–193, 201–
    220
Character education
    seven minimum essentials,
    196–197

Civilizations
    study for educational content,
    170–179
College of liberal arts
    difference from university, 34
Commager, Henry Steele
    social change in America, 53–
    54
Communication
    instruction of the gifted, 161–
    169
Conant, James B.
    study of American schools, 5–6
Creative thinking, 8
Creativity
    in gifted children, 134–136
Curriculum
    additions needed for abler
    child, 99
Curriculum
    four-fold category of subject
    matter, 104–106
Curriculum
    for gifted children, 5, 7
    structure, 36–37

Economy
    principle in education, 102–
    107
Education
    as cognitive perspective, 57–
    64

Education
    general, definition, 34–36
Education
    life span concept, 55–57
Education
    present concept, 62
Education of gifted
    social significance, 41–47
Educational Policies Commission
        of 1950
    definition of gifted child, 11
Educational theory
    process, 55–64
    setting in modern world, 49–
        55
Essays, argumentative
    media for instruction, 164
Ethics
    in secondary schools, 202–204

Fact
    concept of value in education,
        58–61

Garrett, Henry E.
    aptitude tests, 33
Genius,
    I.Q. of historically important
        men and women, 23–25
Gifted child,
    characteristics, 10–13
Gifted child
    composite portrait, 16–18
    definition, 3–4, 6, 10–13
    status at midlife, 14–15, 18–23
Gifted children
    age of learning reading, 91–92
    armed forces experiences as
        adults, 19

    capacity for dealing with ab-
        stractions, 103–104
    creativity, 134–136
    indications of intelligence, 91–
        92
    logic of special education, 80–
        81
    need for wider variety of in-
        structional materials, 99–
        100
    segregation for instruction, 90
    teachers for, 108–119
Gifted persons
    adjustment problems, 185–
        189
    mental characteristics, 25–27
Great Books (see Syntopicon)
Guilford, J. P.
    research into nature of crea-
        tivity, 8

De Haan, Robert F.
    traits for leadership, 31
Hollingworth, Leta S.
    education of gifted children,
        14
Hutchins, Robert M.
    adult education, 56–57

Ideas
    use in education, 136–138
Individual differences
    handling in education, 86–101
Intellect
    role in development of gifted
        individual, 127–140
Intelligence
    early indications in the supe-
        rior individual, 91–92
Intelligence quotient (see I.Q.)

I.Q.
  cut off points, 11–13
  estimated for historically im-
    portant people, 23–25
  gifted children, 15
  Stanford-Binet scale, Terman
    revision, 11
Instructional materials
  need for wider variety by
    gifted children, 99–100

Judd, Charles H.
  transfer of training, 63–64

Killion, James R.
  on critical shortage of engi-
    neers, 60
Kilpatrick, William H.
  intelligence and experience,
    62
Knowledge
  instruction in methods and
    sources, 156–159
  role in educational develop-
    ment, 141

Languages,
  in school curriculum, 84–85
Language study
  secondary schools, 165–169
  in school curriculum, 146–151
Leadership
  identifying characteristics, 31

McClelland, David C.
  factors in academic success, 13
  role of talent in society, 12

Marriage
  change in modern world, 51
Mead, Margaret
  questions on education, 5–6
Meaning
  instruction of the gifted, 161–
    169
Mental characteristics
  highly intelligent persons, 25–
    27
Miles, Catherine Cox
  study of gifted children, 15–
    16, 24–25
Minnesota Occupational Scale
  survey of gifted children as
    adults, 18–19
Moral behavior
  instruction of the gifted, 201–
    211

Parliament of Science, 1958, 53, 67
Patrick, Catherine
  analysis of creative thinking, 8
Personal development
  in the gifted, 183–193
Personal integrity
  planning for, 213–220
Personality problems
  gifted individual, 185–193
Philosophy
  in secondary schools, 202–204

Religion
  status in American schools,
    206–208
Russian language
  in school curriculum, 146

Scientific method
  application in training the
    gifted, 194–199

Scientists
    role in modern society, 53–54
Secondary school
    definition, 55
Sex instruction, 82–83
Shorthand
    in training gifted children, 100
Social adjustment
    instruction for the gifted, 201–
    211
Social development
    in the gifted, 183–193
Social leadership, and intelligence,
    31–32
Social parallelism, 83–84
Spanish language
    in school curriculum, 146
Speedwriting
    in training gifted children, 100
Stanford-Binet Scale, I.Q., 11
*Syntopican of Great Books of the West-
    ern World*, 56, 137

Talent in music
    discovery and training, 40
Teacher
    description of top quality
    type, 110, 111

Teachers
    appraisals by gifted students,
    115–116
Teachers
    professional training for teach-
    ing gifted children, 114–115
    qualities for teaching gifted
    children, 108–119
Terman, Lewis M.
    Genetic Studies of Genius, 8, 10,
    13–14
    Revision of Stanford-Binet
    Scale, 11
Textbooks
    quality for good instruction,
    129–133
Thorndike, Edward Lee
    education of the gifted, 42
Transfer of training, 63–64
Typewriting
    in training gifted children, 100

University, difference from liberal
    arts college, 34

Witty, Paul
    definition of gifted child, 10
Working hours
    1890 to 1950, 50